Books Children Love
A Guide to the Best Children's Literature

Books
Children
Love

*A Guide to the Best
Children's Literature*

Elizabeth Laraway Wilson

CROSSWAY BOOKS ● WESTCHESTER, ILLINOIS
A DIVISION OF GOOD NEWS PUBLISHERS

Cover illustration by Jesse Willcox Smith from a poster for the American
Library Association, 1919. Book design by K. L. Mulder.

First printing, 1987

Printed in the United States of America

Library of Congress Catalog Card Number 87-70459

ISBN 0-89107-441-4

This bookful of books is
lovingly dedicated to all
the special people who are
part of the world of childhood,
and to the four young
book-lovers I know best:
Anna, Andrew, Mary, and Catherine.

Table of Contents

Foreword

"Please read me a story," says the eager little person. Or, "Can I sit on your lap?" "Oh, you're stopping at a good place! Couldn't you read just a bit more?" Familiar pleas in any family. The speaker could be a young child who has pulled out a book that is a firm favorite, or an older child speaking for the whole family as they sit sprawled, relaxed and content one evening in the family room with mugs of hot chocolate steaming beside each one. The *Lord of the Rings* has drawn everyone into its life and nobody wants to stop.

Books! Books contain the throb of human life; the magic entrances, fascinates, sets alight imagination, opens doors of interest and curiosity, informs, and triggers questioning. Restless bodies become still and concentrated—thinking is encouraged. Reading out loud together fosters warm ties in human relationships. The experience is shared, and then interesting and meaningful conversation ensues. Developing the ability and desire to pursue reading *is* education. That's why in English universities you don't "study history"; you "read history," or law, or whatever.

Unhappily, our generation suffers from the presence of a compulsive boxlike affair that spews out a time-consuming addiction. T.V.! The personal growth possible through reading, conversation, *life,* is not possible for many children and adults today. The priorities are wrong. Time often isn't left for the really important things in life.

Families and teachers who are concerned know that the number one priority in society is for a functional family unit. This doesn't mean merely a location called "home" where meals are served and the car garaged. Parents have to create something; they have to give priority to "family life"—which takes time, energy, and discipline. This includes, for instance, routines such as mealtimes with shared conversation, cleaning up the yard together, reading through a whole book as a family, time with one child, etc. This is life. This is education. I'm personally very encouraged by the growing numbers of people who realize this, who realize they don't have to be dragged along by the patterns of our increasingly confused society. They realize they are responsible and there are good alternatives that work. One indication of this is the growing number of home-educated children. Another is the fact that new ways of organizing more flexible schools are being found within which the parents share the responsibility and life. Then, we must consider the children whose parents can't or won't give them these riches at home. Can teachers help? *Yes.* With books! Magic that gets through to the most bored and restless child! Yet, it cannot be a "dry" book, such as many textbooks are. It must be an open door that woos the person into something living. I think this "guide" will indicate many such choices.

"Today, we'll not start with any schoolwork. Let's put our chairs in a circle. I have such a good story, I want to share it with you." And the group will bite the bait as you read, say, *The Lion, the Witch and the Wardrobe* by C. S. Lewis. Maybe the class will come alive to the love, romance, and fascination of books. What did they come to school for? To be bored by pages and pages of workbooks? To decide they hate learning? To be tested so that grown-ups can be satisfied making graphs about them or analyzing them on computers? Meanwhile, our children perish. That greatest and most beautiful resource of human life—*the child*—is lost, having been allowed to waste away with malnourished minds. Atrophied people! That is what I see around me in my country. Poor America! And we enjoyed such a good heritage.

This is where our Christian roots gave us a priceless infrastructure. We had the firm undergirding of truth: God's reality as communicated in His Word. Human life with value, love, knowing where we're going, why there is evil and what to do about it. We were given responsibility, free choice, and creativity: all of life—abundant life. God is the God of life, love, and reality. We can enjoy the creativity of other persons, and are to do so. That was what education was all about. And Christians should look for the "real thing," not some shoddy copy. So the child should be led to truly good books: the originals, or classics, if you will.

We live in a fallen world; that is what those of us who believe Christianity think. But that doesn't mean we pretend that our world is a greenhouse of our making. God's people, as we read about them in the Bible, could face what *other* people think, their ideas, their mistakes. That is why you needn't be afraid of other cultures, other viewpoints, when reading books to children.

One sin is to brainwash another person. We are to inform them, teach them the truth. If you are a Christian, this means communicating God's Word to them. It means living as God intended. But we *aren't* to put on blinkers so the child can't understand what other people think. In other words, go ahead and read a wide spectrum of books. Talk over together ideas you don't think are right. Many times a child will comment *themselves* on the content and ideas in a book. This is strengthening.

Interested? Tired of jaded, nonthinking kids and falling literacy graphs? Discouraged about education that doesn't educate? My husband and I searched for answers and came across a great British educator who worked at the turn of the century: Charlotte Mason. She discarded most textbooks in favor of "living books" and life itself. The children thus "brought up" went on to become thinkers, writers, lovers of learning, contented persons. I was so excited by the way these ideas helped our own children that I wrote a book about it, *For the Children's Sake.* Although written from a Christian worldview, the ideas are *true* to all children and life, and many have found them applicable in any case. I believe these ideas are needed more than ever by the children in our inner cities, those with "low self-esteem," those with no "identity" or inner riches. The child of today.

After writing the book I have been inundated with pleas from parents and teachers and adults who say, "I missed out as a kid. Please, I want to start now myself." They all ask: "Can you tell me which are living books? What can we read? Where do we start?"

Elizabeth Wilson spent a year researching books of quality in many categories. Books for younger children, books for older children. *Not* textbooks, but books that you'll *enjoy* reading. Here they are.

If you're new to all this, choose from the literature section first. And good reading to you!

P.S. Keep the treasure hunt going! Once bitten, you'll want to discover many other treasure books *you'll* love.

One other caution: we're all different. Each person is attracted by slightly different books, different writers. Don't expect each book to be right for everybody!

Susan Schaeffer Macaulay

Further Information– Child Light (Child Life)

C harlotte Mason's practical ideas were *so* good, we've tried to go one step further than merely explaining them in the book *For the Children's Sake* (Crossway).

This *guide* is a resource book to the best books Elizabeth Wilson could find. It will go a long way as you begin to put the ideas found in my book into practice in *your* family or classroom. You can even safely "stop school" for a few years and feast on good books and right living! This could give childhood a lot more zest and vigor! Your child wouldn't lose out, by the way.

In about a year's time, guides to grade-related curriculum will be available, published also by Crossway. These will be invaluable to schools and home schools choosing to operate according to these principals. These are being written by Diane Lopez for "Child Light."

Meanwhile, the address of the homegrown "Child Life" organization mentioned at the end of your copy of *For the Children's Sake* should be crossed out. We had to rename "Child Life" due to an unrelated magazine already using the logo! We are continuing under the new name "Child Light."

If you wish to keep in touch with further material available (including tapes on home education, etc.), newsletter, future seminars, write to:

Child Light (Child Life)
Sound Word Association
P.O. Box 2035
Michigan City, Indiana 46350, USA

Susan Schaeffer Macaulay

Introduction

I n a very real sense this book is a part of the ongoing heritage of Charlotte Mason, an English educator (and a Christian) who died in 1920. The connection between Miss Mason's work and *Books Children Love* is discussed below. It seems fitting, however, to acknowledge her at the outset of this Introduction.

Books Children Love was written for parents, teachers and others concerned with the whole-person needs of children. It is a response to a felt need among Christian people for a resource that would provide information on a broad range of reading matter, making use of the many fine secular books available, along with well-written Christian titles.

To fulfill this purpose, hundreds of books are listed (each one of which I read in its entirety) from more than two dozen subject areas, with comments on each book designed to give readers a clear idea of its tone and content. What is more important, however, than the fact that this is an extensive, diversified list is the basis on which the books were selected (to be discussed later in detail) and the background of how the book came to be written at all.

Books Children Love was written in connection with an overall educational philosophy being developed by Susan Schaeffer Macaulay and her husband Ranald Macaulay. (Susan is the daughter of Edith Schaeffer and the late Dr. Francis Schaeffer, founders of L'Abri Fellowship and internationally known writers. Ranald is now overall director of L'Abri. Both he and Susan have also written several widely read books.)

The Macaulays' interest in the education of children sprang from personal experience with their own family and from the heart-cry of hundreds of parents with whom they had talked. Mrs. Macaulay has effectively discussed the basis for their approach to childhood learning in her book, *For the Children's Sake* (Crossway, 1984).

My own involvement with the project came about as the Macaulays and I shared our mutual interest in the education of children and found an unusual degree of unity in our worldview, our theological imperatives and our high view of the place of reading and books in children's lives. With my own background in literature, the opportunity to research and write an extensive children's book list which would be a practical and helpful resource was one that I undertook with great enthusiasm.

An important influence on the Macaulays' thinking was the work and writings of Charlotte Mason, mentioned earlier. One of Mason's foundational concepts was that it was crucially important for all children to be at home with books and to provide them with excellently written, interest-holding books on as wide a range of topics as possible—books that also embodied ideas and ideals in harmony with traditional values and a Christian worldview. Mason called such works "living books," and her own extensive experience as an educator had demonstrated conclusively that when a child has an ongoing relationship with such books, he or she is willingly participating in the most effective form of education.

First of all, Mason said, the reader is having windows opened onto the world God made for man to live in. Knowledge of fine literature and its insights into human nature and experience, knowledge about places, people, events, processes, causes, effects are all absorbed as the child reads—and this holds true whether the book is a well-written story, an equally well-written biography or history, a book showing great artists' paintings, or simply a well-crafted book on how to successfully grow a vegetable garden. (At the same time, the "nuts and bolts" kind of knowledge is also being absorbed: vocabulary is built, reading and spelling skills are greatly aided, and repeated exposure to various models of good writing do much to help the reader learn to put his or her own thoughts into an effectively written form.)

Of even more significance, Mason believed, are the moral and ethical (and often spiritual) values conveyed by books. When a child identifies with either a real or a fictional character in a book who demonstrates courage or faith or honesty or determination or kindness or any one of the qualities so important to nurture in a child's own character, all those values are reinforced in the child's consciousness. When the effects of dishonesty, unkindness, carelessness, hypocrisy and other wrong behavior are observed in the course of a story or in a nation's history, the truth is learned with lasting effectiveness.

Concrete examples are always helpful. A living book may, for example, tell the true story of a life, as Anne E. Neimark does in *Touch of Light*, a biography of Louis Braille, the Frenchman who gave to the blind the first practical means of "seeing" through reading—an enthralling account that carries the reader along with its drama and event. And as the child reads, he or she is not only looking through a new window on the world, seeing and hearing people of another place, another time, finding out what lies behind that one word, *Braille*, but is also being exposed to the values of Louis Braille's courage, honesty, godly faith, love for others and determination to help all the blind in spite of the obstacles he encountered.

In Marguerite De Angeli's *The Door in the Wall* (the title is taken from the Bible, Revelation 3:8), the reader is taken on an exciting fictional adventure in medieval England with a boy newly crippled by a strange illness, unexpectedly separated from family and friends, trying to come to terms with his lameness and attempting to find his parents. Again, it's the story, the setting, the fine writing that hold the interest of the young reader; but at the same time solid values are being reinforced, helpful ideas are introduced, and the child's lifelong supply of general knowledge is being enjoyably increased.

Other living books show a child in detail how to prepare for a backpacking trip, how to care for pets, how to learn more about nature, how to create a great variety of crafts. Still others share exciting discoveries about early Viking landings in North America, or enter the world of artists and their paintings, telling about the artists' lives, explaining ways of looking at pictures that help a child to better enjoy, understand and appreciate them.

The examples just given mention only a few of the list's subject areas. With good reason, Charlotte Mason equated the use of "living books" with the spreading of a lavish feast, full of flavor and nourishment, before children. *Books Children Love* attempts to offer such a feast and to encourage parents, especially, to look for more living books.

In that connection, it is important to emphasize that *any* list such as this one is essentially unfinished, both because no such list can possibly include all the fine books available, and also because excellent new books are written each year. It is hoped that this list will be used simply as a start, and that once parents and others become more aware through the book's pages of the richness and diversity waiting for their children in the world of books, they will continue to seek out on their own the kind of books to which they have been introduced, or reminded of, in this volume.

Another matter of interest and importance is the criteria used in the selection of the books. The first criterion was the essential starting-point, that a book must readily catch and hold a reader's interest. Then, depending upon the category and purpose of the book, it should do some or all of the following: provide a "magic carpet" to transport a child to faraway places; offer fascinating insights into lives different from his own; give sheer joy or wholesome entertainment; increase understanding of that which is true and real; incorporate significant ideas or issues in a natural and credible manner; stimulate imagination and creativity; encourage logical thought, curiosity and questions; provide clear, accurate information on a specific topic.

The second criterion relates to the literary quality of the writing itself. This is, of course, inextricably bound up with the qualities mentioned above, for it is writers with gifts of imagination, understanding, and vision, a superior grasp of language use and a pleasing style, who are able to create books that do the things we have just talked about. In this regard, it has been important to distinguish between "good intentions" and fine writing. The fact that a writer may wish to convey either some worthwhile truth or some exciting experience (or both) does not in itself qualify his or her work as good, and I have excluded books of any category in which the writing is poor. This does not mean that I have confined the list only to books of the very highest literary excellence; there is a good proportion of such books, but also a solid representation of material which is very good in relation to its function and which, though it may not be timeless literature, is well-crafted and effective.

The final criterion applied has to do with the implied values of the writer as revealed in his or her work. The list includes books by both Christian and non-Christian writers, and a wide range of people in varying circumstances are found in the books, some of them children in very difficult situations. It is important for children to have an informed awareness and an ever-growing understanding of reality as it exists outside their own immediate experience. I have, however, chosen not to include books which reflect a perverse view of human life, which exploit deviant behavior or which undermine or attack basic Judeo-Christian moral and ethical values.

It will be obvious at this point that the importance of moral and spiritual values and of the inseparable relationship between the reading of good books and the acquiring of a good education are concepts which inform this book throughout. I make no apologies, therefore, for including comments in the book notes about specific values that a particular book reinforces, or about ways to tie a book in with an academic course of study.

If *Books Children Love* brings children and fine books together, it will have served its essential purpose. It is a book that was written with love: love for children with their wonderful questing minds, their lives of yet-undreamed, unshaped possibilities; love for language, for ideas, for imagination, for knowledge, for all that is a part of the inexhaustible richness of the world of books; and, above all, with a love for God, and for all He has made and done and given—truth, beauty, love, infinite diversity—for He called it very good.

Elizabeth Wilson
Pasadena, California

Notes on the Book's Organization

S ome comments on the way in which the book is organized, and a few suggestions about locating books may prove helpful.

As the Table of Contents indicates, the books are divided into subject areas. In each category, books are arranged alphabetically as in a library, with the author's last name first. (The one exception to this is in the *Biography* section in which, also as in a library, the books are arranged alphabetically by the last name of the person about whom the biography is written; that name appears in a capital-letter heading above each entry.) Following the name of the writer is the name of the book, then various items of information designed to help the reader. The numbers shown in parentheses are suggested grade levels (e.g., ps = preschool). These levels, however, are not to be taken in a rigid sense or as a restricting guide as to when a child should be ready for a certain book. This varies widely with individual children, and suggested grade levels should never be used in a way that will either discourage or limit a child's reading.

In the literature sections the books are grouped in three levels for the convenience of the reader; Level I, covering ps-2, Level II, grades 3, 4 and Level III, grades 5, 6-up. As to the categories of literature, a few words of explanation about two of them might be helpful. *Fantasies* includes works (other than fairy tales, myths and legends) which are not limited by pragmatic reality, and in addition to stories that completely transcend space, time, or the world as we know it, also includes all stories about animals who behave as human beings (Frog and Toad, for example). The *Historical* category includes all realistic stories written either *about* or *during* any time before 1920. In other words, books by writers such as Alcott or Montgomery were not historical when they were written, but they have now become so, whereas stories by Sutcliff or Harnett are being written in modern times about the past and are also historical.

In reference to the publishers listed, it should be noted that most of the older, children's classics are published by a number of different publishers. I have simply shown the name of the company that published the edition I read; a quick check of *Books in Print* in your library's reference section will reveal currently published editions. As to whether a book is in or out of print: while some titles remain consistently in print, others drop out (and sometimes back in) every year. Fortunately a great many out-of-print titles remain on library shelves. The *OP* in a book listing indicates it is out of print—and by the time the book list is in use, others will also have gone out of print.

A good book is worth trying to track down, and if your local library doesn't have a particular book, by all means explore the use of special requests and interlibrary loans.

To purchase a book not in the store, place a special order if the book is in print, or ask your bookseller to give you the names and addresses of agencies that make a speciality of finding out-of-print books. Finally, if a particular book seems unavailable no matter what avenues you have tried, do some research on what book might be available that would not only be similar in subject matter, but that would also meet the criteria for selection discussed in this Introduction.

☐*1* Animals:
Domestic Animals,
Pets, Zoo Animals

☐ Bellville, Rod and Cheryl Bellville. *Large Animal Veterinarians.* Carolrhoda Books, 1983, 32 pp. (2-6).
With photographs and brief text, the writers describe the work of veterinarians who care for cattle, sheep, pigs and goats. Correct medical terms are used, with the phonetic pronunciation shown in parentheses following the word.

☐ Caras, Roger. *A Zoo in Your Room.* Harcourt, Brace, Jovanovich, 1975, 96 pp. (5-up).
Naturalist and television personality Roger Caras has written a lively, often humorous guide to the care of a wide variety of creatures. Since the habitat that will be their home is very important, the writer gives quite a bit of attention to the creation of attractive terrarium homes for these pets. He also lists animals that should *not* be kept as pets, even though some pet stores sell them.

☐ Fields, Alice. *Pets.* Franklin Watts, 1981, 48 pp. (2-up).
An attractively illustrated general approach to keeping a pet. Children are encouarged to fit the pet to their own environment (not, for example, to try to keep a Great Dane in an apartment). A number of possible pets are pictured and discussed and guidelines as to care and feeding are given.

☐ Freedman, Russell. *Farm Babies.* Holiday House, 1981, 38 pp. (k-3).
A photo-text description of eleven kinds of farm animals during their first days of life. In addition to the usual lambs, calves, etc., the writer has also included the farm puppies, kittens and young barn owls.

□ Haley, Neale. *Birds for Pets and Pleasure*. Delacorte, 1981, 210 pp. (6-up).

> A detailed guide for the serious bird raiser, covering every aspect of the care, training and breeding of cage birds. This is solid text with a thorough discussion of each topic. An extensive appendix focuses on the different species of pet birds and their particular dietary and other needs.

□ Hess, Lilo. *Small Habitats*. Scribner's, 1976, 49 pp. (3-up).

> Primary listing under *Horticulture*.
>
> Along with "how-to's" for creating a variety of terrarium environments, brief instructions are given for the care of turtles, lizards, toads and other small creatures.

□ Hewett, Joan. *Watching Them Grow*. Little, Brown & Co., 1978, 64 pp. (3-up).

> Told in narrative, journal-entry form, this is the story of the San Diego Zoo's animal nursery and the work of Loretta Owens, a night nurse there. Appealing photos illustrate this enjoyable account of the tender, loving care given the baby animals who, for one reason or another, aren't being cared for by their mothers.

□ Jaspersohn, William. *A Day in the Life of a Veterinarian*. Little, Brown & Co., 1978, 74 pp. (3-up).

> The writer has made what he thinks of as a "documentary film in book form" for children. In photos and text he shows the work of a real veterinarian, Dr. David B. Sequist, Jr. Dr. Sequist has his own veterinary hospital in Vermont and cares for farm animals as well as all kinds of household pets. The book provides good general information on the topic for children and is especially helpful for a child who thinks he or she might someday want to become a veterinarian.

□ Maxwell, Gavin. *The Otter's Tale*. Dutton, 1962, 124 pp., OP (4-up).

> The warm, appealing story of Mijbil, Edal and Teko, pet otters, and their life with writer Gavin Maxwell.

This true story is not only excellent because of its interest-holding story quality and irresistible photographs, but it indirectly makes an important point about the amazing possibilities that exist in relationships between people and animals—when the people are informed, concerned, and willing to meet the animals' needs. The lengths to which Maxwell goes make it quite clear that the ownership of an animal should involve a serious commitment. Fortunately, most pets don't have the extensive needs of an otter, but as a child reads of Maxwell's responsible care of his delightful pets, he or she can also see in a new way that, whether it involves a hamster, a lizard, a dog, cat, or other pet, a choice should always be made: either a faithful commitment to learn about and meet the animal's needs, or a decision not to undertake the responsibility at all.

□ North, Sterling. *Rascal: A Memoir of a Better Era.* Dutton, 1963, 189 pp. (4, 5-up).
A longtime favorite story of the writer as a boy and of his irresistible, mischievous companion, the racoon Rascal. The story is also a warm evocation of life in a small Midwest town in 1918.

□ Reynolds, Michelle. *Critters' Kitchen: Cooking for Your Pets.* Atheneum, 1979, 56 pp. (4-up).
When thirteen-year-old Michelle's parents bought a small farm, she was finally able to have all the pets she wanted. She decided that they deserved to have their diet varied and to be given specially prepared foods from time to time. The book contains her "fancy food" recipes (all checked out for nutritional content by a veterinarian) for a wide variety of pets.

□ Ricciuti, Edward R. *Shelf Pets: How to Take Care of Small Wild Animals.* Harper & Row, 1971, 132 pp. (5-up).
The writer discusses which wild animals are appropriate to keep as pets, then details the housing, feeding and general care of more than twenty different animals, including frogs, crickets, spiders and salamanders. Illustrated with black and white photos.

□ Roy, Ron. *What Has Ten Legs and Eats Cornflakes?* Illus. by Lynne Cherry. Houghton Mifflin, 1982, 48 pp. (ps-3).

>Written to be read easily by early readers (or read to preschool children), this nicely done little book discusses three small pets that can be kept in an aquarium (minus water) or other comparable enclosure: land hermit crab, gerbil, chameleon. Care and feeding instructions are simply and clearly stated.

□ Simon, Seymour. *Pets in a Jar: Collecting and Caring for Small Animals.* Viking, 1975, 96 pp. (4-up).

>A child who likes to observe the behavior of a small species of wildlife, and who would enjoy creating an environment in which such a little creature could thrive, will find this book most helpful. The two opening chapters focus on general selection, collection and care notes. Simon then goes on, in six separate chapters, to focus individually on fifteen kinds of possible "pets in a jar." Planarians, tadpoles, earthworms, crickets and hermit crabs are just a few of the possibilities. An experienced elementary and junior high science teacher, Simon brings a good background of factual knowledge to his writing. All the animals discussed in the book have been kept and observed in either Simon's classrooms or at his home.

□ Thomson, Ruth. *Understanding Farm Animals.* Illus. by Joyce Bee. Usborne, 1978, 32 pp. (3-6).

>A colorful, up-to-date survey of all the usual farm animals with a great deal of factual information given in short paragraphs placed under illustrative pictures. Published in England, there are some minor differences in terminology from American usage, but not enough to hamper the usefulness of this enjoyable and informative book.

□ Weber, William J., D.V.M. *Wild Orphan Babies.* Holt, Rinehart & Winston, 1978, 159 pp. (5-up).

>A veterinarian with years of experience in caring for orphaned baby wild animals, Weber has written a thorough manual for children to use when caring for such

foster pets. He also emphasizes the importance of releasing the recovered animals into the wild, and tells how to do the freeing process gradually while the animal is still young enough to adapt to life on its own. Black and white photos illustrate the text.

Wittenberg & Sarber StL

2 Art and Architecture

☐ Chase, Alice Elizabeth. *Looking at Art*. Crowell, 1966, 119 pp., OP (5-up).

In this competent, simply expressed introduction to art appreciation, the approach is objective and largely without distorting biases. The writer is obviously more at home with traditional art, and the book's final chapter, "The Artist in the Twentieth Century," leaves something to be desired. Overall, however, it is a useful and worthwhile treatment. Two other helpful books by the same author (also, unfortunately, out of print) are *Famous Artists of the Past* and *Famous Paintings*.

☐ Cummings, Richard. *Make Your Own Model Forts and Castles*. McKay, 1977, 122 pp.

Primary listing under *Crafts, Hobbies and Domestic Arts*.

The seven projects of this book are based on actual historical fortifications. Interested students could be directed to further research which would provide discussions of architectural details related to the period of history in which the forts were built. Actually building one or more models would further serve to expand practical architectural knowledge.

☐ Denny, Norman and Josephine Filmer. *The Bayeux Tapestry*. Atheneum, 1966, OP (4-6 and up).

The story of the Norman Conquest is portrayed on the famous Bayeux Tapestry (not really a tapestry but embroidery on linen). The book's introduction describes this work of art—which is pictured section by section on the pages of the book—and comments on its background and form. The artistic conventions of the time, the way in which events are portrayed, the clothing and other accouterments all provide material of interest from the artistic point of view. The text that accompanies the pictures is especially well written, with an excellent, wide-ranging vocabulary and fine literary style.

□ Fisher, Leonard Everett. *Alphabet Art.* Scholastic Book Service, 1978, 61 pp. (5-up).

See further notes on this book under *Langauge* category.

An unusual compilation, the book includes large two-page spreads of thirteen different alphabets (Arabic, Gaelic, Thai, for example) and is rich in a variety of artistic qualities. Each alphabet is introduced with an illustration and an inscription written out in the related language. The layout of the alphabets invites the reader to attempt to graphically duplicate these fascinating, strange symbols. An excellent choice for an art unit related to calligraphy.

□ Fisher, Leonard. *The Seven Days of Creation.* Holiday House, 1981, 30 pp. (ps-up).

Primary listing under *Bible Stories and Spiritual Teaching.*

Artist Leonard Fisher has created his own unique graphic interpretation of the Genesis account of creation. Emergent shapes and bold splashes of color accompany the Biblically worded text. The creativity and beauty of the paintings add another dimension to children's perception of God's creation as a masterwork of art.

□ Glubok, Shirley. *Art and Archaeology,* Harper & Row, 1966, 48 pp. OP (3-up).

Primary listing under *History.*

This beautifully done book contains many illustrations of outstanding art objects found during archaeological excavations. The text relates the objects to the era and culture of the people who made them, discussing the distinctive qualities of each artifact.

□ Goffstein, M. B. *Lives of the Artists,* Farrar, Strauss, & Giroux, 1982, 48 pp. (ps-up).

In pithy, unrhymed verse, Goffstein looks briefly at five very different artists and captures the essence of each one's distinctive life and work. A full-color and a black-and-white painting are shown for each artist. A unique and unconventional approach that is simply to be experienced; some will respond to it warmly, and others will look askance!

□ Haldane, Suzanne. *Faces on Places: About Gargoyles and Other Stone Creatures.* Viking, 1980, 40 pp. (3-7).
Here is a nicely put together introduction to architectural ornaments. Combining history and anecdotes, the writer tells how some of the fanciful creatures and comic faces seen on buildings are made. Excellent photographs illustrate each part of the concise text, and children will thoroughly enjoy applying the knowledge newly gained from Haldane's book as they start focusing on gargoyles and other carvings on the buildings of their own communities or those seen on family travels.

□ Hawkinson, John. Two books: *Collect, Print from Nature* (3-up); *More to Collect and Paint from Nature,* OP (3-up); both Albert Whitman Co., 1963, 38 pp.; 1964, 40 pp.
Ideas for watercolor painting are given using models from nature: leaves, flowers and birds, for example. The first book also suggests such ideas as printing with leaves and spatter printing. The second book offers more information and instruction on watercolor techniques and equipment than the first does.

□ Kasuya, Masahiro. *The Beginning of the World.* Abingdon, 1982 (ps-up).
Primary listing under *Bible Stories and Spiritual Teaching.*
Using softly shaded watercolors, Kasuya's artistic vision selects exquisite details in portraying the wonder of creation. The story itself is simply told in contemporary language. Giving children the opportunity to contrast this book with that of Leonard Fisher (see entry above) will provide a valuable example of different ways of seeing artistically.

□ Kurelek, William. *Lumberjack*. Houghton, 1974, 48 pp. (all ages for art).

> Also listed under *Biography* and *History*.
>
> A foremost Canadian painter, Kurelek has created a vibrant gallery of paintings to accompany his story of what it was like to be a lumberjack a little more than thirty years ago. Vivid colors, simplicity of line, and authentic detail all characterize Kurelek's warm, realistic portrayals. This artist's work should be included in any study of modern painting, not only because of the quality of his work, but because the personal faith that informs his perspective gives his work a dimension to which Christians can thoroughly relate.

□ Kurelek, William. Companion volumes: *A Prairie Boy's Winter; A Prairie Boy's Summer*. Tundra Books, 1973, 48 pp.; 1975, 47 pp. (all ages for art).

> Also listed under *Biography* and *History*.
>
> As in *Lumberjack*, colorful full-page paintings face each page of text in these reminiscences of the artist's boyhood on the Canadian prairie near the U.S. border. Visual and verbal pictures combine to make the world of the 1930s live again.

□ Kurelek, William. *A Northern Nativity*. Tundra Books, 1976, 48 pp. (all ages for art).

> Twenty striking paintings accompany the unique text of this lovely book. Each scene pictures Joseph, Mary and the baby Jesus in a setting that was contemporary in the era of the 1930s Great Depression. At a long-ago Christmastime when he was twelve, the artist dreamed that Christ had come bodily to other places, other cultures. His radiant paintings symbolize the truth that Jesus did, indeed, come to all peoples for all times. (Obviously, the book should be approached as artistic symbolism, not as Biblical doctrine or history.)

□ Linder, Leslie and Enid. *The Art of Beatrix Potter*. Frederick Warne, 1955, 336 pp. (all ages).

> This lovely book focuses on Beatrix Potter's art, and includes more than three-hundred reproductions of her drawings and paintings. Each section of the book is

opened with the Linders' notes on the history of the specific group of pictures and on the development of Potter's work. Selections from her childhood art are followed by later work in several categories: interiors, landscapes, plant studies, microscope work, fungi drawings and animal studies. These, in turn, are followed by drawings which represent fantasies and a variety of ideas Potter had for stories.

□ Macaulay, David. *City*. Houghton Mifflin, 1974, 112 pp. (5-up).

Macaulay has created detailed drawings and descriptions of the building of a Roman city. The construction specifications are so clear and complete that the reader can fully visualize the roads, aqueducts and buildings taking shape; certainly a miniature model city could be built from the information given. Macaulay, of course, uses the architectural approach to convey a broad range of information about the culture and daily customs of the first-century Romans. The accompanying text is as concise and crisp as the splendid drawings.

□ Macaulay, David. Three books: *Castle; Cathedral; Pyramid*. Houghton Mifflin, 1977, 74 pp.; 1973, 77 pp.; 1975, 80 pp. (5-up).

See the above listing for Macaulay's book *City* for a description of his technique and the broad purpose of this splendid series of books. On the architectural level, Macaulay's work is superb, capable of both informing and inspiring.

□ Macaulay, David. *Unbuilding*. Houghton Mifflin, 1980, 78 pp. (5-up).

Using the same meticulous techniques as in his other books, Macaulay reveals both architectural and historical/cultural reality; in this case, instead of showing initial construction he depicts what would be revealed if the Empire State Building were dismantled, step by step.

□ Macaulay, David. *Mill*. Houghton Mifflin, 1983, 128 pp. (5-up).

> Another wonderful joining of architecture and history is seen in this further book of David Macaulay's. Spanning the years from 1810 to 1974, Macaulay focuses on four imaginary but typical textile-related mills built in New England at intervals during that time. The writer can take even such apparently unexciting subject matter and render it fascinating. Not only are his drawings and descriptions so lucid that buildings (or models) of the earlier structures he depicts could be constructed simply by following his text, but also the reader is made aware of the technological and social changes that are taking place with the passing years.

□ Marshall, Catherine. *Catherine Marshall's Story Bible*. Chosen, 1982, 192 pp. (ps-up).

> Primary listing under *Bible Stories and Spiritual Teaching*.
>
> Children will be inspired by the imagination and creativity shown in the seventy-seven brilliantly-colored illustrations, all done by children six to ten years old. All the children were members of a Geneva, Switzerland art class conducted by Michèle Kenscoff.

□ Raboff, Ernest. *Paul Klee: Art for Children*. Doubleday, 1968, 32 pp. (3 or 4-up).

> This is one of a series for children on artists and their work. The text helps children to expand their vision of what an artist has done in a given piece of work. The well-done material points out composition, shapes, purpose, etc. Following is a list of other artists in the series: Buonarroti, OP; Chagall; da Vinci; Dürer, OP; Gaugin; Picasso; Raphael, OP; Rembrandt; Remington; Renoir; Rousseau; Toulouse-Lautrec; Velasquez, OP.

□ Reynolds, Graham. *Constable's England*. The Metropolitan Museum of Art, New York/George Braziller, 1983, 184 pp. (all ages).

> Published in connection with a special exhibition of Constable's paintings at New York's Metropolitan Mu-

seum of Art, Reynold's book offers excellent color
plates of more than sixty of Constable's superb English
landscapes. Each one is accompanied on the facing page
with information about the painting and its setting.
Next to repeated visits to a museum or art gallery to
view several examples of a specific artist's work, such a
book is the best way for a child (or adult) to become familiar with that artist's choice of subject and medium
(oils, watercolors, pastels, for example), his or her distinctive painting techniques, and the unique vision conveyed by the artist. A substantial introduction to the
book provides information on Constable's life and
work. (Also see comments on this book in the *Additional Resources* note at the end of this *Art and Architecture*
section.)

□ Rudstrom, Lennart. Three books: *A Family; A Home; A
Farm;* paintings by Carl Larsson. Putnam, 1979, 32
pp.; 1974, 31 pp.; 1976, 34 pp. (all ages).
These books offer splendid paintings of family, home
and farm scenes in the artist's homeland of Sweden.
Simple, one-page-facing-each-painting text comments
on Larsson's life and the subjects of his paintings. The
text is suited to young readers, but the books can be
used with all ages in relation to the art. The work of
this prominent Swedish artist of the late nineteenth and
early twentieth centuries has recently become very popular in the United States. A number of his paintings are
now reproduced on calendars, note cards and a variety
of other materials. Their popularization, however, does
not detract from their very real artistic value. (The
books could also be used in connection with a study of
Swedish culture.)

□ Scheffer, Victor B. *The Seeing Eye.* Scribner's, 1971, 47 pp. (5, 6-up).

> Beauty in form, texture and color seen in nature. Scheffer's lovely photographs encourage a more thoughtful observation of the natural world and a greater sense of the aesthetic qualities in the things observed. The writer is a literary naturalist, biologist and photographer. His comments offer new ways of seeing and he has included a short chapter at the end, "How the Camera Can Help Your Seeing Eye," giving practical suggestions for nature photography. (This can also be used in connection with work in natural science.)

□ Tudor, Bethany. *Drawn from New England: Tasha Tudor.* Philomel, 1979, 95 pp. (5-up).

> Primary listing under *Biography.*
>
> This is a lavishly illustrated biography of the famed artist by her daughter. The book contains many examples of Tasha Tudor's work, as well as a wealth of family photographs and snapshots. Particularly significant from the artistic perspective are the descriptions of Tudor's love of her work, of its growth and development, and the way in which she fulfilled her artistic promise without compromising her determination to live a simple country life.

Additional Art Study Resources

Additional sources for art study materials may be found among adult materials and used by parents or teachers with their children. Following are some possibilities.

□ *The Library of Great Painters.* Harry W. Abrams, Inc.

> This series offers large, extensive (and expensive) volumes on such artists as Rembrandt, Vermeer, Velázquez, Michelangelo, da Vinci and many others. Each volume contains brief biological information on the artist and a number of reproductions of his paintings with accompanying commentary. For example, the Rembrandt volume includes 108 reproductions, forty-eight of them in color.
>
> The cost of this type of book makes it impractical

for most families to own any number of such books, and when libraries have them at all, they may be on the reference shelves rather than available for borrowing. (If necessary, schedule times to look at the books there with your child.)

☐ *The Library of Art*. Time-Life Books.
This series is completely out of print and is no longer available from the publisher or in bookstores. This is unfortunate, as the cost of the books when they were being offered for sale was much more moderate than that of, for example, the Abrams series (see above) and other similar works. Many libraries, however, have some of the Time-Life books in circulation in their collections.

Other suggestions:

A substantial number of art books focusing on a specific artist are published each year. Some of these are in paperback as, for example, *Leonardo da Vinci* by Bruno Santi (Scala/Harper, 1981, 78 pp.). Any generalized bookstore, including the chain outlets which seem to be everywhere, has a section on art books. Look these shelves over periodically for possible reasonably priced materials.

Also, browse in the art sections of both the children's and adults' departments of your local library. Many works now out of print are still on library shelves, as noted in connection with the Time-Life art books.

A special note to parents and teachers:

The ideal material to use in familiarizing children with a particular artist's work is the small portfolios which were used in art study by the English schools directed by Charlotte Mason (see this book's Introduction). Each portfolio measured approximately 8 × 10 inches and contained brief biographical information, small but excellent color reproductions of six or so of the artist's most representative work, and brief comments on each painting itself.

These fine materials were published in England, but are no longer available there, nor was I able to find anything of the kind being published in the United States. The nearest approximation would be for a parent or teacher to create portfolios by ordering small folio prints and combining them with informational materials researched in a library. (Unfortunately, even publishers of folio prints seldom offer as many as six different reproductions of each artist's work.) Following are the names and address of suppliers, but do be aware that the suppliers may not want to fill small orders for single copies of a number of prints; but if not, they might be willing to tell you where you can purchase individual quantities. (It helps greatly to send a stamped, self-addressed envelope with your queries.)

Art Extension Press
Box 389
Westport, CT 06881
Phone: (203) 531-7400

Graphic Arts Unlimited, Inc.
225 Fifth Avenue
New York, NY 10010
Phone: (212) 255-4805

Finally, query letters to major art museums, such as the Metropolitan Museum of Art, New York, might produce helpful sources of small reproductions of specific artists' work. (Remember to send the S.A.S.E. mentioned above.) The book listed in this section on Constable's painting, *Constable's England* by Graham Reynolds (Metropolitan Museum of Art, New York/George Brazziler), is exactly the sort of thing found in the little portfolios I have described above, except that the book, of course, is on a grand scale. Try to see this book in a store or library and use it (on a small scale) as your model. It is the closest thing I have seen to embodying the spirit of those marvelous little portfolios of the past.

③ Bible/Spiritual Teaching

☐ Aylward, Gladys (as told to Christine Hunter). *Gladys Aylward, the Little Woman*. Moody Press, 1970 (6-up).
Primary listing under *Biography*.
    There are many lessons in faith, endurance and obedience to God's purposes in this story of courageous little Gladys Aylward and her missionary work in China.

☐ Becker, Joyce. *Bible Crafts*. Holiday House, 1982, 120 pp. (all ages).
Primary listing under *Crafts, Hobbies and Domestic Arts*.
    Craft projects which help to make the events and people of the Bible come to life for children are clearly detailed in this helpful book.

☐ Booth, Julianne. Two books: *Books of the Old Testament; Books of the New Testament*. Concordia, both 1981, 32 pp. (1, 2).
    These are rhymed, brightly illustrated picture books for early readers briefly describing the books of the Bible. They can provide excellent reinforcement for systematic memorization of the books of the Bible.

☐ Brown, Fletch. *Street Boy*. Moody Press, 1980, 152 pp. (5-up).
    In this fictional but very credible story, Brown tells of an appealing youngster, Jaime Jorka, from the slums of Manila who has a burning desire for a better life. The writer has done an excellent job of picturing Jaime's wretched home-life: brutal, drunken father; screaming, money-demanding mother; assorted grubby siblings— and his other life as a sharp, streetwise little thief and scrounger, cruising the market area, ever alert for what he can grab. The hopelessness he has been feeling about

breaking out of his miserable, half-starved existence is at
its height when he encounters the young missionary
whose wallet he has previously stolen. He is amazed to
be invited to a week at Camp Light, a Christian out-
reach specifically for street boys. Distrustful and wary,
sure that *no* one cares unselfishly for others, Jaime skep-
tically decides to take a chance and go. What he sees in
the lives of the helpers there (many former street boys
themselves) convinces him that what they are saying
about the love of God and salvation in Christ is true,
and Jaime finds a new life within, even though the old
framework of the ghetto is still around him. (A sequel,
Street Boy Returns, continues Jaime's story.)

□ Bunyan, John. (Annotated by Warren Wiersbe.) *The
Annotated Pilgrim's Progress*. Moody Press, 1980 (all
ages).

This helpful edition of Bunyan's classic story of the
Christian walk has marginal annotations throughout
which define the meaning of archaic or difficult words
and explain the many differences and allusions which
may be obscure to most readers. The notes are easy to
follow, for the word(s) is underlined in the text, then
shown in darker type at the head of its note in the marginal column on each page. *Pilgrim's Progress,* which
used to be widely read by children, has almost disap-
peared from their knowledge in recent decades, largely
because its seventeenth-century language has intimidat-
ed several generations of people whose reading experience has not included material in the language of the
past. The spiritual value of Bunyan's wonderful allegory
cannot be overstated, and once children become involved in the lively dialogues, the frequent humor and
the sense of a strenuous, hazardous pilgrimage toward a
glorious goal, they take it to their hearts. Children
should certainly have the opportunity at some point to
read this classic of faith in its original form. A recent
adaptation (see below) which retains Bunyan's words
and catches something of the tone of the complete work
may be a good first step that can lead to a later appreciation of the book in its entirety—for which purpose
the annotated edition we've just discussed would be an
excellent choice.

□ Bunyan, John. Edited by Oliver Hunkin. *Dangerous Journey.* Illus. by Alan Perry. Marshall Morgan and Scott/Eerdmans, 1985, 126 pp. (3-up).

> This lavishly illustrated adaptation of *Pilgrim's Progress* is a good way to introduce children to Bunyan's vivid depiction of the Christian journey from the "City of Destruction" through "the wilderness of this world" to the joys of the "Celestial City." Hunkin has edited with care, and the result is a readily understandable narrative that uses Bunyan's own words and preserves a clear sense of the original's dramatic action, its shrewd depiction of human nature, and the many guises of temptation. There is suspense, peril and humor aplenty, with each page illuminated by Alan Perry's splendid color illustrations.

□ Cassandre. *Life When Jesus Was a Boy.* Judson Press, 1981, 48 pp. (3-up).

> Primary listing under *Reference.*
>
> Packed with information in a pleasing, well-illustrated form, this helpful book is another of the valuable resources available today which give children a greater understanding of many of the things they read or hear about in the Biblical account of Jesus' life here on earth. When the customs and objects of Bible times are familiar to children, it is much easier for them to grasp the reality of Jesus' life and the full meaning of all that He did.

□ Cioni, Ray and Sally. *The Droodles Ten Commandments Story Book.* David C. Cook, 1983, 63 pp. (2-4).

> The Cionis have used the cartoon-styled Droodles to illustrate ten brief, contemporary stories. Each story focuses in sequence on one of the Ten Commandments, relating its concept to an issue or situation that most children have either experienced or observed. A helpful concluding section written by Edith Schaeffer offers tips for parents and teachers on using the book effectively.

□ Coleman, William L. *Who, What, When, Where Book About The Bible*. David C. Cook, 1980 (1-6).

This is a colorful, well-put-together collection of interesting and sometimes surprising facts from the Bible. Some of these are in puzzle or riddle form. Each entry is brief and the book lends itself to reading aloud to younger children; those who are competent readers can enjoy browsing through on their own.

□ *Cool: How a Kid Should Live*. Tyndale House, 1974 (4-up).

This is a tremendously effective book of daily readings for children in an attractive "handbook" format. Using passages from *The Living Bible,* verses on a related topic have been brought together in hard-hitting paragraphs that present Biblical guidelines for living. There is no "talking at" the reader, no tedious effort to sound "with it" or flip. The simple, direct *Living Bible* language is easily understood, and, unlike some materials in which the groupings of verses seem lacking in coherence or weak in impact, those in *Cool* form a powerful (and legitimate) linking of Biblical statements that make the central point a living force. There is an entry for each day of the year, an extensive use of relevant photos, and a brief space on each page for notes of any kind the reader wants to record. Chapter and verse references for all material in each entry are shown in fine print at the bottom of the page. A wide range of ages can profitably use this book, including a few children below the grade 4 level and, in the other direction, some beyond junior high (the book's primary target age).

□ Knapp, John III. *Pillar of Pepper*. David C. Cook, 1982 (ps-3).

Primary listing under *Literature: Poetry and Rhymes*.

These lively nursery rhymes that relate to Biblical events and characters are original creations, not parodies of classic children's rhymes. Children will enjoy the rhymes' rollicking style while their familiarity with Bible people is reinforced.

□ Lawson, Audrey and Herbert Lawson. *The Man Who Freed the Slaves: The Story of William Wilberforce.* Faber and Faber, OP (5-up).

> Primary listing under *Biography*.
>
> The Lawsons have written an exceptional story of the English aristocrat who dedicated himself to living out his Christian faith by pressing for justice and mercy in the treatment of the oppressed and poor. Born to wealth and comfort, and gifted with talents and a magnetic personality, Wilberforce set aside personal ambitions and gave of himself sacrificially. All that he had was to be used of God in service to others. This inspiring account of Christianity in action is, unfortunately, not an easy book to find. It is included in the list because of its excellence and is well worth making a special interlibrary loan request to obtain.

□ Macaulay, Susan Schaeffer. *How to Be Your Own Selfish Pig.* David C. Cook, 1982 (6-up).

> Written primarily for teenagers, this cogent, lively book can also be helpful for preteens who are particularly thoughtful, questioning and mature. The "bottom line" realities of Christian belief are explored in an appealing and direct way. Valid questions are raised—and answered—not with pat formulas, but with reasoned, Biblical truth that can be lived out in the nitty-gritty of everyday life.

□ Macaulay, Susan Schaeffer. *Something Beautiful from God.* Crossway, 1980, 93 pp. (all ages).

> A sensitive, beautifully written and illustrated book on the Christian view of human life: its sanctity, dignity and intrinsic worth. Not simply theoretical, the book provides examples from life and practical answers to the kinds of questions faced by real people. This book can be read to and discussed with younger children, and can be read for themselves by those a little older.

□ Magnusson, Sally. *The Flying Scotsman.* Quartet Books, 1981, 191 pp. (5-up).

> Primary listing under *Biography*.
>
> This inspiring story of the life and work of Eric Liddell, Olympic runner and missionary now widely

known through the film *Chariots of Fire,* embodies important spiritual truths. These are not in any sense "preached" at the reader, but Liddell lived his faith in a remarkable way, and the writer has conveyed most effectively the beliefs and principles on which his life was based.

□ Marshall, Catherine. *Catherine Marshall's Story Bible.* Chosen, 1982, 192 pp. (ps-up).
An unusual book that combines the colorful art (seventy-seven unique illustrations) of six- to ten-year-old students of a Geneva, Switzerland art class, and thirty-seven favorite Bible stories told in the vivid style of one of America's most prominent Christian writers. Children will not only find the stories freshly appealing, but will have their own creativity inspired as they see the graphic interpretations of other children.

□ Mickelson, Berkeley and Alvera. *The Family Bible Encyclopedia.* 2 vols. David C. Cook, 1978 (all ages).
See listing under *Reference* for brief description of this "starter" encyclopedia.

□ Murphy, Elspeth Campbell. Two books: *God Cares When I'm Sorry; God Cares When I'm Worried.* David C. Cook, 1981, 24 pp. (ps-2).
These little books simulate a child's conversations with God about dealing with guilt over wrongdoing and coping with anxiety. The text is brief, in a picture-book format with attractive illustrations. These do quite well in dealing with spiritual issues without a lot of unnatural preachiness. Part of a series; some titles are more effectively done than others.

□ Prokop, Phyllis S. *The Sword and the Sundial.* David C. Cook, 1981 (5, 6).
Primary listing under *Literature, Level III, Realistic Stories—Historical.*
This dramatic story of King Hezekiah (opening with the last part of the rule of his father Ahaz) clearly

demonstrates the possibility of human choice. Ahaz chose not to obey God, not to be faithful to Him; Hezekiah loved God and chose to serve Him. The consequences of their choices underscore truths which are just as significant today as they were almost three thousand years ago.

□ Robertson, Jenny. *The Ladybird New Testament Storybook.* Zondervan//Ladybird, 1982, 160 pp. (1, 2).
Over one hundred well-told stories from the Gospels, Acts and the Epistles are included. Each story is short and concise, accompanied by colorful illustrations.

□ St. John, Patricia. Books by this writer, Moody Press.
See listings under *Literature, Level III, Realistic Stories— Modern* for books by St. John. These stories have a clear, specifically Christian message that is well integrated into the flow of events, and they encourage young people to apply belief and a willingness to do God's will to the problems and decisions they must deal with in daily life.

□ Spier, Peter. *Noah's Ark.* Doubleday, 1977, 48 pp. (ps-up).
Spier's wonderful illustrations are a feast for the eye and the imagination. Except for a brief frontispiece quotation ("But Noah found grace in the eyes of the Lord") and a delightful translation of the poem "The Flood" by Jacobus Revius (1586-1658), Spier's book is without text. But his unique, incredibly detailed drawings make the beloved story live again in a fresh, vivid evocation. Not intended as a complete recounting of the Biblical story, the book's focus on the graphic aspects of the ark, the flood and the animals provides a supplement to the complete story that will delight readers of all ages.

□ Vander Schnier, Nettie. *The Golden Thread*. Moody Press, 1983, 175 pp. (6-up).

Primary listing under *Biography*.

This exciting and inspiring biography of a young Dutch woman who survived the Nazi occupation during World War II, includes the story of Nettie's spiritual pilgrimage along with the daily events of her life. The story moves from Nettie's childhood that is shadowed by her mother's emotional illness, to her teenage bitterness and rebellion, and then to belief and faith—and to the continuing growth that developed in the grindingly hard war years.

□ Vos, Catherine F. *The Child's Story Bible*. Eerdmans, 1983, (1935), 382 pp. (1, 2—or up to 4 if desired).

All of the narrative portions of the Bible are told in a way children can understand. The stories are completely true to the Scriptures on which they are based, but the writer has also included some explanatory material, just as a parent would do in making the story clear to a child. An excellent way to begin to instill a comprehensive knowledge of the Bible as a whole in the minds of young students.

Creation: two picture books of the Genesis account

□ Fisher, Leonard. *The Seven Days of Creation*. Holiday House, 1981, 32 pp. (ps-up).

□ Kasuya, Masahiro. *The Beginning of the World*. Abingdon, 1982 (ps-up).

These beautifully done books will appeal to many children of all ages. Aside from their aesthetic value, the graphic visualizations greatly enhance children's grasp of the wonder of creation. Too often, attempts to explain the beginning of the world to children are associated with unattractive, chart-like drawings in which none of the magnificence, cosmic power and sheer beauty of God's handiwork are even hinted at. It is important from the start of their lives for children to have a sense of reality about the fact that God *made* their world and to associate Him with its wonder and beauty.

The two very different artistic visions of Fisher and Kasuya are also helpful in expanding children's sense of the diversity and richness not only of the world itself, but also of the variety of valid perceptions God has given to individual people. Fisher's style is more abstract, with bold sweeps of line and color accompanying the traditional Biblical language of the text. Kasuya, on the other hand, tells the creation story in her own words and brings it to visual life with detailed watercolors in delicate pastel shades.

Illustrated Bibles and Bible Selections

□ *The Gospels Illustrated* (illustrations by Joseph De Velasco). David C. Cook (all ages).
>This unusual book combines the King James Version of the four Gospels with a wealth of drawings that reflect the varied perspectives on people and events that are recorded in the different Gospels. No matter how many modern translations or paraphrases of the Bible a child has access to, it is a great loss in his or her life not to be familiar with the sonorous, majestic language of the King James Bible. Reading this book is one way a child can become familiar with the beloved traditional King James Version.

□ *The Illustrated Bible Dictionary.* Tyndale House, 1980 (all ages).
>Primary listing under *Reference.*
>This lavishly illustrated three-volume set provides a wealth of information on Biblical terms, objects and people. It is a splendid source of wide-ranging information on the Bible.

□ *Jonah.* Illustrated by Kurt Mitchell. Crossway, 1981, 27 pp. (ps-up).
>A splendid picture-story book with the complete text from the Bible, *New International Version.* The delightful illustrations are scrupulously true to the Biblical account (for example, a huge fish, not a whale, swallows Jonah) and make the story live for young children.

□ *Nelson's Bible Encyclopedia for the Family.* Nelson, 1982 (all ages).

> Primary listing under *Reference.*
>
> Grouped under twenty main categories, this excellent volume gives a wealth of information about the Bible, Bible lands, customs, etc. Beautifully illustrated.

□ *NIV Pictorial Bible.* Zondervan (4-up).

> Using the *New International Version* translation as text, this volume adds indexes, a Bible-reading guide, and extensive informational notes illuminated by five hundred full-color illustrations. Background material on the customs of Bible times, on related history and geography, etc., provide helpful reference sources.

⌐4 Biography

ALCOTT
☐ Meigs, Cornelia. *Invincible Louisa*. Little, Brown & Co., 1933, 260 pp. (6-up).

This is the classic biography of Louisa May Alcott, the much-loved author of *Little Women* and other favorite stories which are still being read almost one hundred and twenty years after their first appearance. In her courageous, selfless life, Alcott quietly embodied the strong, loving qualities of family devotion that are so evident in her writings. At the same time, she was far ahead of her day in supporting the right of young women to make independent choices and to live useful, authentic lives, free of the strictures of social patterns which were often artificial and oppressive. By nature active and impatient, Louisa was also intelligent and acutely sensitive. As a child of only eleven, she began to realize that her family needed care in a way that her loved but ineffectual father never managed to do. Louisa took upon herself the responsibility of someday being able to give each one the security and opportunity they so desperately needed. She not only fulfilled her childhood dream, but she left in her books the heritage of a strong, idealistic response to living that continues to warm and inspire successive generations of readers.

ALEXANDER
☐ Krensky, Stephen. *Conqueror and Hero: The Search for Alexander*. Illus. by Alexander Farquharso. Little, Brown & Co., 1981, 67 pp. (3-7).

This concise overview of Alexander's life follows his meteoric path of conquest and the gradual dissolution of his character. Krensky's assessment of the methods Alexander used in establishing his far-flung empire indicates that in spite of the pride and increasing sense of self-importance which marred his later years, Alexander was more than a military genius; he also had a much broader worldview than did most of his contemporaries. His practice of combining the best of various cultures was not generally accepted, however, and after his death the practice was not widely continued. A clear, comprehensive view of one of history's dominant figures.

ANGOULÈME

□ Powers, Elizabeth. *The Journal of Madame Royale*. Walker & Co., 1976, 150 pp. (5-up).

This moving account is based largely on the journal kept by Marie Thérèse Charlotte, daughter of Louis XVI and Marie Antoinette (her married name was Angoulème) and on firsthand writings of others close to the royal family. The princess (as the daughter of the king, the French titled her Madame Royale) was fourteen when the French Revolution started and she and her family were imprisoned. Three years later she was released to exile in Austria. Her parents had been guillotined, and her young brother had died under mysterious circumstances. In her journal Marie Thérèse writes not only of her present experiences, but also of the past and her life with her family before the eruption of the unchecked violence that marked the Revolution. Hers is a view of those tragic events from an unusual and enlightening vantage-point. The perspective is personal, and thus largely subjective, but whatever the political failings or cultural blind spots of the French royalty, it seems unarguably true that they were subjected to degrading and inhumane treatment, behavior that was particularly unjust in the case of helpless children.

ARCHIMEDES

□ Bendick, Jeanne. *Archimedes and the Door of Science* (Immortals of Science Series). Franklin Watts, 1962, 143 pp., OP (5, 6-up).

Note: Unfortunately, this excellent series is now out of print. With a few fine exceptions, contemporary children's biographies of the great figures of the past, while often well and attractively done, almost universally conform to current public school standards as to reduced vocabulary, short sentences and paragraphs, and greatly reduced overall content. Copies of the books in this series (others of which we also list) are still on the shelves of many libraries. It is well worth making an interlibrary loan request for any of these books. Not a great deal is known about the personal details of the life of the great third century B.C. Greek mathematician, Archimedes. Records of his discoveries and inventions and of a few personal characteristics remain, however, and the biographer has fitted these into the known material on the period's customs and events. It is worth noting that although mathematics was the subject in which Archimedes immersed himself, he made many related scientific discoveries and invented a number of practical machines and processes, copies of which are still being used today. In many ways, Archimedes helped to establish the scientific mode of inquiry and thus all branches of science are strongly indebted to him. Good literary quality and a lively, humorous style characterize this well-told biography.

AYLWARD

□ Aylward, Gladys (as told to Christine Hunter). *Gladys Aylward, the Little Woman*. Moody Press, 1970 (6-up). This version of the story of Gladys Aylward and her work in China is Aylward's own account as told to Hunter, a professional writer. Shorter, less dramatized, and with a much stronger and more specific emphasis on Aylward's evangelistic work than Alan Burgess's *The Small Woman* (see below), this book adds a new dimension to her story. Both books should be read to fill in the complete picture. Burgess, a far more skilled writer, includes much more material and wonderfully recreates scenes, settings, and atmospheres and conveys far more of the feel of China than does Hunter. On the other hand, Hunter touches much more fully on Aylward's primary purpose in being in China: the winning of people to personal faith in Christ. A recommendation would be to first read (or read aloud sections from) *The Small Woman*, which gives so much more of an authentic feel of the Chinese places and people, then go on to

Gladys Aylward, the Little Woman, probably a more literally factual account as to some aspects of Aylward's life, but less rewarding in the literary sense.

□ Burgess, Alan. *The Small Woman.* Dutton, 1957, 256 pp. OP (adv. 5, 6-up or parent/teacher read-aloud).

The enthralling story of Gladys Aylward, a young English parlormaid who was impelled to go as a missionary to China. Rejected at the end of a three-month probationary period at the China Inland Mission Training School in England (Gladys couldn't do well in the theology class, for example), she finally decides to go on her own. Hearing of an elderly, widowed independent missionary in North China who needs help, Gladys writes. The reply indicates that if Gladys can get herself there, they can try working together. Unable to afford steamship fare, Gladys pays three pounds down on a train ticket to China via Siberia. Each month the amount paid toward her ticket increases and finally, in October, 1932, she is on her way.

On the long journey, danger, hardship, fear—and amazing deliverances—become everyday occurrences, a fitting prelude to her unique ministry in China. An absolutely gripping story, with the authentic flavor of a China that no longer exists.

BELL

□ Quackenbush, Robert. *Ahoy! Ahoy! Are You There? A Story of Alexander Graham Bell.* Illus. by author. Prentice-Hall, 1981, 36 pp. (1-4).

This is a contemporary-style biography of the inventor of the telephone. It is brief, humorously written and illustrated with clever cartoon drawings. Children will enjoy the lively introduction to the famous Mr. Bell, but one shouldn't expect it to go into depth on any aspect of his work.

BLACKWELL

□ Clapp, Patricia. *Dr. Elizabeth.* Lothrop, 1974, 156 pp., OP (6-up).

Written as though it were being told by Elizabeth Blackwell herself, this is a splendid story of the indomitable little woman who became the first woman doctor since ancient times. Her life is a story of moral conviction, courage, and dedication. Blackwell wasted no time in hostility, confrontations or bitterness about the prejudice and obstacles she faced. She simply persisted, quietly and immovably, in doing the things that would provide better medical care and open opportunities for other women to be part of her endeavor.

Interestingly written and with a significant theme, Clapp's biography of Blackwell is an excellent accompaniment to the study of American history of the latter half of the 19th century or to a science unit on medicine.

BOONE

□ Daugherty, James. *Daniel Boone*. Illus. by author. Viking, 1939, 94 pp., OP (4-up).

It is in the spirit of an epic adventure that Daugherty has written the story of Daniel Boone. Through vibrant, sometimes poetic language, the reader learns to know the strong, restless man whose life was a significant part of the American heritage. Daugherty's bursting-with-life illustrations complement the vigor and inspiration of the excellently written biography.

□ De Gering, Etta. *Wilderness Wife*. McKay, 1966, 138 pp., OP (5-up).

The story of Rebecca Boone, the tall, dark-haired girl who followed her famous husband, Daniel Boone, wherever he led and in the face of frequent misfortunes simply said quietly, "We'll make do, Daniel." But the Boones' life together held much of joy and achievement as well, and they lived to enjoy an old age surrounded by children and grandchildren. They and others like them are an important part of our history, and most of the famous men whose exploits are still recounted could not have accomplished what they did without the courageous, spirited women who partnered them.

BOWDITCH

☐ Latham, Jean Lee. *Carry On, Mr. Bowditch*. Houghton
Mifflin, 1955, 251 pp. (5, 6).

> A biography in story form, this account of the life and
achievements of Nathaniel Bowditch (born in New
England in 1773) reads like fiction. But in addition to
holding the reader's interest with the suspense, tragedy
and triumph of Nathaniel's life, the book also offers excellent historical background on the young American
nation. Fine values reflected throughout.

BOYLE

☐ Sootin, Harry. *Robert Boyle: Founder of Modern Chemistry*
(Immortals of Science Series). Franklin Watts, 1962,
133 pp., OP (6-up).

> In Sootin's well-researched biography, Boyle emerges
as an individual, a man living in the seventeenth century
with a family background intimately involved with the
turbulent issues of the day. Many interesting sidelights
in this regard, and on his family in general, are included. In addition to his dedication to scientific inquiry
and to the open dissemination of all new scientific discoveries, Boyle was also a devout Christian who believed there was no conflict between religion and science, but that on the contrary it was God who had
designed the natural laws men were slowly discovering.
The writer has included details and diagrams of a number of Boyle's experiments. These will interest science-
minded students, but could be omitted by the general
reader.

BRAILLE

☐ Neimark, Anne E. *Touch of Light: The Story of Louis
Braille*. Harcourt, Brace, Jovanovich, 1970, 186 pp. (4-
6).

> The poignant, inspiring story of the man who invented
the system of raised dot symbols that enables the blind
to read. At the age of three, Louis accidentally pierced
an eye with a sharp tool in his father's harness-making
shop. Resulting infection eventually led to complete
blindness. Gifted intellectually and musically, and with
an exceptionally kind, considerate nature, Braille

learned readily himself just from hearing material read to him or being shown how to play a particular piece of music. But he not only longed for access into the wider realms of printed materials; from early boyhood onward he had a sense of God-given mission, an inner drive to find some method whereby all the blind could read. He found the answer, but an important aspect of the story is the fact that although Braille had demonstrated the effectiveness of his system when still only a boy himself, it was many years before the government and the people in charge of the school where he first studied, then taught would recognize it, sanction its use, or try to develop its potential. A valuable early lesson for readers in one of life's hard-to-accept realities.

BRAND

□ Wilson, Dorothy Clarke. *Ten Fingers for God*. Nelson, 1965, 247 pp. (6-up).

The enthralling story of Dr. Paul Brand and his work in restorative surgery and related rehabilitation of leprosy victims. The son of missionary parents in India, Brand was educated in England and in his early years considered that the last thing he would ever do would be to become a doctor. In an unusual pattern of events, he was prepared for the remarkable contribution he was to make to thousands of lives. This biography wasn't written for children and is longer and more detailed than a majority of fifth or sixth graders would want to read through on their own. Some advanced readers would prove to be exceptions to this. But in general, a broader use with children would be to read sections aloud, something the book lends itself to quite well in its narrative that moves from one specific phase of Brand's life to another. Older children will be fascinated by Brand's medical discoveries and by the dramatic changes his surgery made in his patients' lives.

The same biographer has also written the story of Dr. Brand's indefatigable mother, widowed as a young woman, but who remained in India, continuing to minister to the remote hill people until her death at ninety-five. (*Granny Brand: Her Story*, OP).

BRIDGMAN

☐ Hunter, Edith Fisher. *Child of the Silent Night*. Illus. by
Bea Holmes. Houghton Mifflin, 1963, 124 pp. (1-4).
Simply but effectively written, this is the story of how a
little deaf and blind girl learned to read and to commu-
nicate. Using raised letters of the alphabet on labels at-
tached to familiar objects (a cumbersome and limited
method, but Braille had not yet been accepted even in
its own inventor's country, and was unknown as yet in
America) Laura's teachers at the Perkins School for the
Blind began the difficult task of educating Laura Bridgman. This was in 1837, preceding the education of the
more widely-known Helen Keller by some years. Excellent reading for young students and a fine way to encourage greater understanding of those handicapped in
vision or hearing.

BURBANK

☐ Quackenbush, Robert. *Here a Plant, There a Plant,
Everywhere a Plant Plant! A Story of Luther Burbank*.
Illus. by author. Prentice-Hall, 1982, 35 pp. (2-5).
Another brief, streamlined "80's-style" biography, this
time of plant genius Luther Burbank. The writer's fast-
moving, humorous style serves to introduce Burbank in
an appealing way, but for a fuller treatment of his life
and work in books written for children, it appears necessary to search library shelves for some of the older,
now out-of-print biographies.

CARTIER

☐ Syme, Ronald. *Cartier: Finder of the St. Lawrence*. Illus.
by William Stobbs. Morrow, 1958, 95 pp. (3-7).
Not long after the voyages of Columbus to the New
World, hardy French seamen began regularly to make
annual fishing trips to Newfoundland. Most of them
had no interest in exploring the land that was so near,
but Jacques Cartier, the finest seaman of them all, believed it was a country that could perhaps be settled by
Frenchmen. Eventually he was commissioned by the
commander of the French navy to explore the large river Cartier had seen—perhaps it was that mythical passage to the Pacific Ocean that many explorers looked
for in vain. Cartier had discovered what was later

named the St. Lawrence River and journeyed up its waterway as far as the present city of Montreal, noting the fine trees, plentiful game and beautiful meadows. He experienced the bitter cold of Canadian winter and the uneasiness of the Indians, and though he still thought of Canada as a place that would one day be settled by the French, he was not sorry to return and settle down in France. But although it was another fifty years before those French settlers came, Cartier had laid the foundation with his discovery of the St. Lawrence. A well-written, medium-length account.

CARVER

□ Holt, Rackham. *George Washington Carver: An American Biography*. Doubleday, 1943, 342 pp. (all ages).

This is the inspiring story of a gifted black American. Born into slavery, Carver became free while still a very small child, at the time of the Emancipation Proclamation. A modest man dedicated to improving the lot of his people, and of the South in general, Carver became an agricultural chemist and discovered hundreds of uses for the peanut, soybean and sweet potato. Additionally, he developed many products from cotton waste and taught farmers how to increase agricultural yield through soil improvement and diversification of crops.

COLUMBUS

□ Dalgliesh, Alice. *The Columbus Story*. Illus. by Leo Politi. Scribner's, 1955, 32 pp., OP (1-3).

A brief, well-written beginning biography of Columbus. It is a good choice for reading aloud; helpful as initial background for the study of American history, or as related to European exploration of the New World.

□ d'Aulaire, Ingri and Edgar Parin. *Columbus*. Illus. by author. Doubleday, 1955, 56 pp. (k-4).

As in their other large, picture-and-text biographies, the d'Aulaire's have combined literary excellence with art in a delightfully effective way. Lively and realistic, Columbus's story is told with wonderful little touches that encourage analysis and thought. For example, near the end of the book we read, "Many people say that Columbus was poor and forsaken in his old age. That is not true. He wasn't poor, but he was bitter because he was not the richest and mightiest seaman in the world. Columbus was a great man. But he was not a modest man. He wanted too much, and so he did not get enough."

□ Syme, Ronald. *Columbus, Finder of the New World*. Illus. by William Stobbs. Morrow, 1952, 70 pp. (3-7).
A fast-paced story of Columbus's voyages. More realistic than some accounts in recounting the obstacles, disasters and behavior of the Spanish seamen. It could be read to competent second graders and read by some students in grades 2 to 4, depending on their level of ability. The book provides good American history background and may also be related to European exploration of the New World.

DOUGLASS
□ Patterson, Lillie. *Frederick Douglass: Freedom Fighter*. Illus. by Gray Morrow. Garrard, 1965, 80 pp. (2-5).
The inspiring biography of the famous slave who became a leader in the fight to end slavery. Intelligent and courageous, Douglass escaped to the North when he was a young man. Although he started out doing any work he could find at day labor, he next found a regular factory job. Douglass became active in the abolitionist movement and was unexpectedly called on one night to stand up and tell his story. He was recognized as a natural orator, and from that time on spent much of his time traveling with abolitionist groups, speaking out against slavery. He became active in the Underground Railway and also edited an abolitionist newspaper. This is an exciting account of the life of a gifted and dedicated man.

EDISON
□ Cousins, Margaret. *The Story of Thomas Alva Edison*. Random House, 1965, 175 pp. (5-9).
The life of Edison (certainly one of history's most gifted—and nonconforming—men) makes highly interesting reading in this full-length biography. From early childhood on, Edison was uniquely his own person.

Strong-willed, vigorous, curious and not at all concerned about what other people thought of him, he fit no mold and had he lived in the highly structured society of today, one can only speculate what might have become of him. As it was, he spent just three months in school, was tutored informally by his mother for about three years, and at twelve was out working a full day. Afflicted most of his life by deafness, this increased his tendency toward living a solitary life of preoccupation with his intense interest in scientific experiments and study. There was nothing planned, ordered or conventional about Edison's life; his restless, questioning mind constantly drove him on. He drifted from job to job; at every opportunity he plunged into research, worked night and day, made remarkable discoveries, took on new projects. Eventual recognition, continuing fame and honors, marriage, children, periods of wealth— nothing essentially changed this unique man and his burning compulsion to know more and to develop more and more devices that would contribute to the comfort and enjoyment of the world's people.

EQUIANO
□ Kennerly, Karen (adapted by). *The Slave Who Bought His Freedom*. Dutton, 1971, 121 pp. (5, 6-up).

An unusual true story of a young African boy sold into slavery in 1757, when he was twelve. Kennerly has put into more contemporary language the African Equiano's own story which he wrote in England in 1789.

In a quiet, low-key way Equiano tells of his harrowing experiences. This story brings home the horror of slavery and of racial bigotry in a valid way. No effort to be sensational is needed—the realities speak for themselves.

FARRAGUT
□ Latham, Jean Lee. *Anchors Aweigh: The Story of David Glasgow Farragut*. Harper & Row, 1968, 273 pp. (5-9).

The adventurous, action-filled life of Farragut, the famous American naval officer, is splendidly told by Jean Latham. Farragut's navy career began in 1810 when he was only nine years old. Captain David Porter, a friend of the boy's father, began the youngster's training, and

others who saw his ability and promise were later in-
strumental in giving him the education in mathematics,
foreign languages and seamanship which he successfully
acquired. Daring, cool in the face of danger, and exceptionally determined, Farragut was put in positions of
leadership from his youth onward. A Civil War hero, he
became a rear-admiral when Congress created the new
rank and bestowed it on him. Two years later he was
made a full admiral. Qualities of courage, determination
and loyalty are reflected throughout this story of Farragut's life.

FIBONACCI

□ Gies, Joseph and Frances. *Leonard of Pisa and the New
Mathematics of the Middle Ages.* Crowell, 1969, 127
pp., OP (6-up).
Primary listing under *Mathematics*.

A fascinating account of the life and work of a brilliant Italian mathematician (early thirteenth century).
His book on the use of the Hindu/Arabic system of
numbers, the system we use today, played a significant
part in the mathematical revolution that made so many
modern concepts possible. Well written, and full of
colorful sidelights on the culture of the time.

FRANKLIN

□ d'Aulaire, Ingri and Edgar Parin. *Benjamin Franklin.*
Illus. by author. Doubleday, 1950, 48 pp. (2-4).
A splendid biography of Franklin. Lively, accurate,
beautifully written, with a wealth of fascinating detail
about this famous American. Large, lavishly illustrated
picture-book format, but substantial text included. The
book can be used in relation to pre-Revolutionary/Re-
volutionary American history and also to science and
technology (Franklin's inventions and discoveries).

□ Franklin, Benjamin. *The Whistle.* Illus. by George
Overlie. Lerner, 1974 (1779), 32 pp. (3, 4-up).
A wonderful little autobiographical story about not pay-
ing too high a price—for either objects or men's regard. The woodcut illustrations and very attractive
overall graphics pleasingly enhance the 200-year-old
words of wisdom.

GORGAS

□ Judson, Clara Ingram. *Soldier Doctor*. Scribner's, 1942, 151 pp. (4-9).

The enthralling story of General William Gorgas whose untiring and gifted work in public health rid the world of yellow fever and brought relief to countless people from a variety of other ills which his effective help either entirely eliminated or greatly reduced. Written in a lively, fast-moving narrative style, the biography starts with young Willie as a high-spirited ten-year-old during the last year of the Civil War. Even at that early age, William is determined to be a soldier, but he has no idea of the role he will eventually play as an army doctor. Because they are Southern people, William and his family experience some years of great privation following the end of the war; and even when his father becomes a university faculty member, there is little to spare for William's medical training. Persistence and industry, but most of all a kind, patient and unpretentious nature, characterized this man who did so much for the world's welfare and of whom so few people today have even heard.

GRENFELL

□ Ready, Dolores. *Wilfred's Hospital Ship*. Winston Press, 1977 (1, 2).

A lively, brief, picture-book account of Grenfell's missionary work in Labrador. This could be tied in with a social studies unit that included Labrador, or simply used as a supplement for reading.

HAYDN

□ Lasker, David. *The Boy Who Loved Music*. Viking, 1979, 48 pp. (2-5).

An easy-reading biography of Franz Joseph Haydn, the famous Austrian composer who was dedicated to music from childhood on. The struggles of his early years gave place to long-lasting work for the princes Esterházy, and it was during this time that Haydn became a close friend of Mozart's. Symphonies, sonatas and oratorios are among the beautiful forms of music that are a heritage from this much-loved composer.

HEZEKIAH

□ Prokop, Phyllis S. *The Sword and the Sundial.* David C. Cook, 1981 (5, 6).

> Primary listing under *Literature, Level III, Realistic Stories—Historical.*
>
> A fictionalized story of the dramatic life of Hezekiah, an eighth century B.C. king of Judah. The story is based on the Biblical account, with material added where the Bible is silent.

JENKINS

□ Jenkins, Peter and Barbara. *A Walk Across America; The Walk West: A Walk Across America 2.* Morrow, 1979, 288 pp.; 1981, 349 pp. (6-up).

> Peter Jenkins was a warm, outgoing young man, but he was troubled. Was America as terrible as so many people were saying it was? Peter decided to find out for himself by walking across the land and in the process becoming acquainted with as wide a variety of people as possible. Starting in upper New York state, he walks his way south, stopping to work when necessary, finding interesting, worthwhile people everywhere. The end of the second book finds him at the sea, the edge of the land in Florence, Oregon. The miles (over 4700) and the years (more than five) have not only convinced him of the wonder and beauty of America, but have profoundly changed his life. On his journey and while in the deep South he has become a born-again Christian and, later, has met and married Barbara, an attractive seminary student. Together they continue Peter's quest, often under less than ideal conditions. Wonderful true stories of people and adventure and the natural world, sometimes touching, sometimes very funny—all illumined by the warm, strong spirits of Peter and Barbara.

KELLER

□ Davidson, Margaret. *Helen Keller.* Illus. by Vicki Fox. Scholastic, 1973, 94 pp. (k-3).

> A lively account of the life of Helen Keller written for early readers. The writer has focused effectively on the highlights of Keller's life, with a high proportion of the book dealing with her childhood and youth. Children

are given a good introduction to the inspiring story of the little blind and deaf girl who became an educated and articulate woman.

□ Graff, Stewart and Polly Anne. *Helen Keller*. Illus. by author. Dell, 1966, 80 pp. (2-6).
  The Graffs' approach to the life of Helen Keller, although definitely an "easy read" book, has a somewhat broader scope than Davidson's (see above) and tells more about Keller's adult years. Since these were such significant years, reading both books would round out the picture helpfully. The language in this account, though simple, is a bit more sophisticated than that of Davidson.

KURELEK
□ Kurelek, William. 2 books, companion volumes: *A Prairie Boy's Winter; A Prairie Boy's Summer*. Tundra Books, 1973, 48 pp.; 1975, 47 pp. (4-up, read to some in 2, 3). See also *Art* and *History*.
  Fine evocations of what it was like to grow up on a Canadian prairie farm in the 1930s. The son of a Ukranian immigrant, Kurelek went on to graduate from college, and then, to the dismay of his father, to become a painter. From the other side of the years of struggle and conflict, the renowned artist remembers his boyhood and a distinctive way of life unknown to today's children.

□ Kurelek, William. *Lumberjack*. Houghton Mifflin, 1974, 48 pp. (4-up, read to some 2, 3).
  The noted Canadian artist describes life in the lumber camps of another era. Working as a lumberjack in 1946 and again in 1951, Kurelek's artist's memory retained even small details of that life. Simply, yet vividly told, the account preserves verbally (and pictorially) a way of life forever gone. (Lumbering is one of those processes that has completely changed over the past thirty-five years.) Both the fine text and the wonderfully realistic paintings (one on each facing page) take the reader to another time and place.

LA FLESCHE
□ Brown, Marion Marsh. *Homeward the Arrow's Flight.* Abingdon, 1980, 175 pp. (5, 6-up).
> A moving and interest-holding story of Susan La Flesche, raised on an Omaha Indian reservation and one of a remarkable family dedicated to helping their people. Susan finds that her calling is to aid the reservation Indians medically. Graduating from medical school at the head of her class, Susan becomes the first American Indian woman doctor in history. One of the most appealing aspects of the book is the lively, strong-willed, warm-hearted personality of its central character, the indomitable Dr. Susan. But Brown's account of Susan's years of education in the East also include much about the lives of Susan's family members: her father Iron Eyes, her sisters and brother—gifted, dedicated people all.

LEE
□ Commager, Henry S. *America's Robert E. Lee.* Houghton Mifflin, 1951, 111 pp. (6-up).
> Considered by many to be the greatest general of the Civil War, Robert E. Lee was both a great and a good man. He had always disliked slavery and had set his own slaves free before the Civil War. He felt great loyalty to the United States—the Union. But his deepest roots were in the state of Virginia where generations of his family had lived, and which was the home of literally hundreds of his close family connections. If Virginia seceded and came under attack by the Union, he felt he had no choice but to fight in her defense, agonizing though the decision was for him. Commager tells the story of Lee and of his part in the tragedy of the Civil War.

LIDDELL
□ Magnusson, Sally. *The Flying Scotsman.* Quartet books, 1981, 191 pp. (5-up).
> An inspiring biography of Olympic runner and missionary Eric Liddell (most recently of *Chariots of Fire* fame). The approach is journalistic rather than literary, but it is good journalism, treating its subject with integ-

rity and accuracy. Liddell's warmth, Christian commitment, transparent simplicity, and unselfish love for others come through strongly—yet there is nothing stuffy, self-righteous or preachy either in Liddell himself or in the tone of the book. A remarkable man, one who truly lived his deeply held faith, Liddell's life story is both highly interesting and spiritually challenging to read.

LINDBERGH

□ Collins, David R. *Charles Lindbergh: Hero Pilot*. Illus. by Victor Mays. Garrard, 1978, 80 pp. (2-5).

When he was still only a boy, Charles Lindbergh became interested in flying. In his first year of college, he decided that most of what he was studying had no interest at all for him. He left school and rode his motorcycle to Nebraska where an airplane company was looking for student pilots. From that time on his life was inseparably bound with flying. Collins tells the eventful story of Lindbergh's life and of the flight across the Atlantic that made history and forever linked the airplane and Lindbergh in the minds of millions of people.

LONGFELLOW

□ Holberg, Ruth Langland. *An American Bard: The Story of Henry Wadsworth Longfellow*. Harper & Row, 1963, 168 pp. (6-up).

The most popular American poet in his day, Longfellow is still read to some extent, though literary critics have not looked kindly on his work for many years. Simple, straightforward, usually strongly rhymed and often sentimental, the poetry of Longfellow belongs largely to the past. But part of our American literary heritage are such treasured pieces as "The Village Blacksmith," "Paul Revere's Ride," "The Courtship of Miles Standish," "Evangeline," "The Story of Hiawatha" and others. Holberg tells the story of the gentle, book-loving man whose chief desire from boyhood on had been to write poetry. For some years it was necessary for Longfellow to earn a living as a professor of modern languages, first at Bowdoin, then for many years at Harvard, and his writing of poetry had to be done "on the side." His life was darkened twice by the

death of a loved wife, but in spite of tragedy and loss
he retained his warm, outgoing spirit. Before he was fifty, his poetry had become so popular that he was able
to leave teaching entirely and devote himself solely to
his literary career, honored widely both in Europe and
at home.

LUTHER

□ Nohl, Frederick. *Martin Luther: Hero of Faith.*
Concordia, 1962 (6-up).

A narrative account of Luther's life and a clear state-
ment of the important evangelical beliefs which he pro-
claimed. Written in a brisk, informal style, the book includes personal anecdotes and a chapter on Luther as a
family man. Since, however, years of Luther's life were
spent in theological protest and debate, there is a great
deal of material relating to such matters. Teachers/par-
ents will need to determine the most helpful ways to
use this biography, one of which would be to focus on
selected excerpts after having preread the material themselves.

MAGELLAN

□ Syme, Ronald. *Magellan: First Around the World.* Illus. by
William Stobbs. Morrow, 1953, 71 pp. (3-7).

An excellent early-grades biography of the indomitable
Magellan, the Portuguese seaman who had the vision to
realize that it was possible to sail completely around the
world. Well-educated and born to a family of wealth
and standing, Magellan became so enthralled with the
idea of sailing to strange new lands that as a young man
he went to sea as a common sailor in order to start his
life of exploring by sea. Eventually he was given com-
mand of a ship, and all the while he was listening to accounts of newly discovered routes, of adventurous voyages to places that had never before been reached by
ship. Gradually his conviction grew: there *must* be an
ocean west of America, and beyond that lay the lands of
the Far East. And *he* would find the passage to that
western sea. Syme tells the exciting story of that expedi-
tion and of the vindication of Magellan's belief.

MAYO
□ Goodsell, Jane. *The Mayo Brothers*. Illus. by Louis S. Glanzman. Harper & Row, 1972, 44 pp. (2-5).

A well-done biography of the famous Mayo brothers for early-grades readers. Always very different from each other in appearance and personality, the brothers were nonetheless close lifelong friends. Both became doctors, following in the footsteps of their father, and later developed the world-famous Mayo Clinic. This brief book is only an introduction to the Mayos' lives and work. Interested older students may want to look for adult-level books on these gifted, dedicated doctors and their clinic.

NEWTON
□ Knight, David C. *Isaac Newton: Mastermind of Modern Science* (Immortals of Science Series). Franklin Watts, 1961, 153 pp., OP (6-up).

A detailed and well-written account of the life of Sir Isaac Newton (1642-1727), one of history's most important scientists. Knight includes many lively anecdotes, as well as the facts about Newton's studies and discoveries. In addition to Newton's scientific genius, he was also a devout Christian and a humble, unassuming man, absorbed in his lifelong search for knowledge rather than the pursuit of fame or power.

PENN
□ Foster, Genevieve. *The World of William Penn*. Scribner's, 1973, 192 pp. (5-9).

Primary listing under *History*.

In this "horizontal history" of the world of Penn's day, his own biography is briefly told, interspersed with accounts of people and events occurring more or less concurrently in different parts of the world. One of the most honorable and humane of men, Penn had more than his share of misfortune, but has left a heritage of goodwill and brotherly love that surround his memory to this day.

POTTER
□ Aldis, Dorothy. *Nothing Is Impossible.* Atheneum, 1969, 156 pp. (3-7).

> Shy, lonely and dominated by self-centered parents who had little or no understanding of a child's needs, Beatrix Potter nonetheless had an inner core of strength and determination—and a well of interest and talents that overflowed in spite of her narrowly restricted life. From the time she had been a small girl, Beatrix had kept little animals as pets. She also had a great love for the natural world and a remarkable talent for drawing. All of these aspects of her life came together with the delightful, whimsical quality of her imagination. Dorothy Aldis has written a warm and sympathetic account of the life and work of one of the most famous of children's writers.

ROOSEVELT, THEODORE
□ Foster, Genevieve. *Theodore Roosevelt: An Initial Biography.* Scribner's, 1954, 106 pp. (4-up).

> Foster has infused this biography with the warm, straightforward, energetic personality of Theodore (Teddy) Roosevelt. Even as a child plagued by asthma, Roosevelt never focused on his ills, but made consistent efforts to build himself up physically, kept himself involved in active projects, and, when forced to spend time in bed, used it to read widely, particularly in history and science. In the course of his active life, Roosevelt was a rancher, explorer, heroic military commander, state governor, and then President of the United States. Through it all he was a devoted husband and father, never so happy as when the whole family were together in their home, Sagamore Hill. Many readers will want to know more of the life of this many-sided, warmly human man.

SINGER
□ Singer, Isaac Bashevis. *A Day of Pleasure.* Farrar, Strauss & Giroud, 1969, 221 pp. (6-up).

> The noted Jewish author has collected a number of his autobiographical stories of his childhood in Poland and grouped them in this volume. The stories are, of

course, beautifully written, but more than that, they open a window into the lives of Hasidic Jews (Singer's father was a rabbi) in Poland preceding and during World War I. It is a world of which most Americans are completely ignorant and the reader is jolted by its strangeness, appalled by its poverty—an extreme poverty that, in the Western world, seldom coexists with scholarly study and the discussion of intellectual ideas as it does in this account. Some teachers and parents may want to read selections aloud, omitting the theological questions the writer had as a boy. Others will want advanced students to read this for themselves and discuss the problems raised. The questions are ones they will eventually encounter—or be asking for themselves.

STOWE

□ Johnston, Johanna. *Harriet and the Runaway Book.* Illus. by author. Harper & Row, 1977, 80 pp., OP (1-4).

The story, in brief, of Harriet Beecher Stowe and of her writing of *Uncle Tom's Cabin.* Stowe's emotion-filled story of the evils of slavery had an immeasurable impact on public sentiment in the North, motivated countless people to take a firm antislavery stance, and unquestionably furthered the cause of freedom for the slaves. Easy reading.

TALLCHIEF

□ Tobias, Tobi. *Maria Tallchief.* Crowell, 1970, 32 pp. (2-6).

Primary listing under *Dance.*

A brief, generously illustrated biography of Elizabeth Marie Tallchief, the beautiful Indian girl who became the prima ballerina Maria Tallchief. As a teenager, Maria had to choose between music and dance, and then to work very hard in her chosen art of ballet. She danced successfully for some years. But after she had a little daughter she very much missed being with her family; so she left dancing in order to stay home with her husband, an engineer, and her little girl, Elise Maria.

TUDOR

□ Tudor, Bethany. *Drawn from New England: Tasha Tudor.* Philomel, 1979, 95 pp. (5-up).

> The daughter of artist Tasha Tudor has written a fascinating text-and-picture biography of her famous mother. Choosing a rural life in New England, the artist accomplished her work of writing and/or illustrating more than sixty children's books, while taking an active part in growing and preparing food, caring for animals—and rearing four children. Written with the intimate knowledge only a member of the family would possess, and illustrated with family photographs and snapshots (and many of the artist's book illustrations, paintings and drawings) the book is not only a delight to read, but presents an inspiring picture of a gifted artist who remained true to her deep convictions as to how her life should be lived.

TYNDALE

□ Drewery, Mary. *Devil in Print.* McKay, 1966, 216 pp. (5-up).

> Primary listing under *Literature, Level III, Realistic Stories—Historical.*
>
> The book is not primarily a biography of Tyndale, but he is one of the central figures in this story of a young boy who helps Tyndale in a day when translating the Bible into English was heresy punishable by death.

□ O'Dell, Scott. *The Hawk That Dare Not Hunt By Day.* Houghton Mifflin, 1975, 222 pp. (6-up).

> Primary listing under *Literature, Level III, Realistic Stories—Historical.*
>
> Not primarily a biography of Tyndale, but he is a very significant figure in the story. His courage and dedication are clearly portrayed as he risks his life (which he ultimately sacrifices) to put the Bible into English and make God's Word available to the common man.

VANDER SCHRIER

□ Vander Schrier, Nettie. *The Golden Thread*. Moody Press, 1983, 175 pp. (6-up).

The inspiring and suspenseful story of a young Dutch woman who survived the unbelievable hardships and dangers of the Nazi occupation during World War II. Nettie's story starts in her early childhood, some years before war strikes Holland, a childhood troubled by the deaths of a sister and brother, and the effect these deaths had on her mother. Later, the untimely death of her beloved father, the only parent who showed her tenderness and warmth, turns Nettie into a sullen, embittered teenager, full of rage against life and against God. An unexpected encounter with the Salvation Army has a life-changing impact on Nettie, and it is with faith and courage that she faces the war years with their seemingly endless variety of miseries, including near-starvation. Her account of the bombing of Rotterdam and of the suspenseful years that followed make exciting reading, as well as adding another segment to the reader's knowledge of World War II history.

VERNE

□ Freedman, Russell. *Jules Verne: Portrait of a Prophet*. Holiday House, 1965, 256 pp., OP (6-up).

This wonderfully interesting account of the life and work of Jules Verne reads almost like fiction itself. The gifted imagination and intense energy of the man who vividly wrote of men sailing *Twenty Thousand Leagues Under the Sea,* of traveling *Around the World in Eighty Days,* and of countless other adventures were so strong that eighty years after his death a reader can sense their power. Freedman has effectively portrayed Verne and commented perceptively on the keenness of his vision. Verne combined indefatigable reading about science and technology with the storyteller's powers of invention. The result of this combination captured the imaginations of countless young readers, a number of whom went on to build submarines, undertake explorations, break "round-the-world" time records, and become space-age scientists.

WASHINGTON, BOOKER T.

☐ Washington, Booker T. *Up from Slavery*. Doubleday, 1963
(1901), 243 pp. (5-up).

> The classic autobiography of an outstanding American,
> Booker T. Washington. Born a slave just before the out-
> break of the Civil War, Washington, though soon freed,
> struggled desperately to obtain an education and to
> help his people achieve a quality of life that would pro-
> vide opportunity and personal dignity. He became an
> educator and a worker for civil rights.
>
> Washington was honored repeatedly for his achieve-
> ments, and was the founder of the outstanding black
> college, Tuskegee Institute.

WASHINGTON, GEORGE

☐ d'Aulaire, Ingri and Edgar Parin. *George Washington*.
Illus. by author. Doubleday, 1936, 55 pp. (1-4).

> This is an excellent introductory biography of Washing-
> ton. It could be read to preschool and first grade stu-
> dents, self-read by competent second grade and up stu-
> dents. It has a large picture-book format with
> wonderful illustrations, but also includes a substantial
> amount of text.

WESLEY, JOHN

☐ McNeer, May and Lynd Ward. *John Wesley*. Abingdon,
1951, 55 pp. (4-up).

> An interest-holding account of the life of John Wesley,
> one of the founders of Methodism. A small, almost frail
> man who twice fought off tuberculosis, Wesley con-
> stantly expended his energy in his service to God and
> his fellowman; yet he lived (and continued preaching)
> until he was eighty-eight. McNeer has included excel-
> lent background material on the eighteenth-century
> England of Wesley's time, complemented by Ward's
> carefully researched illustrations done in full-color. The
> book focuses on Wesley's efforts to effect social reforms
> and to minister to the needy. The evangelical aspects of
> his ministry are virtually omitted, but the book offers a
> fine introduction to John Wesley and his family and is a
> tribute to his faith and tremendous accomplishments.

WILBERFORCE

□ Lawson, Audrey and Herbert Lawson. *The Man Who Freed the Slaves: The Story of William Wilberforce*. Faber and Faber, OP (5-up).

Born to wealth and comfort, with great natural gifts and personal charm, Wilberforce as a young man dedicated his life to serving God and his fellowman. One of the causes he worked for most of his life was the outlawing by England of the slave trade and the abolition of slavery. Both were accomplished, the latter part of the process just two days before he died. During his life, Wilberforce also concerned himself with the needs of many other poverty-stricken or oppressed groups: chimney sweeps, children factory workers, lawbreakers being punished far too severely, the unevangelized in foreign lands, even ill-treated animals. For forty-five years he served in Parliament, persistently pressing for justice and mercy for those in all walks of life. The Lawsons' biography of Wilberforce tells in a lively narrative manner the story of this great and good man. (Unfortunately, this book is not easy to find, but is well worth the effort to track it down through interlibrary loan.)

WILDER

□ Wilder, Laura Ingalls. *On the Way Home*. Harper & Row, 1962, 101 pp. (3-up).

After the death in 1957 of the much-loved author of the Little House books, a diary she had kept in 1894 was discovered among her things. The entries record the journey of Almanzo and Laura as they left South Dakota and traveled to Mansfield, Missouri, the place where they were to spend the rest of their long lives. The Wilders' only child, Rose Wilder Lane, has framed the diary account with opening and closing chapters that put the journey in context and provide a setting for the glimpses of frontier life given in the journal.

□ Wilder, Laura Ingalls. *West from Home*. Harper & Row, 1974, 124 pp. (4-up).

>In 1915, Laura (who later wrote the Little House books) visited her daughter, Rose Wilder Lane, in San Francisco. Her letters home to her husband, Almanzo (whom she called Manly), during her two-month stay were found among Rose's things several years after the latter's death in 1968. Wanting to share her experiences with Manly, Laura writes of her trip west and of her impressions of San Francisco.

□ Zochert, Donald. *Laura*. Contemporary Books, 1976, 260 pp. (6-up).

>A thoroughly researched account of the life of Laura Ingalls Wilder, author of the beloved Little House books. The book is well worth reading in relation to the quantity and variety of factual material presented, but as a biography it leaves something to be desired. In spite of the writer's dutifully sympathetic approach to Laura's life, there is an intangible lack, a kind of underlying remoteness. As a result, there is too often a strong sense that Zochert has simply tried to pass on as much as possible of the material he has researched (what items were being sold in the stores in the communities near where Laura and her family lived, what the names of some townspeople were, and other trivia) while never really quite understanding Laura or her family. Even biographies, if they are to give the reader a sense of a life as it was lived, must have an essential empathy and a "story" quality which Zochert's careful compilation of facts and respectful tone just don't convey.

SIX EIGHTEENTH-CENTURY AMERICAN PIONEERS
□ Steele, William O. *Westward Adventure: The True Stories of Six Pioneers*. Harcourt, Brace, Jovanovich, 1962, 188 pp. (5-up).

>Spanning the eighteenth century in chronological order, the writer has told of the adventurous treks, in what was then the American West, of six widely different people (one of them a woman captured by Indians). Each person, none of whom is famous or remembered, emerges as a distinct individual, with his (or her) own

reasons for making the hazardous journeys. Certain qualities, however, of determination, ingenuity and endurance seem common to all, and the ways in which each person pursued his or her particular goal make fascinating, thought-provoking reading.

FAMOUS MATHEMATICIANS

□ Stonaker, Frances Benson. *Famous Mathematicians.* Harper & Row, 1966, 118 pp. (4-9).
    Listed also under *Mathematics.*

    Easy-reading accounts (in brief) of the lives and work of eleven famous mathematicians, from ancient times onward. This is an excellent way to introduce students to these men whose work contributed so significantly to major developments in the history of civilization, men about whom all students should have at least a basic core of general knowledge.

⑤ Crafts, Hobbies and Domestic Arts

☐ Allison, Linda. *Trash Artists Workshop.* Pitman Learning (all ages).
> A collection of things to make from throwaway materials. On the whole, the objects made are actually either useful or truly creative, active fun, rather than being the sort of paper plate/doily things that seem to exist solely as projects for small children to carry home to fond parents. (An occasional such decoration may be welcomed, but it is nice to see the kinds of ideas in this more practical collection.) Directions are clear, drawings to illustrate abound, and a list of likely "trash" sources is included.

☐ Barwell, Eve. *Disguises You Can Make.* Lothrop, Lee & Shepard, 1977, 111 pp. (3-up).
> Instructions for making more than two dozen disguises using masks, makeup and a variety of easy-to-make-or-find accessories. Splendid for costume parties, skits, or just "dressing up" play.

☐ Becker, Joyce. *Bible Crafts.* Holiday House, 1982, 120 pp. (all ages).
> A fine collection of things to make, related to well-known stories of the Old Testament. A wide variety of craft techniques are used in this enjoyable book.

☐ Beede, Gretchen. *Simple Sewing.* Illus. by G. Overlie. Lerner, 1975, 32 pp. (1-4).
> A brief introduction to sewing that starts with the basic tools and stitches, then gives complete instructions for four fairly simple projects. (Younger children will definitely need adult help.)

□ Boxer, Arabella. *Wind in the Willows Country Cookbook.*
Scribner's, 1933, 117 pp. (5-up).
> A charming book of English recipes for older children.
> It includes "Bubble and Squeak," "Toad Hall Trifle,"
> "Steak and Kidney Pie," and many more. The book is
> enhanced by some of the Shepard illustrations and fa-
> vorite passages from *Wind in the Willows* (see *Litera-
> ture, Level II, Fantasies*).

□ Brown, Osa. *Metropolitan Museum of Art Activity Book.*
Random House, 1983, 88 pp. (4-up).
> An attractive group of crafts, models, toys, games and
> mazes to make and do, all inspired by treasures now in
> the Museum's collection. A quite special book.

□ Chorzempa, Rosemary A. *My Family Tree Workbook:
Genealogy for Beginners.* Dover, 1982, 64 pp. (4-up).
> A practical workbook in which to record family data as
> to parentage and ancestry. For those with a developing
> interest in genealogy, the book provides a solid start-
> ing-point: guidance on how to go about tracing ances-
> tors and a short bibliography of related resource books.
> For those who don't care to pursue such a quest, the
> workbook simply gives each child a compact listing of
> family information that might readily be referred to in
> later years for the kind of factual information often re-
> quested for school assignments, passports and high-se-
> curity jobs.

□ Cobb, Vicki. *The Secret Life of School Supplies.* Illus. by Bill
Morris. Lippincott, 1981, 82 pp. (3-up).
> Fascinating facts behind the origins of everyday materi-
> als such as paper, ink, pens, chalk, paste, glue, erasers
> and more. Children can make their own versions of
> these supplies. Clear instructions and explanations of
> how and why materials can be combined to produce
> the desired results help to ensure success in the projects.

□ Cone, Ferne Geller. Two books: *Crazy Crocheting.*
Atheneum, 1981, 101 pp. (4-6) and *Knutty Knitting
for Kids,* Follett, 1977, 159 pp. OP (4-up).
> Both books include basic instructions and then launch
> out into creative projects and experiments. Lots of ideas

for crazy shapes, wall hangings, hand puppets, etc. as well as some things to use and wear. Imagination, creativity and just plain fun are the operative terms.

□ Cooper, Terry and Marilyn Ratner. *Many Hands Cooking: An International Cookbook for Girls and Boys.* Crowell, 1974, 50 pp. (4-up).
A tasty and up-to-date selection of recipes from a variety of cultures. Attractively illustrated and with clear, easy-to-follow instructions.

□ Corrigan, Barbara. *I Love to Sew.* Doubleday, 1974, 139 pp. (4-7).
The writer, who has taught many children and adults to sew, has written a basic manual on sewing that is both enjoyable and practical. Illustrated throughout with drawings and photographs, the book guides the young sewer through a range of projects which gradually increase in difficulty.

□ *Betty Crocker's Cookbook for Boys and Girls.* Western Publishing, 1984 (1975), 96 pp. (4-up).
A good selection of practical recipes in a step-by-step format, using clear, helpful illustrations. A variety of basic information is also given as to equipment, terms, and cautions.

□ Cummings, Richard. *Make Your Own Model Forts and Castles.* McKay, 1977, 122 pp. (5, 6-up).
All seven projects are based on actual historical fortifications. They range from simple to fairly complex. Detailed instructions are given. Fine simply for developing skills and for pleasure, but also excellent as history-related projects.

□ Emal, Janet and Barbara Kern. *Kids Cook Microwave.* HP Books, 1982, 80 pp. (3-up).
A no-frills, clearly stated little book that addresses a contemporary reality. Many kids need to know how to properly use a microwave oven. Not only the format, but also the choices of the recipes is basic and provides just the kind of guidance needed.

□ Félix, Monique. *Yum Yum! I'll Be My Own Cook.* Green
Tiger Press, 1983, 32 pp. (3-up).
> A wonderful picture cookbook with almost thirty rec-
> ipes, given in a fresh, graphic manner sure to appeal to
> young cooks. The illustrations (color drawings) are fun
> simply to look at.

□ Herda, D. J. *Model Boats and Ships.* Franklin Watts, 1982,
63 pp. (4-up).
> Helpful instructions for achieving the best results in
> making boat and ship models. Both tabletop and radio-
> controlled types are discussed. Although basic instruc-
> tions come with model kits, anyone who has ever tried
> to use one realizes that, for the beginner at least, more
> help is often needed. Herda gives some background on
> the history of boats and ships, discusses techniques in
> building plastic and wood models, offers tips on paint-
> ing and finishing, and concludes with a chapter on ra-
> dio-controlled models that sail and race.

□ Hogrogian, Nonny. *Handmade Secret Hiding Places.* Illus.
by author. Overlook Press, 1975, 48 pp. (all ages).
> Ideas for the youngster who longs for a little hideaway
> he can construct in a hurry. Clever illustrative drawings
> accompany brief instructions for making a pole bean
> teepee, a dugout, a between-the-chairs hideout, and sev-
> en other secret hiding places.

□ Johnson, Hannah Lyons. *Let's Make Soup.* Lothrop, Lee
and Shepard, 1976, 26 pp. (3-up).
> Detailed, photographically illustrated instructions on
> making old-fashioned beef and vegetable soup, from
> making the stock (broth) on up. Suggestions for vari-
> ations, and instructions for making chicken soup are
> also included.

□ Kirkman, Will. *Nature Crafts Workshop.* Pitman Learning
(3-up).
> A varied collection of craft and study projects using
> plants and animals. Hatching eggs in a home-made in-
> cubator and growing personalized pumpkins are just
> two of the more than forty projects.

□ Lasky, Kathryn. *The Weaver's Gift*. Frederick Warne, 1980, 64 pp. (all ages).

This is *not* a how-to book, but rather a wonderful birth-of-a-lamb-to-beautifully-woven-blanket account of the way wool is grown, sheared, spun, and woven. The sheep in this book are raised by a young Vermont couple, and the many accompanying pictures were taken by the author's husband, a former *National Geographic* photographer.

The book is more than a documentary on wool and weaving, for the writer captures the effort, the love, the satisfaction inherent in true craftsmanship. An added virtue of the book is its combination of clarity and simplicity with an effective vocabulary and style that doesn't talk down to the reader.

□ Lightbody, Donna M. *Braidcraft*. Lothrop, Lee & Shepard, 1976, 96 pp. (4-up).

A practical, clearly illustrated manual that includes a variety of braided projects that are genuinely attractive and useful. Braiding is one of the easiest crafts to master, and readers will be surprised to learn the variations that are possible and the satisfying results that can be achieved by even a rank amateur.

□ Maginley, C. J. *Models of America's Past and How to Make Them; Historic Models of Early America and How to Make Them*. Harcourt, Brace, Jovanovich, 1969, 144 pp; 1947, 156 pp. (4-7).

Both of these books give instructions, detailed materials lists, and drawings on how to make models of a wide variety of early American buildings, furniture, accessories, bridges, vehicles and more. Generally speaking, a substantial amount of adult help would be needed, but the books do provide specifications for many objects. Something to keep in mind: the writer specifies dimensions but does not discuss the scale he is using. Thus, if the model-maker wanted to use a particular scale, such as the 1-inch to 1-foot scale most common among current miniature makers, he might need to make some changes in dimensions.

□ Mariolti, Mario. *Hanimals*. Green Tiger Press, 1982, 36 pp. (2-up).

A clever little wordless book entirely made up of color photographs of the human hand (and often the forearm as well) immersed in a base color (water-based paint), then drawn upon with other colors to simulate an animal or bird. The hand and fingers are, of course, held in specific positions. The effects are both amazing and amusing, the sort of thing to encourage imagination and creativity.

□ May, Rosalind G. *Exciting Things to Make with Wool, String and Thread*. Harper & Row, 1977, 45 pp. (3-up).

A particularly well-done book of instructions for a variety of projects. The step-by-step directions are pictured clearly and attractively. Wool wrapping, braiding, finger weaving and gluing wool are only some of the types of yarn/string/thread craft included.

□ Meyer, Carolyn. *Miss Patch's Learn-to-Sew Book*. Harcourt, Brace, Jovanovich, 1969, 96 pp. (5-up).

A pleasingly written step-by-step introduction to sewing, for girls old enough to work with detail, follow instructions and stay with a project to its completion. Instructions are very clear and detailed—in fact, the language would be easily understood by a younger child, but the projects are more challenging than she could manage. Instructions for a nice variety of items are given.

□ Perl, Lila. *Hunter's Stew and Hangtown Fry: What Pioneer America Ate and Why*. Houghton Mifflin, 1977, 176 pp. (6-up).

A fascinating glimpse into pioneer history in America from the perspective of the eating habits of various groups and regions. The writer not only relates food to the events of the time, but traces the development of early kinds of cooking into contemporary eating styles. Twenty authentic pioneer recipes are included.

☐ Perl, Lila. *Slumps, Grunts, and Snickerdoodles: What Colonial America Ate and Why.* Houghton Mifflin, 1975, 128 pp. (6-up).

> The writer offers thirteen authentic Colonial recipes, but this is much more than a cookbook. In providing background information on corn oysters, shoo-fly pie, snickerdoodles and other foods, Perl also tells her readers much about the cultural history of the day.

☐ Pfrommer, Marian. *On the Range: Cooking Western Style.* Atheneum, 1981, 95 pp. (4-6).

> A collection of hearty recipes of the kind of flavorsome food most youngsters enjoy—and enjoy cooking. General cooking instructions and cautions are followed by the recipes, all marked to indicate degrees of complexity from "Tenderfoot," to "Range Rider," to "Bronc Busters." Fun to read, make—and eat.

☐ Purdy, Susan. *Christmas Cooking Around the World.* Franklin Watts, 1983, 96 pp. (4-up).

> A collection of delicious Christmas foods to make from countries around the world. Recipes have clear, easy-to-follow directions.

☐ Purdy, Susan and Cass R. Sandak. Civilization Project Books Series, Franklin Watts, all 1982, 32 pp. (4-6). Ancient Egypt, Ancient Rome, Ancient Greece, Aztecs, Eskimos, North American Indians.

> This series offers craft projects which reflect historical/cultural aspects of life among the cultures indicated in the books' titles. Each book has ten to twelve projects, with instructions and diagrams/illustrations. A brief summary of the country's history and people opens each book. Excellent for use with related social studies classwork and also for crafts fans in general.

□ Rasmussen, Richard and Rhonda Lee. *The Kids'
Encyclopedia of Things to Make and Do.* Oak Tree, 1981,
244 pp. (all ages).
Over two hundred pages of ideas range from experiments and projects related to air (movement, weight,
pressure, etc.) to home-designed wrapping paper. The
suggestions are short, simple and workable rather than
elaborate and complicated. Sufficient information is
given, then the child is on his or her own, free to create
as imagination leads.

□ Rubenstone, Jessie. Three books: *Knitting for Beginners;
Crochet for Beginners; Weaving for Beginners.* Harper &
Row, 1973, 64 pp.; 1974, 64 pp.; 1975, 80 pp. (3, 4).
Clear, step-by-step instruction for beginners. Each pro-
cedure is illustrated in helpful photos, and directions are
given for the kind of simple, uncomplicated articles the
new knitter, crocheter or weaver can handle successfully.

□ Schwartz, Paul D. *You Can Cook.* Atheneum, 1976, 192
pp. (5-up).
A well-put-together book of basic recipes for older children who have some idea of how to handle cooking
techniques. Soups, main courses, vegetables, salads,
breads and desserts are all included, as well as separate
sections on breakfast suggestions and other menu ideas.
Careful instructions accompany each recipe, and an especially helpful feature is the listing in the front of the
book of general cooking hints, measurements and definitions.

□ Shapiro, Rebecca. Two books: *Wide World Cookbook; A
Whole World of Cooking.* Little, Brown & Co., 1962, 58
pp.; 1972, 70 pp. (5-up).
Each volume contains one or more distinctive but sim-
ple-to-make recipes from several dozen different countries. Hard-to-obtain ingredients have been avoided,
and children who are flexible about trying new foods
can have a delightful time working their way through
the varied flavors of these international dishes.

☐ Sisson, Edith A. *Nature with Children of All Ages.*
Prentice-Hall, 1982, 195 pp. (all ages).
> Primary listing under *Teaching Resources.*
>
> Sisson's book includes some enjoyable nature-relat-
> ed craft projects and hobbies.

☐ Thompson, David. *Easy Woodstuff for Kids.* Gryphon
House, 1981, 115 pp. (all ages).
> The writer combines his love for fine carpentry with his
> interest in children. The book's projects are all ones he
> has worked through many times with children and his
> lists of materials, instructions and illustrations are clear
> and detailed. The twenty-seven projects range from
> simple to somewhat complex. Beginning projects using
> sticks, nuts and berries can be done by quite young
> children. At the next level are birdhouses, trivets and
> wood jewelry, with still-more-advanced undertakings
> suggested for older children.

☐ Tunis, Edwin. *Colonial Living.* Harper & Row, 1957,
155 pp. (5-up, or all ages with adult guidance).
> Primary listing under *History.*
>
> The book contains information and drawings relat-
> ed to Colonial American artifacts. Useful either for his-
> tory-related projects or recreational crafts.

☐ Tunis, Edwin. *Indians.* Harper & Row, 1959, 157 pp.
(4-up, or all ages with adult guidance).
> Primary listing under *History.*
>
> An excellent source of detailed information and
> drawings and even some specific instructions for mak-
> ing Indian objects. Good for either history-related pro-
> jects or recreational crafts.

☐ Walker, Barbara. *The Little House Cookbook.* Harper &
Row, 1979, 240 pp. (adult/child project).
> A wonderful book of frontier foods from the Little
> House books. Walker has researched each one, adapted
> the recipes to contemporary measurements and equip-
> ment, yet retained their authentic qualities. A rich vari-
> ety of background information on cooking, eating and
> kitchens is also included, along with specific references
> to the foods as mentioned in the various stories.

□ Walker, Les. *Carpentry for Children*. Overlook Press, 1982, 208 pp. (2-up).
>A birdhouse, coaster car, puppet theater, raft and doll cradle are just a few of the projects for which plans are included in this 200-page book. It is generously illustrated with photographs, drawings and diagrams along with the writer's step-by-step instructions.

□ Walker, Les. *Housebuilding for Children*. Overlook Press, 1977, 174 pp. (2-up).
>Plans, diagrams and instructions for use in building six different child-sized houses: tree, wood-frame, junk-yard, post and beam, factory-built and glass. A crew of ten children ages seven to ten built all six of these one fall, and the writer photographed them in the process. More than ninety photographs and 150 line drawings are included.

□ Weiss, Harvey. *How to Run a Railroad: Everything You Need to Know About Model Trains*. Harper & Row, 1977, 127 pp. (5-up).
>A clear, well-written manual on model railroading that a young reader can readily understand. After thoroughly discussing general information—kinds of trains, how they work, track plans, etc.—the writer then describes the step-by-step process he himself went through in building his own layout. Photographs, drawings, and diagrams illustrate every page, and detailed instructions are given for constructing buildings, bridges, mountains, etc. This is one of an excellent series of books by the same writer on making models. Others are on airplanes, ships, cars.

Three helpful manuals for beginning stamp collectors:

□ Herst, Herman, Jr. *Fun and Profit in Stamp Collecting*. Dutton, 1962, 168 pp. (adv. 6-up).

□ Hobson, Burton H. *Getting Started in Stamp Collecting*. Sterling, 1982, 160 pp. (6-up).

□ Olcheski, Bill. *Beginning Stamp Collecting*. Mckay, 1976, 135 pp. (6-up).

Eight helpful ethnic cookbooks

□ A series of Easy Menu Ethnic Cookbooks. Lerner, all 1982-83, 46 pp. (5-up).
> Clear, colorfully illustrated recipes for each country are in the following separate volumes. Preceding the recipes is information on the particular country, its food and customs, and comments on special ingredients. About eighteen recipes are given in each book.

□ Ling, Yu. *Cooking the Chinese Way*

□ Hill, Barbara. *Cooking the English Way*

□ Waldee, Lynne M. *Cooking the French Way*

□ Weston, Reiko. *Cooking the Japanese Way*

□ Bisignano, A. *Cooking the Italian Way*

□ Coronado, Rosa. *Cooking the Mexican Way*

□ Munsen, Sylvia. *Cooking the Norwegian Way*

□ Christian, R. *Cooking the Spanish Way*

6 Dance

☐ Ancona, George. *Dancing Is.* Dutton, 1981, 48 pp. (1-up).

> In photographs and brief text, Ancona shows a wide variety of dance forms and mentions some of the reasons people dance. He has effectively captured the spirit of movement-to-rhythmic-music, the freedom and joy that can be expressed in dance. A brief description of each dance pictured is included at the end of the book.

☐ Baylor, Byrd. *Sometimes I Dance Mountains.* Scribner's, 1973, 44 pp. (k-3).

> Dancing as a means of expressing a wide range of emotions or movements found in the natural world is the theme of this photographic book. A young girl dancer is shown interpreting wind, rain, flowers, frogs, fire ". . . because a dance can say anything," Introduces children to some of the possibilities of this form of expression.

☐ Berger, Melvin. *The World of Dance.* S. G. Phillips, 1978, 190 pp. (6-up).

> A survey-style history of dance, ranging from the earliest known forms to those of the present, both as artistic expression and as social activity. Berger takes the position that dance forms reflect existing culture, springing "from people's basic beliefs and activities." Clear and concisely stated, the value of the book is informational rather than literary.

□ Davis, Jesse. *Classics of the Royal Ballet*. Coward, McCann, Geoghegan, 1980, 81 pp. (4-up).

> The stories of six favorite ballets are told in sequential photographs and with brief textual notes by ballet critic Mary Clarke. (The notes also include a page on the history of each classic and comments on dancers especially related to specific roles.) The following ballets are shown: *The Nutcracker; Swan Lake; La Fille Mal Gardée; Giselle; Romeo and Juliet; The Sleeping Beauty.* Many readers not previously enthralled with the idea of ballet will find themselves interested in seeing some of the stories portrayed here.

□ Diamond, Donna (adapted and illustrated by). *Swan Lake*. Holiday House, 1980, 32 pp. (2-6).

> Basing her story on the original script used in the creation of Tchaikovsky's classic ballet, Diamond tells the beautiful and tragic story in the style of a Russian fairy tale.

□ Elliott, Donald. *Frogs and the Ballet*. Illus. by Clinton Arrowood. Gambit, 1979, 57 pp. (all ages).

> Using frogs (as they used alligators in the companion volume on the symphony orchestra, *Alligators and Music*), the writer and illustrator present clear directions and marvelous drawings on basic ballet positions and movements. Preceding the main body of the book is a serious foreword about ballet and a listing of the basic categorizations of ballet performance. There is both charm and humor in Elliott's method of presenting information, and this is a delightful book.

□ Fonteyn, Margot. *A Dancer's World: An Introduction for Parents and Students*. Knopf, 1979, 128 pp., OP (6-up).

> The great ballerina Margot Fonteyn offers advice based on her own extensive experience to children who want to study ballet, and to their parents who will be an important element in the endeavor. Clear, practical and well-written, the book should be of value to all parents and children interested in dance training, whether ballet or other forms of dance. (Fonteyn comments in the book on modern dance, folk, ethnic, jazz and tap.)

□ Godden, Rumer. *The Tale of the Tales: The Beatrix Potter Ballet*. Frederick Warne, 1971, 208 pp. (5, 6-up).

The fascinating story of the making of the film *Tales of Beatrix Potter*, (done in ballet form). Included in the book are stills from the film (which combined several Potter stories), a text woven of selections from the stories themselves, and drawings of the way the film was sequenced. Juxtaposed with the latter are the related scenes from Potter's books. The remarkable fidelity to Potter's work that was maintained in the film can thus be clearly seen.

□ Gross, Ruth Bellow. *If You Were a Ballet Dancer*. Dial Press, 1980, 48 pp. (k-5).

Using a question-answer format throughout, Gross supplies a wide variety of information about the day-to-day routines and responsibilities of a ballet student and of performing ballet artists. Generously illustrated with relevant photographs and with a simply written text, the book should answer most of the questions those considering taking ballet lessons or seriously training in that art may have.

□ Hammond, Mildred. *Square Dancing Is for Me*. Lerner, 1983, 47 pp. (3-up).

A well-illustrated introduction to this popular form of folk dancing. Elementary-age children are photographed actually doing each step, and "how-to" text accompanies each group of pictures.

□ Haney, Lynn. *I Am a Dancer*. G. P. Putnam's, 1981, 64 pp. (6-up).

Through words and photographs, the writer gives an objective view of what it means to take serious training for ballet. The focus is on three actual students, a girl and two boys, only one of whom is completely committed to ballet as a career. Informative, detailed and well expressed.

□ Hansen, Rosanna. *The Fairy Tale Book of Ballet*. Grossett
& Dunlap, 1980, 77 pp. (1-7).
> Another photographic/text treatment of favorite ballets:
> *Swan Lake, The Sleeping Beauty*, and *The Nutcracker*.
> Along with the pictures and comments on each story,
> Hansen has also included information on ballet posi-
> tions and techniques, the stories from which the ballets
> were taken, the writers and composers, some of the
> stars of the ballet. Photographically the book has a plus in
> its generous proportion of color photos; on the other
> hand, the pictures are all a little less sharp and clear
> than many of Jesse Davis's wonderful black and white
> pictures in *Classics of the Royal Ballet*.

□ Mara, Thalia, with Lee Wyndham. *First Steps in Ballet*.
Doubleday, 1955, 64 pp. (3-up).
> A much-used book for more than thirty years, Mara
> not only details a wealth of basic barre exercises for
> home practice (not intended as a guide for self-instruc-
> tion but as an aid in home practice for the ballet stu-
> dent), but also includes a helpful foreword for parents.
> In this, she emphasizes the importance of having only a
> bona fide teacher of ballet for a child, and specifies
> ways by which a teacher's qualifications can be deter-
> mined. Comments on what constitutes a well-structured
> class and program are also noted.

□ Nelson, Esther L. *Dancing Games for Children of All Ages*.
Sterling, 1973, 72 pp. (ps-up).
> Each of the over thirty-five dance games is described
> step-by-step and accompanied by simple piano arrange-
> ments of the music for each dance. Nelson gives good
> suggestions throughout as to how to involve reluctant
> participants, how to develop variations, etc. Some help-
> ful comments about using the material with retarded or
> otherwise handicapped children are also included.

□ Streatfeild, Noel. *A Young Person's Guide to Ballet*.
Frederick Warne, 1975, 120 pp. (3-up).
> Children's writer Streatfeild has created a quite compre-
> hensive treatment, focusing primarily on ballet (basic
> steps, history, famous ballet dancers and schools), but
> she also discusses other forms of dancing. Streatfeild

approaches her topic by following the progress of two real children, Anna and Peter, in their dance training. The text, though factual, has a pleasing literary quality, and there are fine drawings and photographs to illustrate the material being discussed. This is a particularly good book for any and all children to read, for it is not written exclusively for those with a strong involvement in dance. As Streatfeild says to conclude her preface, "What this book tries to tell you is that, quite apart from a career, dancing is a lovely thing to be able to do and, because you have learnt something about it, watching dancing will give you pleasure all your life."

□ Tobias, Tobi. *Maria Tallchief.* Illus. by Michael Hampshire. Crowell, 1970, 32 pp. (2-6)

Tall and beautiful, Maria Tallchief, with her Osage Indian heritage, was a leading ballerina for some years. One of her most famous parts was that of a magical wild bird in *Firebird.* This brief biography tells Maria's story, from her early childhood in Oklahoma, through the years of her training and performing, and to the happy ending when she "hung up her toe shoes" and stayed home to be with her husband and little daughter.

□ Walker, Katherine Sorley. *Ballet for Boys and Girls.* Prentice-Hall, 1979, 93 pp. (3-7).

Sorley, a ballet critic for the London *Daily Telegraph,* has written a pleasing and (considering its picture-text format and relative brevity) surprisingly comprehensive discussion of ballet. The focus is not exclusively technical, but a good deal of basic information is given, as well as some of the history of the art, etc. The outstanding feature of the book is the effectiveness of the many photos which perfectly exemplify what the writer is saying and which seem to capture fully the grace and the "flying" effect which is so appealing in the ballet.

□ Zeck, Gerry. *I Love to Dance.* Carolrhoda Books, 1982, 63 pp. (1-5).

A documentary picture-story of ten-year-old dancer Tony Jones. Tony studies both ballet and contemporary dance with teachers and dance organizations in Minneapolis, Minnesota, and in the book we see and read about the variety of training and performance he is involved with. All of the preparation and instruction are vitally important for an aspiring dancer, but of primary importance is the fact that this is what Tony most enjoys and most wants to spend his time doing.

⁷Drama, Skits and Other Performances

☐ Barwell, Eve. *Disguises You Can Make*. Lothrop, Lee & Shepard, 1977, 111 pp. (3-up).
> Primary listing under *Crafts, Hobbies and Domestic Arts*.
> Instructions are given for a variety of disguises.
> These could be used in skits or impromptu children's theatricals. The section at the beginning of the book on "materials" includes tips on makeup and other theatrical supplies that could be used helpfully in making actors up for more serious kinds of dramatic projects.

☐ Berger, Melvin. *Putting on a Show*. Franklin Watts, 1980, 64 pp. (5-up).
> A concise general guide to theatrical production. The book can be read simply as information on another area of experience, one the average person has little contact with. Or it can be used as a guide for school classes or other groups who want to put on a show of some kind. Although Berger briefly discusses all aspects of the steps taken in putting on a professional style of production, his information can also be adapted to much simpler projects.

☐ Brown, John Russell. *Shakespeare and His Theatre*. Illus. by David Gentleman. Lothrop, Lee and Shepard, 1982, 64 pp. (6-up).
> In comparison with the similarly titled book by Hodges (listed below), Brown's treatment of the subject is more suited to older children. He attempts to deal with a greater variety of related matters, assumes a good deal of knowledge and sophistication on the part of his readers, and the book doesn't have the easily-followed pattern of organization which characterizes the Hodges work.

On the other hand, Brown includes much material not touched on in Hodges's book; thus both are helpful in understanding the background, setting and technical aspects of the theater of Shakespeare's time. As in Hodges's book, there is a special focus on the Globe Theatre with which Shakespeare was so closely associated.

Pleasing drawings in color enliven each page, although not as helpfully described and identified as are those in Hodges's book. Brown's book would be a good one to read a year or two later than Hodges's, particularly after some of Shakespeare's plays have been read and discussed and tie-ins with the related historical period have been made.

□ Carlson, Bernice Wells. *Let's Find the Big Idea.* Abingdon, 1982, 128 pp. (3-6).
Nineteen skits, playlets and plays are included, all based on fables. Helpful hints as to how to go about putting on these small productions are also given. The little dramas are not only enjoyable to do, but offer positive reinforcement of basic values in a form children will welcome.

□ Godden, Rumer. *The Tale of the Tales.* Frederick Warne, 1971, 208 pp. (5, 6-up).
Primary listing under *Dance.*

The story of the making of the film *Tales of Beatrix Potter,* which was done in ballet form. The details of its production, the way in which the film faithfully followed the characterizations, the "look" of Potter's work are of special interest to those attempting to work with staging, producing, etc.

□ Haley, Gail E. *Costumes for Plays and Playing.* Methuen, 1978, 134 pp. (3-up).
A splendid resource book for those who want to dress for a part, however simply or elaborately, using materials readily at hand in home or school. The subject is covered in great detail, and these details are amply illustrated. Whether children simply want to play make-believe for fun or a parent/teacher needs ideas about

costuming children for a skit or play, Haley's book offers practical, effective help.

□ Hodges, C. Walter. *Shakespeare's Theatre*. Illus. by author. Coward, McCann, 1964, 103 pp. (4-up).
Starting with the traveling entertainers of medieval times, then discussing the early religious pageants and plays, Hodges traces the emergence of acting as a profession and the building of theaters in which plays could be presented. A number of theaters are mentioned, but the book's special focus is on the Globe Theatre in which Shakespeare had a part interest and in which his plays were performed.

Hodges's own attractive illustrations combine well with his clear descriptions of the way scholars think the Globe Theatre was laid out, and how a specific play (in this case, *Julius Caesar*) may have been presented.

The book provides an excellent introduction to the way in which the dramatic form evolved in England and the framework within which Shakespeare's work, so significant in English literature and in the development of modern drama, first reached an audience.

□ Krementz, Jill. *A Very Young Circus Flyer*. Knopf, 1979, 100 pp., OP (3-up).
An appealing, true, photo-text story of a young circus "flyer" (trapeze artist). Nine-year-old Tato Farfan is the youngest member of the Flying Farfans, a Ringling Bros. and Barnum & Bailey Circus family. The book not only reads well, but writer Krementz has included many little informational details related to circus life: the care of the animals, how to get up on an elephant, etc. Its larger value for children is the opportunity it offers to expand their awareness of another way people live. Our understanding increases as we become more knowledgeable about the world's diversity.

□ McCaslin, Nellie. *Act Now! Plays and Ways to Make Them*. S. G. Phillips, 1975, 120 pp. (4-up).
A personal approach to acting, addressing itself to the individual. Anyone with the desire to do so has the basic qualities necessary to act, says the writer, and guides the reader through ways of thinking and doing that re-

sult in acting. When a person can put themselves into a story, a role, they are acting, and McCaslin moves the reader toward participation, including several informally structured plays. An excellent and helpful introduction to becoming a participant in acting.

□ Meyer, Charles R. *How to Be a Clown*. McKay, 1977, 51 pp. (4-7).
Clowns have always appealed to a large number of children, and Meyer's book will appeal to clown fans. The writer traces the history of clowning, discusses the various types of clowns, clown makeup, costuming, and (briefly) clown acts and routines.

□ Nolan, Paul T. *Folk Tale Plays Round the World*. Plays, Inc., 1982, 248 pp. (4-up).
A fine collection of sixteen one-act, royalty-free plays adapted from folk tales of countries the world over. "Robin Hood and the Match at Nottingham," "A Leak in the Dike," "The Skill of Pericles," and "Johnny Appleseed" are just four of the plays included.

□ Speaight, George. *A History of the Circus*. A. S. Barnes & Co., 1980, 216 pp. (6-up).
A detailed study of the circus and its development and present form in Europe, England, and the United States. Speaight takes his subject seriously, and the book is packed with detailed information, anecdotes, stories of famous performers. Not everyone's field of interest, but full of appeal for some.

□ Wyler, Rose and Gerald Ames. *It's All Done with Numbers*. Doubleday, 1979, 128 pp. (5, 6-up).
Primary listing under *Mathematics*.
A collection of "magic" tricks to perform involving prediction, lightning calculation, etc., all done with numbers. Successful performance depends on the dramatic flair and showmanship of the performer. Some suggested "patter" to accompany the tricks is given.

$\boxed{8}$ Geography and History

☐ Allan, Tony. *Pharaohs and Pyramids*. Usborne, 1977, 32 pp. (2-6). Time-Traveler Series.

> See the immediately following entry, for *Rome and Romans* in this same series, for a description of the approach. This is useful supplementary material.

☐ Amery, Heather and Patricia Vanags. *Rome and Romans*. Usborne, 1976, 32 pp. (2-6). Time-Traveler Series.

> A detailed captioned-drawing survey of daily life and house and city layouts in first-century Rome. Full of clusters of information, the book is more suited to reference or browsing than to primary curriculum use. Lively and attractive, the book could be usefully coordinated with other in-depth material on ancient Rome.

☐ Benchley, Nathaniel. *Sam the Minuteman*. Illus. by Arnold Lobel. Harper & Row, 1969, 62 pp. (ps-1).

> An I Can Read book with a controlled vocabulary and short, simple sentence structure. Sam goes with his father and other farmers as they encounter the British troops at Lexington, Massachusetts. (That confrontation became the start of the American Revolution.) Allowing for its "early reader" style, Benchley has done a good job of including some drama and characterization in this little book.

☐ Blackmore, Richard D. *Lorna Doone*. Buccaneer, 1981 (1869), 345 pp. (6-up).

> Primary listing under *Literature, Level III, Realistic Stories—Historical*.
>
> Rural life in seventeenth-century England (with some events in London) form the background for this

☐ 99

lovely old classic romance. Daily life conditions and social patterns of the story illumine English history of the
period.

□ Blos, Joan W. *A Gathering of Days*. Scribner's, 1979, 144
pp. (6-8).
Primary listing under *Literature, Level III, Realistic Stories—Historical*.
This fictional journal of a young New England girl
is set in about 1830. It captures effectively the speech
and flavor of the time and could help to amplify a study
of that period of American history.

□ Bowyer, Carol. *The Children's Book of Houses and Homes*.
Usborne, OP (3-up).
A captioned-picture survey of a wide variety of shelters
in which people live across the world. Like all such
books, the information is brief and specific, not in any
way taking the place of in-depth study. The value of
such material is in opening up possibilities for further
research and study, for giving students a broad view of
the diversity that exists in the structures people call
home.

□ Brady, Esther Wood. *Toliver's Secret*. Crown, 1976, 166
pp. (3-5).
Primary listing under *Literature: Level II, Realistic Stories—Historical*.
Lively adventure at the time of the American Revolution. Ellen Toliver must carry a message under hazardous circumstances that is destined for General Washington.

□ Brown, Marion Marsh. *Homeward the Arrow's Flight*.
Abingdon, 1980, 175 pp. (5, 6-up).
Primary listing under *Biography*.
American Indian, woman doctor, 1880s.

□ Bulla, Clyde Robert. *The Beast of Lor*. Illus. by Ruth
Sanderson. Crowell, 1977, 54 pp. (1-4).
Primary listing under *Literature: Level I, Realistic Sto-
ries—Historical*.

A brief, especially well-done story of a young Celtic boy in Roman Britain.

□ Burgess, Alan. *The Small Woman*. Dutton, 1957, 256 pp., OP (Adv. 5, 6-up or parent/teacher read-aloud).
Primary listing under *Biography*.
Includes excellent historical and cultural geography material on China in the 1930s and 1940s.

□ Butwin, Frances. *The Jews in America*. Lerner, 1980, 120 pp. (5, 6).
One of Lerner's In America series. The book gives quite a thorough treatment (within the limits of its modest length) of the place the Jews have had in the development and life of the United States. Excellent for a supplement to the study of American history.

This series offers a long list of ethnic-group titles, making it possible for students of almost any national background to find material on the contributions their particular ancestral category of people have made to the United States.

□ Cairns, Trevor. *The Birth of Modern Europe*. Lerner, 1975, 99 pp. (5, 6-up).
Published in the United States by Lerner, this is the seventh in the Cambridge Introduction to History series originating in England. It focuses on the political, cultural and religious movements in Europe from 1500-1715. The writer's approach is objective as he deals with the controversies and conflicting factions of history. The material is well-written, lavishly illustrated and effectively presented.

□ Cairns, Trevor. *The Middle Ages*. Lerner, 1975, 99 pp. (5, 6-up).
Another in the Cambridge series mentioned above. Again one is impressed with the comprehensive, intelligent approach, which is detailed, clear and informative. As is the case with other books of the series, the graphics are excellent.

☐ Cassandre. *Life When Jesus Was a Boy.* Judson Press, 1981, 48 pp. (3-up).

Primary listing under *Reference.*

Includes much material that would be helpful in a primary grade study of ancient history.

☐ Cates, Edwin H. *The English in America.* Lerner, 1978, 176 pp. (5, 6).

One of thirty-one titles in Lerner's In America series. This one gives a brief but effective overview of the part the English had in the founding and developing of this country. This would be an excellent supplement for use with the study of American history.

☐ Ceserani, Gian Paolo. *Marco Polo.* Illus. by Piero Ventura. G. P. Putnam's, 1982, 34 pp. (3-6).

A brief, beautifully illustrated account of Marco Polo's travels and his stay in China at the court of Kublai Khan. The text, although it simply sketches the outlines of Polo's experiences, manages to include a variety of fascinating details. Piero Ventura's drawings of the exotic settings in which Polo lived are packed with colorful, minutely precise (and authentic) details that perfectly complement the stories of the world of the powerful Khan. When, after many years, the Polos (Marco, his father and his uncle) returned home, much of what they told was disbelieved. It was only after Marco Polo's death that the world began to realize that most of his seemingly fanciful stories were all true. A good introduction to Marco Polo, and a useful book to use as a supplement to world history or geography in the medieval period.

☐ Chamberlain, Barbara. *Ride the West Wind.* David C. Cook, 1979 (5, 6).

Primary listing under *Literature: Level III, Realistic Stories—Historical.*

A story based on an actual voyage, one of the worst experienced by colonists sailing for the New World.

□ Clapp, Patricia. *Dr. Elizabeth*. Dutton, 1974, 156 pp. OP (6-up).
   Primary listing under *Biography*.
   Includes good historical background as to medical and related conditions in America in the latter half of the nineteenth century. Elizabeth Blackwell became the first woman doctor since ancient times. The picture is broadened by the fact that Blackwell never lost her childhood love for the England in which she started life; all of her older years were spent there.

□ Commager, Henry S. *America's Robert E. Lee*. Houghton Mifflin, 1951, 111 pp. (6-up).
   Primary listing under *Biography*.
   Commager's biography of the brilliant Civil War general Robert E. Lee includes a substantial amount of Civil War history, told in an interest-holding narrative form.

□ Cooke, Jean et al. *Archaeology*. Franklin Watts, 1977, 48 pp. (5-up).
   The story of famous (and some less well-known) archaeologists, their discoveries, and some of the methods used in the work of archaeology. A substantial amount of information, along with a wealth of color illustrations is packed into this relatively brief book. It provides a good overview/introduction. Students in whom it sparks an interest will want to start on a wider program of more detailed reading about specific sites.

□ Cummings, Richard. *Make Your Own Model Forts and Castles*. McKay, 1977, 122 pp. (5, 6-up).
   Primary listing under *Crafts and Hobbies*.
   Contains seven projects based on actual historical fortifications.

□ Dalgliesh, Alice. *The Columbus Story*. Illus. by Leo Politi. Scribner's, 1955, OP (1-3).
   Primary listing under *Biography*.
   Good supplemental material for use with study either of American history or European history in the era of the exploration of the New World.

□ Dalgliesh, Alice. *The Courage of Sarah Noble.* Illus. by
   Leonard Weisgard. Scribner's, 1954, 52 pp. (1-3).
   Primary listing under *Literature: Level I, Realistic Stories—Historical.*
   Based on the true story of an eight-year-old girl
   who goes with her father into the wilderness to keep
   house for him until he can build their new home and
   send for the rest of the family (which includes a young
   baby).

□ Dalgliesh, Alice. *The Thanksgiving Story.* Illus. by Helen
   Sewell. Scribner's, 1954, 32 pp. (1-3).
   A well-written story of the first Thanksgiving and the
   events leading up to it, told from the perspective of a
   fictional family, the Hopkinses. American history supplement.

□ Daugherty, James. *Daniel Boone.* Illus. by author. Viking,
   1939, 94 pp., OP (4-up).
   Primary listing under *Biography.*
   Daugherty, more than many writers, creates the feel
   of what it must have been like to push into new territory, to live intimately with the Indians, to be a significant part of American history. This is not simply the
   story of one famous man, but of a whole way of life at a
   particular time and in a particular region of our nation.

□ Daugherty, James. *The Landing of the Pilgrims.* Random
   House, 1981, 160 pp. (4-up).
   Starting with the reasons for the devout Christian
   group known as Separatists to leave England and seek a
   new home across the sea, Daugherty has written a spirited account of the whole enterprise: the years in Holland, the weary weeks at sea in the Mayflower, the first
   near-starvation years in the Plymouth settlement, the
   friendly (and the hazardous) contacts with the Indians,
   and the gradual establishment of a stable community.
   Daugherty's account not only reads like a story, but it
   conveys the courage, vision and faith of the diverse
   group of determined settlers.

□ d'Aulaire, Ingri and Edgar Parin. *Columbus*. Illus. by
author. Doubleday, 1955, 56 pp. (k-4).
> Primary listing under *Biography*.
>
> The careful research that goes into a d'Aulaire biog-
> raphy is reflected in the illuminating historical details
> that are woven naturally into the fabric of Columbus's
> story. The book provides splendid complementary ma-
> terial for use with related history curriculum.

□ d'Aulaire, Ingri and Edgar Parin. *Benjamin Franklin*.
Illus. by author. Doubleday, 1950, 48 pp. (2-4).
> Primary listing under *Biography*.
>
> Splendid American history supplement focusing on
> Franklin, one of the nation's significant early leaders.

□ De Angeli, Marguerite. *The Door in the Wall*. Doubleday,
1949, 111 pp. (3-up).
> Primary listing under *Literature: Level II, Realistic Sto-
> ries—Historical*.
>
> In late medieval England a boy crippled after an ill-
> ness learns to find purpose in life. This well-researched
> book provides good details as to the customs of its
> time. There are castle and monastery scenes depicting
> everyday routines, a military attack on a castle and so-
> cial and family interaction.

□ de Gering, Etta. *Wilderness Wife*. McKay, 1966, 138 pp.,
OP (5-up).
> Primary listing under *Biography*.
>
> De Gering has included much detail taken from let-
> ters and early accounts. These details of daily living lend
> reality and authenticity to the history of the period, and
> a book focusing on the wife of the famous Daniel
> Boone is particularly welcome, as it adds a new dimen-
> sion to what we know about the era.

□ Denny, Norman and Josephine Filmer. *The Bayeux
Tapestry*. Atheneum, 1966, OP (4-6 and up).
> The famous embroidery known as the Bayeux Tapestry
> portrays the Norman Conquest in a long, continuous
> strip. Denny and Filmer's book discusses the events as
> shown, in a carefully researched historical framework.

Sparkling, interest-holding, and excellent from a literary standpoint, the book offers rich detail and excellent background as a supplement to the study of early English history.

□ Dicks, Brian, consultant editor. *The Children's World Atlas*. Celestial Arts, 1981, 128 pp. (4-6).

This enjoyable book is much more than the conventional atlas. One section introduces basic concepts of mapping (starting with the immediate environment), then moves on to successively larger units. It then explains (with a generous use of diagrams, etc.) the structure of our planet, its landforms, bodies of water, other natural features, and discusses climate, weather, vegetation. The second part of the book examines briefly the countries of the world. A surprising amount of information is included in a colorful, attractively illustrated form. It's the sort of book that most children love to browse through. In addition, a number of relevant practical projects are given, with complete instructions—e.g., "Making a Rain Gauge," "Making an Australian Hat," "Making Gazpacho."

□ Drewery, Mary. *Devil in Print*. McKay, 1966, 216 pp., OP (5-up).

Primary listing, *Literature: Level III, Realistic Stories— Historical*.

William Tyndale's translating of the Bible into English at a time when this work is banned, is a central theme of Drewery's fictional story of a young boy who must flee from England for political reasons. Good historical background is woven into the story.

□ Fairservis, Walter A., Jr. *Mesopotamia: The Civilization That Rose Out of Clay*. Macmillan, 1964, 126 pp., OP (6-up).

Black-and-white photos and drawings illustrate this informative pictorial survey of Mesopotamia's history, art and architecture. These are of special interest to many readers because Mesopotamia (geographically next door to Babylon) is a land of Bible times.

□ Foster, G. Allen. *The Eyes and Ears of the Civil War.* Harper & Row, 1963, 168 pp. (6-up).

A lively account of the various means of communication and information transmission used during the Civil War, including signal flags, the telegraph, couriers on horseback, observational balloons and several categories of espionage. The writer is a specialist on the Civil War period and includes a great variety of information (often with a humorous note) in this different-from-the-usual perspective of those turbulent years.

□ Foster, Genevieve. *Theodore Roosevelt: An Initial Biography.* Scribner's, 1954, 106 pp. (4-up).

Primary listing under *Biography.*

Although principally focused on the life and character of Theodore Roosevelt, this biography also includes significant historical background related to national and world events either directly involving Roosevelt, or on which comment is made.

□ Foster, Genevieve. Two books: *George Washington's World; Abraham Lincoln's World.* Scribner's, 1977, 347 pp.; 1941, 348 pp. (5-up).

Each of these books tells, in a lively narrative style, some of the events (both large and small) going on in the United States and other parts of the world at various stages of its central character's life. For example, when Lincoln was a boy, David Livingstone was working long hours in a Scottish cotton mill, Charles Dickens worked for a time in a shoe blacking factory in London, and Simon Bolivar became the "great liberator" of some of the South American countries from the domination of Spain. The writer doesn't attempt to cover all of the world all of the time, or to recount continuous biographies of Washington or Lincoln. But the books help to give a broader perspective than many students have previously been aware of, and would be especially helpful as supplementary material during the study of specific periods of American history.

□ Foster, Genevieve. *The World of William Penn*. Scribner's, 1973, 192 pp. (5-9).

A combination of history and biography told in a lively, narrative style that gives a broad-horizon view of significant events during the years of William Penn's life (1644-1718). The scene moves from Pennsylvania to the Mississippi River, to France, India, England, China and Russia, focusing in each case on specific people and events that affected the course of history.

□ Fritz, Jean. *Early Thunder*. Coward, McCann, Geoghegan, 1967, 255 pp. (5-up).

Primary listing under *Literature: Level III, Realistic Stories—Historical*.

A young Tory boy living in Boston has to decide for himself where his loyalties lie. Offers good historical background on the months immediately preceding the outbreak of the American Revolution.

□ Fritz, Jean. *Brady*. Coward, McCann, 1960, 223 pp. (5-up).

Primary listing under *Literature: Level III, Realistic Stories—Historical*.

This well-written story offers good historical background reading on antislavery sentiment and activity twenty-five years before the outbreak of the Civil War.

□ Fritz, Jean. *The Cabin Faced West*. Coward, McCann, 1958, 124 pp. (3-up).

Primary listing under *Literature: Level III, Realistic Stories—Historical*.

An easy-reading story of late eighteenth-century pioneering based on the lives of real people. The Hamilton family are part of a pioneer settlement in western Pennsylvania, and although there is not a great deal of specific historical event, one brief episode in the book is based on an actual entry in George Washington's diary.

□ Giblin, James Cross. *Chimney Sweeps*. Crowell, 1982, 64 pp. (3-up).

An award-winning account of the chimney sweeping profession with an emphasis on the plight of the young "climbing boys" (sweeps' apprentices) who worked in

England until the last quarter of the nineteenth century. The well-researched material is interesting in itself, and is especially helpful in relation to English literature of the eighteenth and nineteenth centuries in which a reader often encounters the mention of chimney sweeps. Clever drawings of the sweeps of the past combine with photographs of contemporary chimney sweeps (the profession continues to flourish) to illustrate this unusual and informative little book.

□ Glubok, Shirley. *Art and Archaeology.* Harper & Row, 1966, 48 pp., OP (3-up).
A good first treatment for children of major archaeological finds. It focuses on both the idea of learning how ancient peoples lived and also on the objects of lasting value that were retrieved. A number of interesting references are made in relation to Biblically mentioned locations. Generously illustrated.

□ Goodall, John S. *The Story of an English Village.* Atheneum, 1979, 60 pp. (any age from 4-up).
In a series of watercolor paintings, the artist shows the changes at a particular location in England from medieval times (fourteenth century) to the present. Wonderful detail in both interior and exterior scenes. *No text.*

Excellent for use as a supplement in history study. Goodall has done a number of books in the same style, all filled with historically accurate details depicted in wonderful paintings. One of the interesting features of the books' format is the use of half-pages that lift up to show, for example, an interior scene under the page showing the exterior. Some of Goodall's other titles in this kind of book are: *An Edwardian Summer; Edwardian Christmas; Edwardian Entertainments; An Edwardian Season; Victorians Abroad.*

□ Grun, Bernard. *The Timetables of History; A Horizontal Linkage of People and Events.* Simon and Schuster, 1982 (4-up).
Primary listing under *Reference.*

An excellent source of a concurrent view of history. In a columnar form, the book lists, from 5000 B.C. through 1978 A.D., events, developments, etc. under seven headings: History, Politics; Literature, Theatre; Religion, Philosophy, Learning; Visual Arts; Music; Science, Technology, Growth; Daily Life.

□ Harnett, Cynthia. *The Writing on the Hearth*. Viking, 1973, 320 pp. (6-up).
Primary listing under *Literature: Level III, Realistic Stories—Historical*.
A carefully researched story set in fifteenth century England just prior to the Wars of the Roses. Good . background of actual historical events and of social/daily-life patterns.

□ Haugaard, Erik Christian. *Hakon of Rogen's Saga; A Slave's Tale* (Sequel). Houghton Mifflin, 1963, 132 pp.; 1965, 217 pp. (6-up).
Primary listing under *Literature: Level III, Realistic Stories—Historical*.
Fiction, but excellent insight into the harsh life of the Scandinavian people of this period. Vivid depictions of living conditions, customs, outlook on life. Excellent literary quality.

□ Haugaard, Erik Christian. *A Messenger for Parliament; Cromwell's Boy* (Sequel). Houghton Mifflin, 1976, 218 pp. (6-up).
Primary listing under *Literature: Level III, Realistic Stories—Historical*.
Excellent historical material in these fast-moving stories of a young boy on his own who becomes a messenger for Cromwell. Fine literary quality in the writing.

□ Hewes, Agnes Danforth. *With the Will to Go*. Longmans, Green, 1960, 244 pp., OP (5-up).
Primary listing under *Literature: Level III, Realistic Stories—Historical*.
The historical information that is woven into this colorful and eventful story is as exciting as the fictional happenings. It was a time when the great seafaring powers were jockeying for preeminence on the rich trade routes to the East. Such material adds greatly to the interest of history text accounts of the period.

□ Hine, Al and John Alcorn. *Where in the World Do You Live?* Harcourt, Brace, Jovanovich, 1962, 40 pp. (1, 2).
An excellent introduction to basic physical geography and to orienting oneself to the world around. It identifies continents, bodies of water, and defines and shows relationships between units of geographical division (countries, states, etc.).

□ Holbrook, Sabra. *The French Founders of North America and Their Heritage.* Atheneum, 1976, 256 pp. (6-up).
A serious comprehensive history of the French exploration and settlement in North America. Holbrook not only recounts the facts, but acknowledges the debt of other North Americans to the little-remembered efforts of French pioneers. Bringing her account up to 1974, the writer also explains the "two Canada" concept and helps the reader to understand the bilingual (and bicultural) nature of today's Canada. A little beyond the average fifth- or sixth-grader as straight-through reading, but excellent supplementary reading for an advanced student, and also for a parent or teacher who can digest and pass on its information on the seldom-mentioned French contribution to the founding of both the United States and Canada.

□ Holling, Holling Clancy. *Paddle-to-the-Sea.* Illus. by author. Houghton Mifflin, 1941, 63 pp. (3-up).
Primary listing under *Literature, Level II, Realistic Stories—Modern.*
This modern classic tells an intriguing story of a little carved Indian-in-a-canoe that (with the kindly help of many people along the way) floats through the Great Lakes water system and on to the sea. Much of the story involves geographical descriptions, and also includes maps, diagrams of a sawmill, canal lock, lake freighter, etc. Every facing page is a beautiful full-color painting of scenes related to the voyage.

□ Holman, Felice. *The Wild Children*. Scribners, 1983, 151 pp. (5-up).

>Primary listing under *Literature: Level III, Realistic Stories—Modern*.

>Conditions in Russia in the 1920s are graphically portrayed in this excellent story that focuses on one of the bands of wild children that roam the country. Fine supplementary material to a study of post-World War I history.

□ Irwin, Constance. *Strange Footprints on the Land: Vikings in America*. Harper & Row, 1980, 192 pp. (5, 6-up).

>This fascinating, excellently written and carefully re-searched study presents the evidence—some of it now universally accepted, other parts still controversial–of the exploration of North America by Norsemen from about 985 A.D. on. Irwin is careful to avoid jumping to conclusions or to oversensationalize. But the sheer drama of the material and the narrative skill of the writer make the book read like a story. And quite apart from the light it sheds on early American history, it makes a clear commentary on the larger movement of events in the whole history of man. So much rests on the readiness of a given period in civilization to use or understand new possibilities. When ships from Iceland and Greenland were repeatedly making landings in North America, some Europeans actually knew something of this, but there was no sense of need to investigate further; all the focus of world interest was in other directions. At the time of Columbus, however, the European vision had shifted and the hour of expansion to the New World had come. An excellent, thought-provoking book for an advanced student.

□ Jenkins, Peter and Barbara. *A Walk Across America; The Walk West: A Walk Across America 2*. Morrow, 1979, 288 pp.; 1981, 349 pp. (6-up).

>Primary listing under *Biography*.

>The two books form a detailed, intimate look at the real America that doesn't make the headlines. Peter, and later Peter and his bride, Barbara, together, are keen observers and lively recorders of the places they

see and the people they meet. Sharing their journey is a delightful way to see America in a new way. (There are even three maps and many illustrations.)

□ Johnson, Gerald. A trilogy: *America Is Born; America Grows Up; America Moves Forward*. Morrow, 1959, 254 pp., 1960, 223 pp.; 1960, 256 pp., OP (5, 6-up).
A lively, narrative-style account of American history from its days of early colonization to modern times. Johnson presents a comprehensive picture, showing the underlying causes of events, relating conditions in America with those in other parts of the world, etc. The books provide excellent enrichment in a study of American history, offering thought-provoking ideas, many possibilities for research of people and events that are not as familiar as the usual stories.

□ Kennerly, Karen (adapted by). *The Slave Who Bought His Freedom*. Dutton, 1971, 121 pp. (5, 6).
Primary listing under *Biography*.
　　Scenes and events in Africa, West Indies, the United States and England, focusing on a slave captured in Africa as a young boy, and on slavery in general. Because this account is taken directly from the slave's own story, it provides excellent material to read in connection with slavery in the last half of the eighteenth century and with other history of the period.

□ Kramer, Samuel N. *The Cradle of Civilization*. Time-Life Books, Time, Inc., 1967, 183 pp. (6-up).
Comparatively long and extensive in its coverage, this book, focusing on the "fertile crescent" lands of Bible times and the lands of the Tigris and Euphrates rivers, is written in a "for adults" style. The approach is highly secular. For example, the writer states that Judaism was "borrowed" from Mesopotamian myths, etc. The volume does offer much worthwhile information, however, and could be a useful parent/teacher sourcebook.

□ Krensky, Stephen. *Conqueror and Hero: The Search for Alexander*. Illus. by Alexander Farquharson. Little, Brown & Co., 1981, 67 pp. (3-7).
>Primary listing under *Biography*.
>The life of Alexander the Great and the path of history in a large area of the then-civilized world during his lifetime are inextricable. Krensky's concise overview focuses on Alexander's march of conquest and on the changes and far-reaching effects of his empire-building on world history.

□ Kroeber, Theodora. *Ishi: In Two Worlds*. U. of Calif. Press, 1961, 255 pp. (Adv. 6-up).
>Strictly speaking, this is anthropology rather than history, and is an adult book. But it is possible for an advanced eleven-or twelve-year-old with an interest in native Americans. It is also valuable reading for parents or teachers. Ishi was the last North American Indian to live in the wild, the sole survivor of an Indian tribe that became extinct in the first quarter of this century. Befriended by San Francisco-based anthropologists, Ishi gradually revealed the tragic fate of his people. A unique and remarkable glimpse of a culture that no longer exists, and another reminder of the inhumanity with which our native people were treated—right up to modern times.

□ Kurelek, William. *Lumberjack*. Houghton Mifflin, 1974, 48 pp. (4-up).
>Primary listings under *Art* and *Biography*.
>This prominent Canadian artist uses his painting and excellent text to detail a segment of modern history (1946, 1951), lumbering as it used to be done, attitudes and customs of the time.

□ Kurelek, William. Two books: *A Prairie Boy's Winter; A Prairie Boy's Summer*. Tundra Books, 1973, 48 pp.; 1975, 47 pp. (4-up).
>Primary listings under *Art* and *Biography*.
>These books offer excellent insights into social history of the 1930s, farm life on the Canadian prairie.

□ Lacey, Peter (edited by). *Great Adventures That Changed Our World*. Reader's Digest, 1978, 384 pp. (4-up).

Designed for a broad audience, the book is suitable for competent young readers as well as for adults. The focus is on narrative accounts of the explorers and adventurers that pressed beyond the borders of their existent nations and land masses and found new parts of the world—and universe. Starting with the great Phoenecian seaman Hanno and the Greek merchant-mariner Pytheas, the book recounts more than thirty historically significant adventures grouped in nine chronologically sequenced sections. Lavishly illustrated in color and with frequent boxed insets focusing on some related special interest item (a piece on naturalist Georg Steller, for example, in the chapter on Bering's explorations), the book offers a wealth of material, both visually and in the substantial text.

□ Latham, Jean Lee. *Anchors Aweigh: The Story of David Glasgow Farragut*. Harper & Row, 1968, 273 pp. (5-9).

Primary listing under *Biography*.

Because virtually all of Farragut's life was spent in the navy, there is a high proportion of historical material in his biography. Involved in the War of 1812, in extensive cruises at sea, in the War with Mexico, and finally as a hero of naval combat in the Civil War, Farragut's life was intimately involved with events of national significance. Latham's lively writing style balances the personal with the public aspects of Farragut's life, and his vigorous, courageous, determined nature is clearly depicted. Full of action and adventure, Farragut's story offers an excellent source of historical knowledge in a context that reads like fiction.

□ Latham, Jean Lee. *Carry on, Mr. Bowditch*. Houghton Mifflin, 1955, 251 pp. (5, 6).

Primary listing under *Biography*.

This splendid biography provides much authentic background material on the eventful American history of the late eighteenth and early nineteenth centuries. It is full of well-researched details.

□ Lawson, Audrey and Herbert Lawson. *The Man Who Freed the Slaves: The Story of William Wilberforce*. Faber and Faber (5-up).
    Primary listing under *Biography*.
    In addition to telling the inspiring story of Wilberforce, the Lawsons weave in a substantial background of English history during his lifetime. His life spanned highly eventful years: the American Revolution, the French Revolution, the twenty-year war with France and, not least, the years-long struggle to outlaw slavery and to effect various humanitarian reforms. Wilberforce believed that Christian belief should be intensely practical in its outworking, and he was himself a model of this conviction, a stand that profoundly affected history.

□ Leacroft, Helen and Richard. *The Buildings of Ancient Mesopotamia*. Addison Wesley, 1975, 40 pp. (6-up).
    Since archaeological finds of the remains of buildings and the related artifacts are a primary source of information about early civilizations, buildings make good focus for a child's book on the subject. This one has pictures and diagrams of a variety of buildings (many in color) and includes material on what is known of the history of early Mesopotamia, its culture and daily customs.

□ Levenson, Dorothy. *The First Book of the Civil War*. Franklin Watts, 1977, 66 pp. (4-7).
    A simply-told account of some of the causes of the Civil War and of the war itself. The writer takes an essentially fair, objective view and focuses largely on factual events. The terrible loss of life on both sides and the failure of the government to aid in rebuilding the South and in dealing constructively with the needs of the former slaves (freed to poverty and a society in which they had no clear place) are clearly shown.

□ McNeer, May and Lynd Ward. *John Wesley*. Abingdon, 1951, 55 pp. (4-up).
    Primary listing under *Biography*.
    In this interestingly told story of the life of John Wesley, there is much authentic background material on eighteenth-century England.

□ Macaulay, David. *City.* Houghton Mifflin, 1974, 112 pp. (5-up).
> Primary listing under *Art and Architecture.*
>
> Macaulay's minutely detailed description of the building of a Roman city offers a wealth of historical information, along with its remarkable architectural coverage. As archaeology so clearly demonstrates, the buildings used by any civilization reveal a great deal about the culture and daily life of its people. As the reader follows Macaulay's step-by-step description of the city's construction, much that was distinctively Roman is observed—and remembered.

□ Macaulay, David. Three books: *Castle; Cathedral; Pyramid.* Houghton Mifflin, 1977, 74 pp.; 1973, 77 pp.; 1975, 80 pp. (5-up).
> Primary listing under *Art and Architecture.*
>
> See comments above on Macaulay's book *City* for ways in which these books are related to the history of their respective times.

□ Macaulay, David. *Mill.* Houghton Mifflin, 1983, 128 pp. (5, 6-up).
> Primary listing under *Art and Architecture.*
>
> Using four imaginary but typical structures related to the textile industry (built at intervals of about twenty years) Macaulay not only shows technological change from 1810-1974, but also focuses subtly on cultural patterns and labor-management relations over the years.

□ Maginley, C. J. Two books: *Models of America's Past and How to Make Them; Historic Models of Early America and How to Make Them.* Harcourt, Brace, Jovanovich, 1969, 144 pp.; 1947, 156 pp. (4-7).
> Primary listing under *Crafts, Hobbies and Domestic Arts.*
>
> Instructions and ideas for model-making that tie in with early American history as to types of furniture, buildings, bridges, vehicles, accessory equipment, etc.

□ Meadowcroft, Enid L. *By Wagon ad Flatboat*. Harper & Row, 1938, 170 pp. (3-up).
   Primary listing under *Literature: Level II, Realistic Stories—Historical*.

   In this story of pioneers on their way from Pennsylvania to Ohio in 1789, the writer has included a good proportion of historical detail, both as to the new nation and as to day-to-day customs, items in use, etc. No attempt has been made to use the authentic speech of the time, which detracts from the atmosphere of the book. The story does, however, provide worthwhile information in a pleasantly interesting form.

□ Meadowcroft, Enid L. *Silver for General Washington*. Harper & Row, 1967 (1944), 138 pp. (3-7).
   Primary listing under *Literature: Level II, Realistic Stories—Historical*.

   A young brother and sister help the struggling American cause during the winter of Valley Forge. The story provides good historical background on the American Revolution for the younger reading group.

□ Meigs, Cornelia. *Invincible Louisa*. Little, Brown & Co., 1933, 260 pp. (6-up).
   Primary listing under *Biography*.

   This biography of beloved author Louisa May Alcott provides excellent historical sidelights on the New England of the last half of the nineteenth century. Insights on the slavery question and the Civil War are significant topics that are woven into the story of Alcott's life.

□ Monjo, F. N. *The One Bad Thing About Father*. Illus. by Rocco Negri. Harper & Row, 1970, 62 pp., OP (k-2).
   The one bad thing was that "Father" became the President of the United States instead of having chosen to go on with some of the other things he did so well. This is a delightfully written little fragment of fictionalized history for early readers, written as though by Quentin, a son of then-President Theodore Roosevelt. The short account tells of some of the things the lively Roosevelt children did while they lived in the White

House, and of some of the historical events that were going on at that time in the early years of the twentieth century. An informative "Author's Note" at the end of the book tells a little of what later happened to the Roosevelt children.

□ Morgan, Gwyneth. *Life in a Medieval Village*. Lerner, 1982, 52 pp. (5, 6-up).
One of the excellent series of Topic Books produced by Cambridge University Press (published in the U.S. by Lerner). Scholarship and human interest are combined in this concise yet detailed study of medieval village culture. The well-written text is generously illustrated.

□ Neimark, Anne E. *Touch of Light: The Story of Louis Braille*. Harcourt, Brace, Jovanovich, 1970 (4-6).
Primary listing under *Biography*.
Although this is primarily the story of Louis Braille and his invention of the raised dot symbols by which the blind can read, it also provides good supplementary material on cultural and political history in France for the period of 1812-1852. The effect on Braille's family of the impoverishing war being fought in which the French soldiers stripped the small farms and households of livestock, produce, anything at all of value; the hopeless condition of most of the blind of that day; the lack of concern manifested by the government for the needs of its people are all clearly part of Braille's story.

□ O'Dell, Scott. *The Hawk That Dared Not Hunt by Day*. Houghton Mifflin, 1975, 222 pp. (6-up).
Primary listing under *Literature: Level III, Realistic Stories—Historical*.
This exciting story of a young seaman who helped smuggle William Tyndale's Bibles into England has a fine, well-developed historical background. O'Dell brings out the way in which forces of intrigue from all over Europe had gathered to prevent Tyndale from carrying out his mission, and vividly pictures the religious and political turmoil that was on every hand.

□ O'Dell, Scott. *The King's Fifth.* Houghton Mifflin, 1966, 264 pp. (6-up).
Primary listing under *Literature: Level III, Realistic Stories—Historical.*
O'Dell's story is written from an unusual perspective: the hero is a young Spanish map-maker with the conquistadors who ravaged the American southwest in their lust for gold. Good historical insights not often seen from this particular vantage-point.

□ Perl, Lila. *Hunter's Stew and Hangtown Fry: What Pioneer America Ate and Why.* Houghton Mifflin, 1977, 176 pp. (6-up).
Primary listing under *Crafts, Hobbies and Domestic Arts.*
Through the foods they ate, the writer illumines the daily life of the westward-moving pioneers. One of the interesting aspects of the book is Perl's discussion of the distinctive culinary contributions made by specific immigrant groups who settled in various parts of the United States.

□ Perl, Lila. *Slumps, Grunts, and Snickerdoodles: What Colonial America Ate and Why.* Houghton Mifflin, 1975, 128 pp. (6-up).
Primary listing under *Crafts, Hobbies and Domestic Arts.*
Revealing sidelights on the cultural history of the colonists are given in relation to what they ate and why. The specific origins of various regional foods are traced, and geographical and historical background as well as the settler's domestic arrangements are interwoven in the account.

□ Plotz, Helen (edited by). *The Gift Outright: America to Her Poets.* Greenwillow, 1977 (all ages).
Primary listing under *Poetry.*
This excellent collection of poems about America offers a number of possibilities for tie-ins with historical events and personages.

□ Porter, Jane. *Scottish Chiefs*. Scribner's, 1982 (1809), 520 pp. (6-up).

Primary listing under *Literature: Level III, Realistic Stories—Historical*.

A long, highly romanticized story of the Scottish hero William Wallace in the late thirteenth, early fourteenth century period of English-Scottish conflict. Full of idealism, courage, hairbreadth escapes and noble deaths, it nonetheless offers some general historical insights on the period and its events. For advanced readers.

□ Prokop, Phyllis S. *The Sword and the Sundial*. David C. Cook, 1981 (5, 6).

Primary listing under *Literature: Level III, Realistic Stories—Historical*.

This fictionalized story of Hezekiah includes some good background on the political and social conditions of the period, 8th century B.C., in the Kingdom of Judah.

□ Purdy, Susan and Cass R. Sandak. Civilization Project Books Series. Franklin Watts, all 1982, 32 pp. (4-6).

Primary listing under *Crafts, Hobbies and Domestic Arts*.

Craft projects are given (ten to twelve per book) that can be used in connection with history classes. See the primary listing entry for titles of these books which are done on Ancient Greece, Rome, Egypt, the Aztecs, Eskimos and North American Indians.

□ Pyle, Howard. *Otto of the Silver Hand*. Dover, 1967 (1883), 136 pp. (4-6).

Primary listing under *Literature: Level III, Realistic Stories—Historical*.

Germany in the day of the feudal barons. The story shows the harshness of the life under the iron-fisted barons and contrasts it with the peace of the monastery where the story's central character is cared for. Excellent literary quality as well as an authentic historical setting.

□ Rau, Margaret. *Red Earth, Blue Sky: The Australian Outback.* Harper & Row, 1981, 118 pp. (4-up).
A detailed, factual account of life at a variety of locations and situations in the Australian Outback. Written in a straightforward information-giving style, the book is interest-holding and well stated. The material is based on the writer's extensive travel and interviews, and gives the reader a clear picture of life on cattle and sheep stations, in aboriginal settlements, etc. Special topics are also discussed in some detail: a camel farm, the opal mines, etc. The way in which medical care and education are provided in the many remote homes, the natural plant and animal life, the area's ecological needs are all included.

□ Ready, Dolores. *Wilfred's Hospital Ship.* Winston Press, 1977 (1, 2).
Primary listing under *Biography.*
This brief introduction to the missionary work of Dr. Wilfred Grenfell could be tied in with a geography unit that included Labrador.

□ Reynolds, Peter J. *Life in the Iron Age* Lerner, 1976, 51 pp. (5, 6-up).
Another in the Cambridge Topic Books series. Archaeological findings and occasional references in Greek and Roman writings are about the only evidence for the character of life in England during the seven hundred years preceding the birth of Christ. The writer starts by cautioning readers that much of the evidence is circumstantial, and thus many errors could have been made in the tentative conclusions about the Iron Age culture. The speculation, however, is interesting and certainly harmonizes with known facts. Well worth including in an ancient history course.

□ Robinson, Charles A. *The First Book of Ancient Mesopotamia and Persia.* Franklin Watts, 1962, 61 pp., OP (4-up).
Robinson's book is a simple account of the history and culture of these ancient lands. It is illustrated with black-and-white photos and maps. Frequent reference is made to Biblical places or events.

☐ Rushdoony, Haig A. *The Language of Maps.* Pitman
Learning, 1982 (4-6).

> This supplementary paperback includes teacher-directed
> lessons, student-directed activities, maps and related
> graphics, all designed to teach and reinforce map-read-
> ing skills. Much of the information is practical and
> helpful and some of the activities are interesting in
> themselves and would help to fix particular concepts in
> students' minds. Some of the questions and activities
> are more like contrived busywork, a failing that seems
> almost universal in workbooks. Overall, the book offers
> useful content for parents and teachers who prefer not
> to create their own supplementary map-reading activi-
> ties.

☐ Sauer, Carl. *Man in Nature: America Before the Days of the
White Man —A First Book in Geography.* Turtle Island
Foundation, 1975 (1939), 273 pp. (3-5).

> As indicated in the introduction to this book, we have
> not included textbooks in the book list. The unique na-
> ture of Sauer's geography text, however, mandated an
> exception. The writer believes that children will acquire
> a truer and more lasting view of the natural elements of
> the continent (land, water, weather, plants and animals)
> which distinguished one area from another, by first see-
> ing and understanding North America as it was when
> only scattered Indian tribes populated its vast expanse,
> and before the occurrence of the surface layers of
> change brought by man's intervention.
>
> Sauer is not at all unmindful of the significance of
> current social geography (differences in people and
> what they have made and used and changed in any giv-
> en place). He simply wants to start by giving children a
> fundamental approach on which to build a lifetime of
> clear, ordered information about the world in which
> they live, an approach which could be applied to places
> other than North America.
>
> It is impossible, given the necessarily brief nature of
> these notes, to adequately describe the book's content,
> which not only offers factual knowledge, but also draws
> its readers into a contemplation of the natural world
> and encourages creative thinking. At the same time,
> Sauer is not anticivilization, and while dealing fairly

with the positive aspects of Indian life, does not by any means see their lifestyle as idyllic.

In relation to the book's integrity and credibility, it is important to remember that it was written almost a half-century ago, so that the depiction of Eskimo life (spoken of in the book as continuing into the then-present) must be seen to be now as clearly past as that of the prewhite-civilization Indians portrayed in the rest of the book.

Numerous drawings, map-making, climate and weather observation, kinds of vegetation and animal life are integral parts of Sauer's discussion of each section of our continent. Not widely available in libraries, the book is well worth ordering through a local bookstore or directly from the publisher.

□ Sedor, Mary. *Living in Rio de Janeiro*. Wayland Pub., 1981, 52 pp. (4-up).
One of a good British series, Living in Famous Cities. The book is brief, so necessarily somewhat superficial, but it does capture the broad outlines. It shows, for example, the contrast between the living conditions of the affluent and the masses of the very poor. Clear black-and-white photos illustrate each page. The text is straightforward exposition/description. The vocabulary is good, the writing well done in a factual, documentary way. Other books in the series focus on Berlin, Cairo, Calcutta, Hong Kong, Jerusalem, Johannesburg, Madrid, Moscow, New York, Paris, Peking, Rome, Tokyo.

□ Singer, Isaac Bashevis. *A Day of Pleasure*. Farrar, Strauss & Giroux, 1969, 221 pp. (6-up).
Primary listing under *Biography*.
Insights into the life of Eastern European Jews (Poland) during the early twentieth century.

□ Sootin, Harry. *Robert Boyle: Founder of Modern Chemistry*. Franklin Watts, 1962, 133 pp., OP (6-up).
See also *Biography* and *Science* listings.
Boyle's father was the wealthy Earl of Cork, one of the powerful English landowners in Ireland in the seventeenth century. The family was intimately involved in

major political events of the period, and as well as recounting Boyle's contributions to scientific development, the book sheds light on the English role in Ireland, the Royalist-Puritan confrontations, the relatively brief rule of Cromwell, and the Restoration. Boyle's family had connections with both sides of the conflict and the way in which the family interests were affected makes enlightening reading. Brief mentions of cultural patterns and the "advantageous" marriages arranged by the Earl for some of his sons and daughters (at least two of which were disastrously unhappy) show quite clearly the very real situations on which many historical novels have been based.

□ Speare, Elizabeth. *The Bronze Bow.* Houghton Mifflin, 1961, 272 pp. (5, 6).
> Primary listing under *Literature: Level III, Realistic Stories—Historical.*
>
> A well-written, suspenseful story set in Palestine at the time of Christ. Good historical background and details of daily life under Roman rule.

□ Steele, William O. *The Buffalo Knife.* Harcourt, Brace, Jovanovich, 1952, 177 pp. (4-up).
> Primary listing under *Literature: Level II, Realistic Stories—Historical.*
>
> In the framework of an adventure-filled story of two young boys and their families moving west, the writer provides information on early pioneering. While the American Revolution was still being fought in the far eastern part of the country (1782), inland settlers were continuing their local conflicts with Indians, extending farmlands, and ever pressing on to new frontiers. Young Andy and Isaac float more than a thousand miles down (and up) the Tennessee River on a flatboat, encountering a variety of hazards and new experiences on the way, arriving finally at their destination at what would someday become Nashville, Tennessee.

□ Steele, William O. *The Perilous Road*. Harcourt, Brace,
Jovanovich, 1958, 191 pp. (4-up).

Primary listing under *Literature: Level II, Realistic Stories—Historical*.

Steele's well-written Civil War story focuses on a
Tennessee mountain farm family who feel sympathy for
both sides of the conflict. The exception to this family
feeling is eleven-year-old Chris who is enraged at the
Yankee soldiers for taking his family's winter food supplies and their only horse. When Chris's older brother
joins the Union Army, Chris's sense of betrayal is complete. The story offers clear insights on the impact of
the Civil War in people's lives, and of the position oc-
cupied by people who had no immediate large gain in
view no matter which side won or lost.

□ Steele, William O. *Westward Adventure: The True Stories
of Six Pioneers*. Harcourt, Brace, Jovanovich, 1962, 188
pp. (5-up).

Primary listing under *Biography*.

Steele has drawn upon a variety of sources, including firsthand journals and reports, in recounting the
true experiences of six very different eighteenth-century
people who struggled through or around the Appala-
chian Mountains into the "lands of western waters."
These were areas crossed by some of the main inland
rivers in territory that would someday be within Tennessee, Kentucky, and other nearby states. Arranging
the stories chronologically, Steele virtually spans the
century and gives an almost "you are there" feeling to
the reader as he or she reads; there is a sense of the
movement of history: the interaction with various Indian groups, the mixed motives that drew people to the
wilderness, the realities of pioneer life.

□ Stevens, Byrna. *Ben Franklin's Glass Armonica*. Illus. by
Priscilla Kiedrowski. Carolrhoda Books, 1983, 48 pp.
(k-3).

Primary listing under *Music*.

The story of yet another ingenious invention of the
amazing Mr. Franklin. This could be used as an "extra
interest" tie-in with American history of Franklin's
time.

□ Stevenson, Robert Louis. *The Black Arrow.* Airmont, 1964 (1888), 274 pp. (5-up).

Primary listing under *Literature: Level III, Realistic Stories—Historical.*

Stevenson's exciting story should effectively help to illumine the period of the Wars of the Roses, for the history that is absorbed in the process of reading a gripping story is often retained more fully than when it is read in a textbook.

□ Stevenson, Robert Louis. *Kidnapped.* Grossett & Dunlap; *David Balfour* (Sequel). Scribner's, 1948 (1886), 340 pp.; (1893), OP (5, 6-up).

Primary listings under *Literature: Level III, Realistic Stories—Historical.*

In Stevenson's classic adventure tale and its suspenseful sequel, the main focus of the stories is on the lives of the central characters, but a good deal of historical material is an integral part of the background of the stories. (David's friend Alan, for example, is a former Jacobite leader.)

□ Sutcliff, Rosemary. *Blood Feud.* Dutton, 1977, 144 pp. (6-up).

Primary listing under *Literature: Level III, Realistic Stories—Historical.*

A broad sweep of action and adventure based on an actual historical event. (See *Literature* listing.) Scenes in England, Ireland, Denmark, and an extended stay in Constantinople. Splendidly written, with the fine literary quality one expects in a work of Sutcliff's.

□ Syme, Ronald. *Cartier: Finder of the St. Lawrence.* Illus. by William Stobbs. Morrow, 1958, 95 pp. (3-7).

Primary listing under *Biography.*

Cartier's story offers good supplementary material for studies in the history of New World exploration in the early sixteenth century. Aside from the discoveries themselves, Syme's account points up the casual disregard most Europeans demonstrated for the rights or personal dignity of the native Americans. Even Cartier was not free of such callousness, though on the whole he was a reasonably fair and humane person for his day, with attitudes and behavior in marked contrast to the cruelty and greed of Roberval, the nobleman who financed one of Cartier's journeys.

☐ Syme, Ronald. *Columbus, Finder of the New World*. Illus. by William Stobbs. Morrow, 1952, 70 pp. (3-7).
    Primary listing under *Biography*.
    Good supplementary material related to American history and to the New World discovery period of European history.

☐ Syme, Ronald. *Magellan: First Around the World*. Illus. by William Stobbs. Morrow, 1953, 71 pp. (3-7).
    Primary listing under *Biography*.
    The significant period of seafaring exploration from the late fifteenth and on through the sixteenth century was to change forever man's perception of the world and to usher in a new era of history. One of the key figures in these adventure-filled days was Ferdinand Magellan. Convinced that it was possible to start sailing from Spain, find a passage to the ocean he was sure lay west of America, finally reach the Far East, and then sail back to Europe, Magellan gained the backing of the King of Spain and led a voyage of exploration. Although Magellan died in the Philippines, one ship of the expedition and a few of the men finally reached home again. Magellan's belief had been vindicated. For the first time in history, as far as anyone knows, men had sailed around the world—and history was to be profoundly altered in the century that followed.

☐ Tunis, Edwin. *Colonial Living*. Harper & Row, 1976, 160 pp. (5-up).
    The writer provides detailed descriptions and drawings of the equipment of daily living used from about 1564-1770 in America. Tunis does tend to overgeneralize about such things as regional lifestyles, but used wisely the book is a fine supplement to the study of American history in the colonial period.

□ Tunis, Edwin. *Frontier Living.* Harper & Row, 1976, 168 pp. (4-up).

As in his other books on cultural history, Tunis views a variety of locations and groups. In this case he describes the movement to frontier areas, the mode of life of the pioneers, the equipment and tools they used, the clothes they wore, etc. Maps, synopses of specific historical background events and political conditions, and Tunis's excellent illustrative drawings all combine to make this a highly pleasing and informative volume.

□ Tunis, Edwin. *Indians.* Harper & Row, 1959, 157 pp. (4-up).

A detailed sourcebook on American Indian life before the arrival of the white man. Almost 250 drawings illustrate clearly the tools, weapons, houses, etc. used by various tribal groups. Good supplement to study of American history.

□ Tunis, Edwin. *Oars, Sails and Steam: A Picture Book of Ships.* Harper & Row, 1977 (1952), 77 pp. (5-up).

Primary listing under *Science and Technology.*

A fine reference source to tie in with historical material that involves any activity of ships—ships for trade, exploration, fishing, battle, etc. In many of Tunis's books his illustrations complement the text; in this case, the illustrations are preeminent, complemented by relevant text.

□ Tunis, Edwin. *The Tavern at the Ferry.* Harper & Row, 1973, 128 pp. (4-up).

From a quiet farm by the Delaware River owned by Quaker Henry Baker, a ferry and then an inn/tavern gradually developed. Using this focal point and loosely following the Baker family, Tunis has written in great detail about life in colonial America for the hundred years starting in 1687. Rich in detail and background material, the writer illumines an ever-interesting period of American history. Tunis doesn't confine himself to one limited spot and brings in a wealth of information on every imaginable aspect of daily life: clothing, tools, transportation, building styles, as well as on political changes, the development of resistance to British rule, etc. Tunis's fine, authentic drawings illustrate every page.

□ Tunis, Edwin. *Wheels: A Pictorial History.* Harper & Row, 1977 (1955), 96 pp. (5-up).
   Primary listing under *Science and Technology.*
   An excellent reference source on wheeled vehicles (other than trains or trolleys) mentioned in historical material. As always, the fine, detailed drawings accompany a fine, informative text.

□ Tunis, Edwin. *The Young United States: 1783-1830.* Harper & Row, 1976 (1969), 160 pp. (4-up).
   Approaching his material topically and regionally, Tunis surveys customs, events, and social/cultural developments during the first fifty years of the new young nation, the United States of America. A sampling from the nineteen chapter titles ("The Farmers," "The Villages," "The Wilderness," "Inventions and Factories," "The Seafarers and the Countinghouse," "Schools and Colleges") indicates the scope of the material covered. As in his other books, Tunis focuses in a coherent way on countless details and on each page illustrates many of the objects about which he writes.

□ Twain, Mark. *The Prince and the Pauper.* Harper & Row, 1909 (1882), 296 pp. (5-up).
   Primary listing under *Literature: Level III, Realistic Stories—Historical.*
   Twain's famous story about the young prince and the beggar-boy who exchange roles has a strong appeal simply on the story level. But the portrayal of midsixteenth-century life in England offers enlightening background for study of the period's history. Twain's strong consciousness of social injustices is reflected throughout.

□ Updegraff, Imelda and Robert. *Seas and Oceans*. The Children's Book Co., 1983, 28 pp. (3-up).

A concise coverage of various aspects of seas and oceans: currents and waves, the seashore, tides, etc. The content is well illustrated, but there is also a substantial amount of text. An attractive feature of the book is the four half-width pages that appear at strategic points and when turned over show a changed state of progression in some landform, tide level, etc. This book is one of a series, other titles of which are *Earthquakes and Volcanoes, Weather, Continents and Climates, Mountains and Valleys,* and *Rivers and Lakes.* All of these books are good supplementary data on physical geography topics.

□ Urdang, Laurence (editor). *The Timetables of American History*. Simon and Schuster, 1981, 470 pp. (4-up).

Primary listing under *Reference.*

This is a splendid approach to a broadening of students' grasp of history. In a columnar form, *Timetables* shows, year by year, what was occurring at the same time in the United States and elsewhere under four categories: History and Politics; The Arts; Science and Technology; Miscellaneous.

□ Vander Schnier, Nettie. *The Golden Thread*. Moody Press, 1983, 175 pp. (6-up).

Primary listing under *Biography.*

This inspiring story of a young Dutch woman who survives the Nazi occupation during World War II offers good supplementary material on conditions in Holland at that time.

□ Verne, Jules *Michael Strogoff: A Courier of the Czar*. Airmont, 1964, 340 pp. (6-up).

Primary listing under *Literature: Level III, Realistic Stories—Historical.*

Few children's stories of pre-Revolution Russia are available, and while the imaginary adventures of the story's hero are the dominant theme, insights into some aspects of Czarist Russia and into the politics of the era are a part of the background of Strogoff's exploits.

□ Walsh, Jill Paton. *Children of the Fox*. Farrar, Straus &
Giroux, 1978, 128 pp. (5, 6-up).
Primary listing under *Literature: Level III, Realistic Sto-
ries—Historical.*

Three stories of courage and adventure in the Grecian world of the fifth century B.C. The stories are fictional, but the historical events involved are factual, as
are the Athenian general, the Spartan leader, etc.

□ Washington, Booker T. *Up from Slavery*. Doubleday,
1963 (1901), 243 pp. (5-up).
Primary listing under *Biography.*

This story (written in 1901) of the courageous and
effective life of Booker T. Washington, offers valuable
historical material on "the way it was" for blacks during
the post-Civil War years, and on the related cultural and
political conditions prevailing.

□ Wilder, Laura Ingalls. *On the Way Home*. Harper & Row,
1962, 101 pp. (3-up).
Primary listing under *Biography.*

This firsthand account of the Wilders' 650-mile
journey from South Dakota to Missouri reflects a variety of historically interesting facts. In her diary, Laura
mentions small, simple matters that help to give a vivid
picture of life in 1894. The reader is struck forcibly by
the almost unbelievably complete changes that have oc-
curred in virtually every aspect of life since the Wilders
made their journey.

□ Wilder, Laura Ingalls. *West from Home*. Harper & Row,
1974, 124 pp. (4-up).
Primary listing under *Biography.*

A collection of letters to her husband by Laura Ingalls Wilder (author of the Little House books) during
a 1915 visit she made to her daughter in San Francisco.
Laura's keen observations take the reader back to the
time about which she writes, and as always, such comments lend life and reality to the historical facts of the
past.

□ Willard, Barbara. *The Lark and the Laurel*. Harcourt, Brace, Jovanovich, 1970, 207 pp. (6-up).

> Primary listing under *Literature: Level III, Realistic Stories—Historical*.
>
> Set at the time of the accession to the throne of England of the first Tudor king, the suspenseful story includes good historical background and details of late fifteenth-century rural life.

Two illustrated cultural/historical series

□ The Living Past series. Arco, all 1979, 61 pp. (4-6).

> These are captioned-picture format books in which the facts are given succinctly with no particular literary grace. They are informative and attractively illustrated in color and enjoyable as supplementary material.
>
> Windrow, Martin. *The Invaders*—The development of new European civilization from 200 to 1200 A.D., including the fall of Rome, rise of Moslem power, heyday of the Vikings.
>
> Gibson, Michael. *The Knights*—The life, duties, etc., of the medieval knight, and the Crusades in which so many became involved.
>
> Grant, Neil. *The Discoverers*—Accounts of early explorers and the effect their discoveries had on the culture and economy of both the Old and New Worlds.
>
> Goodenough, Simon. *The Renaissance*—Life during the Renaissance, a period which was to have a profound effect on the future development of Western civilization.

□ The "See Inside" series. Franklin Watts. All 1979-80, 29
   pp. (4-up).
   Hughes-Stanton. *See Inside an Ancient Chinese Town*
   (OP).
   Rutland, Jonathan. *See Inside an Ancient Greek Town.*
   Burland, Cottie. *See Inside an Aztec Town.*
   Unstead, R. J. *See Inside a Castle.*
   These brief, attractive and colorful books are not intended as in-depth studies. Instead, in captioned-picture
   form they focus on a wide variety of details related to
   the daily life, special characteristics, etc., of the subject
   community. They are especially helpful in opening up
   possibilities for further inquiry, and in giving a student
   a little of the flavor of a particular culture's distinctive
   features.

⑨ Handicaps and Special Problems

☐ Blue, Rose. *Seven Years from Home*. Raintree, 1976, 58 pp. (4-up).
> Primary listing under *Literature: Level II, Realistic Stories—Modern*.
>
> This story of eleven-year-old Mark offers insights into the emotional disturbances sometimes experienced by an adopted child. (Fiction)

☐ Branscum, Robbie. *For Love of Jody*. Lothrop, Lee & Shepard, 1979, 111 pp. (5-up).
> Primary listing under *Literature: Level III, Realistic Stories—Modern*.
>
> Frankie, a young Arkansas farm girl, struggles with her feelings about her ten-year-old sister Jody who is retarded. A warm, helpful story. (Fiction)

☐ de Paola, Tomie. *Now One Foot, Now the Other*. Illus. by author. G. P. Putnam's, 1981, 48 pp. (1, 2).
> Primary listing under *Literature: Level I, Realistic Stories—Modern*.
>
> Bobbie and his grandpa are close friends. After his grandpa's stroke, it is Bobbie who is able to elicit response from him, encourage him to walk again, and help him as grandpa once helped him. (Fiction)

☐ Gordon, Shirley. *The Boy Who Wanted a Family*. Illus. by Charles Robinson. Harper & Row, 1980, 96 pp. (1-4).
> Primary listing under *Literature, Level I, Realistic Stories—Modern*.
>
> Michael, a young boy who has spent most of his life in foster homes, wants a home and family of his own more than anything else in the world. This happy story of Michael's adoption by a gray-haired, single

woman writer is enjoyable reading as well as a good medium to help children realize that even a child who hasn't been adopted into a traditional situation may still have the hope of finding a loving home. (Fiction)

□ Kamien, Janet. *What If You Couldn't. . . ?* Scribner's, 1979, 83 pp. (4-up).
 This excellent book about disabilities asks the reader to imagine that he or she is the person with the disability, then suggests things the reader can do to feel what it is like to have that disability. Various devices and procedures for helping people with their particular problems are explained. Hearing, impaired vision, other physical disabilities, emotional and mental handicaps are included in the book's coverage.

□ Little, Jean. Two books: *From Anna* and *Mine for Keeps.* Little, Brown & Co., 1972, 203 pp.; 1962, 186 pp. (3, 4-up).
 Primary listings under *Literature: Level II, Realistic Stories—Modern.*
 In each of these books, the central character is coping with a physical handicap—and with the related emotional and social problems. In the first book, Anna's visual impairment is finally discovered, and in *Mine for Keeps,* Sally, a cerebral palsy victim, struggles with the transition from a special boarding school to life at home and in a regular school. Little writes especially well and her books have warmth, humor, perception and depth. (Fiction)

□ Miles, Miska. *Aaron's Door.* Illus. by Alan E. Cober. Little, Brown & Co., 1977, 46 pp. (2-up).
 Primary listing under *Literature: Level I, Realistic Stories—Modern.*
 Pictures and a brief text tell the story of Aaron's emotional withdrawal when he and his younger sister are adopted. How the unconditional love and acceptance shown him by his new parents break through the closed door of Aaron's emotions is the story of this book on the special needs of children adopted after babyhood. (Fiction)

□ Peter, Diana. *Claire and Emma*. John Day Co., 1977, 30 pp. (k-3).

This is a true story about Claire and Emma who are four and two and live in London, England with their mother and their brother Alastair, who is six. Claire and Emma were both born deaf, and this simply written photo-story explains their handicap and tells about the things they have to do to try to learn to speak, to lip-read, and to hear a little with the use of hearing aids.

□ Pollock, Penny. *Keeping It Secret*. G. P. Putnam's, 1982, 112 pp. (4-6).

Primary listing under *Literature: Level III, Realistic Stories—Modern*.

A sixth-grade girl is self-conscious about her hearing aid, particularly when starting school in a new community. Her emotional disturbance affects her attitudes toward others until her parents and teacher help her to work through the problem. (Fiction)

□ Rosenberg, Maxine B. *My Friend Leslie: The Story of a Handicapped Child*. Lothrop, Lee & Shepard, 1983, 48 pp. (1-3).

A picture story of Leslie, with a simple text done as though in the words of Karin, the writer's small daughter, a friend of Leslie's. Leslie was born with severe visual impairment, moderate hearing loss, cleft palate, muscular weakness of her arms and legs and eyelid muscles that have had to be operated on twice to tighten them up. She attends regular school and tries to function as much as possible like her schoolmates. Another good source of information and "consciousness raising" about the handicapped.

□ White, Paul. *Janet at School*. John Day Co., 1978, 25 pp. (k-4).

Five-year-old Janet is a real little girl with a handicap known as *spina bifida*. Janet has a lively, courageous spirit and works hard at trying to do as much as she possibly can. She moves her wheelchair around for herself part of the time; at other times someone pushes it for her. She attends a regular kindergarten class at school and is also learning to walk with the aid of leg braces and a walking frame. Janet's mom, dad and older brother help and encourage her in many ways. This photo-and-brief-text book will help readers to better understand the needs of people like Janet. Two more books in this series are: *Sally Can't See* by Palle Petersen (a twelve-year-old blind girl tries to live as much like a sighted child as she can) and *Don't Forget Tom* by Hanne Larsen (an appealing little six-year-old is mentally retarded).

□ Wolf, Bernard. *Connie's New Eyes*. Harper & Row, 1976, 95 pp. (4-up).

A fine documentary on a young woman, Connie David, who has been blind from birth. Although a full photographic sequence runs through the book, the text is much more substantial and detailed than in many such documentaries. Connie is preparing to start her first full-time job in a few months as a teacher in a school for handicapped children. For years she has wanted to have a guide dog, and now seems the ideal time to realize her dream. The reader is shown—and told about—the care and training of Blythe, the dog that will later be introduced to Connie, and about the month Connie herself spends at The Seeing Eye headquarters being trained to be able to properly use the help of a guide dog. The account then goes on to show Connie's life over a period of months as she enjoys the new independence and freedom brought to her by the help and companionship of Blythe. An excellent and informative book.

□ Wolf, Bernard. *Don't Feel Sorry for Paul*. Harper & Row, 1974, 96 pp. (3-6).

Paul Jockimo, an especially handsome little boy, is just turning seven; but all his life he has had to live with a handicap. He was born with only stumps beyond a flexible right wrist and right heel; his left hand has an enlarged thumb and two webbed-together fingers, his left foot just a heel and a big toe. What went wrong? Not even medical experts can say why this happened, but Paul must learn to live as fully as possible in spite of his substantial handicap. Writer-photographer Wolf perceptively documents two active weeks in Paul's life and accompanies the pictures with a clear, detailed text. Wolf has caught just the scenes, brought out exactly the facts, that help a reader to "feel" Paul's situation, to realize a little of what a struggle he determinedly carries on.

10 Horticulture

☐ Brown, Marc. *Your First Garden Book*. Little, Brown & Co., 1981, 48 pp. (1-6).
> Brown has not only written a clear introductory guide for young gardeners (indoors and out), but he has included a lot of sheer fun in the process. His clever, humorous color illustrations are guaranteed to intrigue kids of all ages, and as to gardening activities, he has included (along with the usual procedures) a variety of entertaining projects: growing sprouts and cress, planting a potato in a bucket, growing peanuts, sunflowers, avocado seeds—and even instructions for a couple of bird-feeders using readily available materials. A glossary, index and list of seed and bulb sources conclude the book.

☐ Herda, D. J. *Making a Native Plant Terrarium*. Messner, 1971, 96 pp. (3-up).
> Step-by-step instructions (with accompanying photos and drawings) for growing native plants in a terrarium. The writer covers the topic simply, but quite thoroughly. In areas where the digging up of native plants is prohibited, a child could substitute small plants purchased at a nursery.

☐ Herda, D.J. *Vegetables in a Pot*. Messner, 1979, 96 pp. (3-up).
> Clear, practical directions for growing vegetables in pots, either indoors or out. These are "child-geared" projects and are not expected to produce large yields of produce. Types of plants, soil preparation, planting, watering, light sources, etc., are all discussed.

□ Hess, Lilo. *Small Habitats*. Scribner's, 1976, 49 pp. (3-up).

All the necessary information for making a variety of terrarium environments in which small animal inhabitants can thrive. Well-illustrated with how-to photos, the book also gives brief care instructions for turtles, lizards, toads and other small creatures.

□ Johnson, Hannah Lyons. *From Apple Seed to Applesauce*. Lothrop, Lee & Shepard, 1974, 48 pp. (3-up).

A detailed account of the life cycle of the apple. This is not a "how-to" for the home gardener, but rather the story of how apple trees are started, cared for and harvested in apple orchards. Grafting, pollination and the role of bees are all described and pictured. The book concludes with a recipe for homemade applesauce.

□ Johnson, Hannah Lyons. *From Seed to Salad*. Lothrop, Lee & Shepard, 1978, 48 pp. (2-up).

Clear, step-by-step instructions on planting and caring for a basic salad-vegetable garden: radishes, leaf lettuce, spinach, scallions, carrots, tomatoes, green peppers and cucumbers. Well-illustrated with photos. Recipes for three kinds of salad dressing conclude the book.

□ Paul, Aileen. *Kids Gardening: A First Indoor Gardening Book for Children*. Doubleday, 1972, 96 pp. (3-up).

A how-to manual on the planting and care of house plants. Fairly extensive, for an introductory book, the contents include suggestions for indoor desert and rock gardens and terrariums, as well as coverage of a variety of potted plants. Illustrations are two-color drawings; glossary, index, and list of the Agricultural College Extension Service address in each state are included. (Advice and free publications are often available from such a source.)

□ Paul, Aileen. *Kids Outdoor Gardening*. Doubleday, 1978, 80 pp. (3-up).

A quite detailed manual on raising flowers and vegetables for the young, beginning gardener. Tools, fertilizers, composting, soil preparation, planting, care, how to combat pests, etc., are all discussed. A list of additional information sources, a glossary, and very complete index make this a handy practical guide. Illustrated with line drawings.

□ Selsam, Millicent. *Eat the Fruit, Plant the Seed.* Morrow, 1980, 48 pp. (3-up).
This is "for the fun of it"(or, for the botanically inclined, "for scientific observation") planting. Instructions for growing the seeds of avocado, papaya, mango, pomegranate, kiwi and citrus fruits are given, accompanied by many photographs both of procedures and of the resulting plants. The plants can be enjoyed as pot plants, but are not expected to become fruit producers in most situations.

□ Selsam, Millicent E. Two books on "snack food" plants: *Popcorn; Peanut.* Morrow, 1976, 48 pp; 1969, 46 pp. (3-up).
The fascinating, detailed history of each plant, and instructions on how to grow it, are accompanied by many fine, informative photographs.

□ Stevenson, Peter and Mike. *Farming in Boxes.* Scribner's, 1976, 64 pp. (4-up).
Good news for kids who don't have a big garden plot space available to them, who live where the soil is extremely poor, or who particularly need to conserve water. The Stevensons' book is all about raising plants in boxes: all that is needed is a sunny spot in which to set them. Instructions for making boxes, a compost pile box and even a 6′ × 7′ frame-and-plastic greenhouse/potting shed/storage structure are given, as well as instructions on soil preparation, planting, growing and harvesting. Written specifically for kids, but some of the building processes are a bit complex and the help of one or more handy adults would ordinarily be required. Illustrated copiously with photos of children at work on the projects and diagrams of construction details. A complete materials list for all projects concludes the book.

□ Tarsky, Sue. Two house-plant books: *The Potted Plant Book; The Prickly Plant Book*. Little, Brown & Co., both 1981, 48 pp. (3-up).

Both of these are very attractive books, with color illustrations on every page. The first book briefly covers basic procedures and then describes and pictures a large number of house plants and their care. The second does the same for a wide variety of cacti and succulents. The books are helpful in introducing children to the range of plant possibilities and to a number of propagation methods, etc. It is important to be aware, however, that in covering so much material and so many plants, the information is sometimes quite limited. This does not diminish the usefulness of the books, which can lead the aspiring young horticulturalist into further, more detailed reading on specific plants and their care.

□ Verey, Rosemary. *The Herb Growing Book*. Little, Brown & Co., 1981, 48 pp. (3-up).

In the same series as the plant books by Sue Tarsky, this is another beautifully colorful book. Plans for outdoor herb gardens, ideas for indoor cultivation, instructions for planting, care and propagation of a large number of herbs are all included. Verey has also added "how-to" information on drying herbs, making a lavender bag, pot-pourri, tea, herb nosegay and a pomander.

□ Walsh, Anne B. *A Gardening Book: Indoors and Outdoors*. Atheneum, 1976, 112 pp. (3-up).

A very well put together handbook for the beginning gardener. Walsh covers all the basic areas of information for a start in either the indoor or outdoor cultivation of plants. Her instructions are detailed and very clear, and each project is begun with a complete list of "things you will need." In addition to the more conventional projects are such things as sprouting bean or alfalfa seeds, making a terrarium, a "hodge podge" windowsill garden, kitchen and herb gardens, and more.

□ Wexler, Jerome. *Secrets of the Venus's Fly Trap*. Dodd,
   Mead, 1981, 64 pp. (4-up).
   > Most of this book focuses on the details of the carnivo-
   > rous plant's structure, and of the way in which it proc-
   > esses its food, but a concluding chapter tells how one
   > can grow his own plant. The photography is outstand-
   > ing, revealing the amazing qualities of this fascinating
   > plant that entraps and consumes live insects.

☐11 Humor

Note: Humorous stories and poems are not listed here, but are included with the *Literature* listings. The notations on each such book mention their humorous quality.

☐ Berger, Melvin and J.B. Handelsman. *The Funny Side of Science*. Harper & Row, 1973, 48 pp. (5-up).
> These are kid-type jokes in the area of science and technology; for example: "Archaeologist: a scientist whose career lies in ruins." All that and amusing illustrations too!

☐ Cerf, Bennett. Two books: *Bennett Cerf's Book of Riddles; More Riddles*. Both illus. by Roy McKie. Beginner, 1960, 62 pp.; 1961, 64 pp. (1-3).
> Kid-style humor, with the benefit of Cerf's taste and style. Children need a goodly portion of this sort of thing; too often, school programs forget to include and encourage humor—something kids love and are benefited by. (Adults too!)

☐ Gounand, Karen Jo. *A Very Mice Joke Book*. Houghton Mifflin, 1981, 47 pp. (3-up).
> A lighthearted collection of jokes and riddles all about well-known mice (such as the best-known mouse of all, Fay *Mouse;* the historic dictator *Mouse*olini, and the writer of the Declaration of Independence, Tom *Mouse* Jefferson). Clever, humorous illustrations on almost every page.

☐ Keller, Charles (compiled by). *Ballpoint Bananas and Other Jokes for Kids*. Prentice-Hall, 1973, 96 pp. (3-7).
> Wacky riddles, ridiculous rhymes, and taunts and teases. (If junior-high-type insult humor isn't for you, just avoid this little book.)

□ Levine, Caroline Anne. *The Silly Kid Joke Book*. Dutton, 1983, 64 pp. (1-3).

Silly questions and silly answers ("Why did the silly kid burn her new coat?" "It was a blazer." Or "Why did the silly kid go out in the rain with her purse open?" "She expected some change in the weather.") Kids love these.

□ Walker, Barbara K. (compiled by). *Laughing Together: Giggles and Grins from Around the World*. Four Winds Press, 1977, 106 pp. (3-up).

Jokes, cartoons, riddles, rhymes and short tales gathered from almost a hundred countries and political or ethnic groups. In some cases, the item is shown in both its native language and English, while the rest are simply in English translations. Observing the similarities (and the differences) in humor from one country or ethnic group to the next expands students' world awareness as well as their literary sense. But most of all, these are kid-type jokes to laugh and have fun with.

□ Watson, Clyde. *Quips and Quirks*. Harper & Row, 1975, 64 pp. (3-7).

For hundreds, perhaps thousands, of years, people have called each other names designed to reveal some peculiarity, quirk or flaw. The writer diligently researched old books and dictionaries and came up with a choice collection of terms for such trying people as boors ("clunch" and "lumpkin" are just two of the synonyms); chatterboxes ("flapjaw," "windjammer" and others put that message across), etc. This is a book for word-fans who have the good sense not to use their newfound, fun-to-say words in inappropriate situations!

□ Ziegler, Sandra K. *Jokes and More Jokes*. Illus. by Diana L. Magnuson. Children's Press, 1983, 47 pp. (1-5).

An enjoyable collection of jokes in several categories. The opening chapter offers examples of jokes from various periods in the past; succeeding chapters focus on jokes about monsters and dinosaurs; then there are Silly Sam and Sally jokes, puns in jokes, jokes from many countries, and more.

12 Language

☐ Anno, Mitsumasa. *Anno's Alphabet.* Illus. by author. Crowell, 1975, 64 pp. (ps-up).

A creative, mind-and-eye-stretching ABC book. A prominent Japanese illustrator and book designer, Anno has also written a number of challenging and widely acclaimed children's books. In this one, each page is full of things to look for and identify. Each letter and its matching object are surrounded on their two facing pages by stylized borders of foliage, flowers, and other almost-hidden details: insects, birds, people, etc. The border for each letter is different, and in each case, the initial letter of everything depicted matches the letter on its page. "A"'s border, for example, contains acanthus, anemone, aster, and tiny ants. There is a glossary in the back in which the things pictured are listed. Other visual surprises are left for the reader to discover.

☐ Carle, Eric. *All About Arthur.* Illus. by author. Franklin Watts, 1974, 32 pp., OP (ps-2).

A delightful ABC book. Each letter has a little paragraph of contemporary-flavored nonsense that is full of words beginning with the subject letter. Fun and linguistically enriching.

☐ Charlip, Remy, et al. *Handtalk: An ABC of Finger Spelling and Sign Language.* Scholastic, 1974, 48 pp. (1-up).

Two methods of talking with hand signals: finger spelling and signing. This book offers just a start, but it does use the same methods used by the deaf. As a game it is enjoyable; as a means of communicating with the hearing-impaired it has a deeper dimension.

☐ Farber, Norma. *As I Was Crossing Boston Common*. Illus. by Arnold Lobel. Creative Arts Books, 1982, 32 pp. (ps-2).

> This is a great little rhyming alphabet book, using the names of real animals most people have never heard of. Fun, and good for word practice, sparking interest in exotic fauna, etc.

☐ Fisher, Leonard Everett. *Alphabet Art*. Scholastic Book Service, 1978, 61 pp. (5-up).

> This elegant book (also listed under *Art*) shows the development of written language by means of excellent graphics. An opening chart shows the nearest equivalents for our alphabet of today in Sinai, Phoenecian, Greek and Roman. The body of the book is made up of the alphabets of thirteen languages still in use today. A brief introduction outlines the development of written language, and a page accompanying each alphabet sketches the history of that language. Splendid enrichment material.

☐ Goodall, John S. *The Story of an English Village*. Atheneum, 1969, 60 pp. (3, 4-up to any age).

> Primary listing under *History*.

> This wordless, chronologically-organized series of scenes offers raw materials for creative stories about the people and places pictured, for papers on social history, on environmental destruction, etc.

☐ Greenfield, Howard. *Sumer Is Icumen In: Our Ever-Changing Language*. Crown, 1978, 67 pp. (6-up).

> A brief, clearly stated account of the origins and development of the English language. The writer explains the basis upon which languages are grouped and how our particular language came into being. He traces the major influences that made changes in English and gives examples of the specific ways the language has changed over different periods of time.

☐ Gwynne, Fred. *The King Who Rained*. Illus. by author. Windmill, 1970, 40 pp. (1, 2-up).

The writer contrasts literal and figurative speech, plays with homonym confusion, etc. Deadpan humor, zany illustrations abound. A wonderful introduction to games with language.

☐ Jackson, Jacqueline. *Turn Not Pale, Beloved Snail: A Book About Writing Among Other Things*. Little, Brown & Co., 1974, 192 pp. (adv. 6-up).

An author and teacher of writing and children's literature, Jackson has written about ways of seeing, hearing, thinking that generate authentic written expression. Informal, personal, perceptive, her sharing of ideas and experiences is a welcome reading experience for the confirmed reader and/or writer, even if the writing is simply the keeping of a journal. An advanced, mature student of eleven or twelve could enjoy and benefit from this book. Parents and teachers who would like to increase their own literary awareness should also find it both enjoyable and helpful. (Yes, in the book Jackson does identify the literary quotation from which the book's title is taken.)

☐ Kraske, Robert. *The Story of the Dictionary*. Harcourt, Brace, Jovanovich, 1975, 67 pp. (4-up).

An outstanding little book on the whats, whens, and hows of dictionaries. How did dictionaries start? What were the first ones like? How are today's dictionaries put together? In addition to answering such questions in a lively, fascinating manner, Kraske concludes his book with a discussion of the English language, including the different words used to describe the same thing, depending on the region of the country one is in.

☐ Laird, Stan. *Hands-On-Grammar: An Instant Resource*. Pitman Learning, 1978 (5, 6-up to all ages).

Primary listing under *Reference*.

A handy, pamphlet-sized little handbook that any parent or teacher should find most helpful. It is not intended to take the place of a grammar text or of a complete handbook. See *Reference* listing for details and suggested use.

□ Miles, Miska. *Apricot ABC*. Illus. by Peter Parnall. Little,
Brown & Co., 1969, 32 pp. (1, 2).
> A splendid rhymed alphabet book, not only using the
> realm of nature to illustrate letters, but rich in alliter-
> ation, superior use of language. Entrancing illustra-
> tions.

□ Pizer, Vernon. *Take My Word for It*. Dodd, Mead, 1981,
128 pp. (6-up).
> A surprising number of words in the English language
> have been derived from the name of a person. Among
> many others, two related to clothing are the *raglan*
> sleeve and the *cardigan* sweater. Pizer not only identifies
> a number of these words that found a way into our lan-
> guage, but he recounts with storyteller detail the full
> background of each such linguistic adoption. A joy to
> browse through, and a broadening experience linguisti-
> cally.

□ Plagemann, Bentz. *How to Write a Story*. Lothrup, Lee &
Shepard, 1971, 64 pp. (adv. 5, 6-up).
> A concise introduction to the art of creative writing.
> The author, himself a writer of fiction, describes the ba-
> sic elements and techniques of story writing. In many
> instances he illustrates his points with brief examples
> from the work of well-known writers. A good start for
> students interested in writing stories themselves, and a
> helpful supplement for language arts classes to give all
> students an idea of the creative writing process.

□ Reid, Alistair. *Ounce, Dice, Trice*. Gregg, 1980 (1958),
57 pp. (any age, depending on individual).
> A wonderful book of words to say aloud and listen to.
> Humorous, clever. Contains groups of words related,
> for example, as to sound, and sound related to meaning.
> *Not ordinary words,* and a few newly created, just for the
> pleasure of their sound.

□ Rowell, Elizabeth H. and Thomas B. Goodkind.
Teaching the Pleasures of Reading. Prentice-Hall, 1982,
256 pp. (adult).
> Primary listing under *Supplementary Teaching Resources.*
>   Hundreds of suggestions for involving kids pleasurably in word-related activities.

□ Sarnoff, Jane and Reynold Ruffins. *Words: A Book About
the Origins of Everyday Words and Phrases.* Scribner's,
1981, 48 pp. (4-up).
> Sarnoff's book is an enjoyable introduction to etymology. An appealing, humor-filled style and sprightly illustrations add to the charm of this informative and entertaining book.

□ Steckler, Arthur. *101 Words and How They Began.*
Doubleday, 1979, 48 pp. (4-up).
> The writer provides students with a good start on the fascinating activity of tracking down the origin of words. Some are a story in themselves.

13 Literature: Level I
Fables, Folk Tales and Fairy Tales

☐ Aesop. *Aesop's Fables.* Illus. by Fritz Kredel. Grossett & Dunlap, 1947, 234 pp. (all ages).
> A fine collection of dozens of Aesop's wise and pithy little tales. These ancient stories-with-a-moral are as timely today as they were centuries ago, and are valuable for children not only for their sheer pleasurableness and the timeless lessons they teach, but also for the literary background they offer. Many of the fables are woven firmly into the fabric of our culture and are frequently alluded to in a variety of contexts. For example, the fox and the "sour grapes" he couldn't reach; the plodding tortoise and the fast but irresponsible hare, etc.

☐ Aesop. *Aesop's Fables.* Illus. by Heidi Holder. Viking, 1981, 25 pp. (all ages).
> A selection of nine favorite fables, beautifully illustrated. The "moral" of each fable is gracefully and concisely stated after each one.

☐ Andersen, Hans Christian. *Hans Andersen: His Classic Fairy Tales.* Illus. by Michael Foreman. Harper & Row, 1978, 185 pp. (1-up).
> A fine selection of the classic Andersen tales most appreciated by children. Beautifully illustrated.

☐ Brown, Marcia. *Stone Soup.* Illus. by author. Scribner's, 1947, 48 pp. (k-up).
> A lively retelling of the old tale. In this version, villagers don't want to help some very hungry soldiers. The soldiers arouse the villagers' interest by saying they're going to make soup with stones. They always *flavor*

their delicious soup with. . . . And the intrigued villagers proceed to furnish the soup ingredients (added to the elegant stones already simmering in the big pot of water!).

□ Garner, Alan. *Alan Garner's Fairytales of Gold*. Illus. by Michael Foreman. Philomel, 1980, 200 pp. (1-up).
Four original fairy tales told in the traditional form. The vocabulary is not extensive, but the overall effect of the language used is excellent. Good triumphs over evil in these well-imagined stories.

□ Grimm, Brothers. Retold and illustrated by Jacquelyn Ilya Sage. *Many Furs*. Celestial Arts, 1981, 32 pp. (1-up).
Fleeing from her evil father, the king, the beautiful princess disguises herself in a coat made of a thousand different furs. Becoming a scullery maid in the kitchen of a handsome prince, she is eventually discovered and lives happily ever after. The illustrations are outstanding, and each double page of text is followed by a double-page illustration.

□ Grimm, The Brothers. *Fairy Tales*. Illus. by Fritz Kredel. Grossett & Dunlap, 1963, 247 pp. (1-up).
A classic collection of Grimm's fairy tales. With a wide variety to choose from, careful selections can be made, avoiding the fiercer or more violent stories in cases where this seems advisable.

□ Lang, Andrew. *The Red Fairy Book*. Viking, 1978 (1890), 371 pp. (2-up).
For a hundred years, children have enjoyed Lang's excellent collections of lovely, classic fairy tales from various cultures. *The Red Fairy Book* is just one of the series which includes *The Blue Fairy Book, The Yellow Fairy Book* and a number of other color-titled volumes.

Literature: Level I
Fantasies

☐ Alexander, Lloyd. *Coll and His White Pig*. Illus. by Evaline Ness. Holt, Rinehart, Winston, 1965, OP (k-2).

> A story for younger children set in the same mythical kingdom of Prydain that Alexander uses in his fine series for older children. Prydain has a Welsh flavor, and the story takes place in the days of enchanters, armored warriors, etc. The use of language is excellent, humor and nice little touches related to animals and garden abound, and the moral tone is splendid, with a good emphasis (subtly done) on being kind and helpful even when it isn't convenient. Fine reading for both children and adults.

☐ Alexander, Lloyd. *The Truthful Harp*. Illus. by Evaline Ness. Holt, Rinehart, Winston, 1967, 26 pp., OP (k-2).

> Another Prydain story for younger readers. An inept, not too powerful king ventures out into his world of castles, knights, etc., as a bard. The king's little hand-held harp has an important part in teaching him the value of being truthful. Other significant values are also brought out in this cleverly humorous little story. Excellent use of language.

☐ Bach, Alice. *The Smartest Bear and His Brother Oliver*. Illus. by Steven Kellogg. Harper & Row, 1976, 34 pp. (1-up).

> A delightfully illustrated story of a studious bear and his happy-go-lucky brother. Much fun is involved in prehibernation eating (a specific detailing of food in mouth-watering style). An important underlying point

is made: When each child is accepted as he is, it becomes easier for him to accept the differences of others and to fit happily into the family lifestyle.

□ Barklem, Jill. *The Big Book of Brambly Hedge*. Illus. by author. Philomel, 1981, 24 pp. (ps-2).

Lovers of the special worlds of the Beatrix Potter stories, of *Wind in the Willows,* will respond to the charm of Brambly Hedge. "There is a hedge . . . made up of elderberry and hawthorn bushes, brambles, wild roses, an ancient oak. . . . There are small front doors half-hidden in the tangled roots, and little curtained windows in the leafy trunks." The busy lives of the mice who live in Brambly Hedge are pictured in delicious detail: little rooms of multilevel tree-trunk homes, the flour mill, the store, cozy firesides. Quite irresistible.

□ Barrett, Judi. *Animals Should Definitely Not Wear Clothing*. Illus. by Ron Barrett. Atheneum, 1970, 32 pp. (ps-2).

Children will love the hilarious pictures and brief text (all in very large, lower-case letters) in this amusing book. Its theme is what would happen if animals (already so appropriately garbed in their own skins) were put into human-style clothes. Great for fun, and for good vocabulary-expanding reading.

□ Berenstain, Stan and Jan. *The Berenstain Bears Go to School*. Illus. by author. Random House, 1978, 32 pp. (ps-2).

This lively picture book is one of a widely popular series designed to provide early readers with stories that teach everyday-life lessons in a format they will enjoy. The delightful Bear family are entertainingly pictured (the clever characterizations and very human facial expressions are great fun) in a wide variety of situations. In *Go to School,* some of the fears and potential problems about school that worry kids are confronted and solved, with much of the tension of such situations defused for readers by the book's irresistible humor. Some of the other titles in the series are: *The Berenstain Bears and the Sitter, The Berenstain Bears' Moving Day* and *The Berenstain Bears and the Messy Room.*

□ Brooke, L. Leslie. *Johnny Crow's Garden*. Illus. by author. Warne, 1903, 48 pp. (ps-up).
> This is a picture book with its own special flavor. The illustrations are unique, often hilarious. The brief, rhymed text throws in words not often found in early-childhood books (children love the sound of them) in lines like these: "Then the Stork/ Gave a Philosophic Talk/ Till the Hippopotami/ Said: 'Ask no further, "What am I"'/While the Elephant/ Said something quite irrelevant/ In Johnny Crow's Garden." This book has been treasured for years by those fortunate enough to have encountered it. Two other "Johnny Crow" titles are equally enjoyable: *Johnny Crow's Party* and *Johnny Crow's New Garden*.

□ Brown, Margaret Wise. *The Little Fur Family*. Illus. by Garth Williams. Harper & Row, 1968, 32 pp. (ps-1).
> A wonderful little book about simple natural joys, family love, the pleasure of venturing forth to the out-doors—and of returning to the total security of home and parents. Fur symbolizes perfectly the soft, deep, infinitely warm atmosphere of love and security created in the book. All of Margaret Wise Brown's books have been loved by children for decades.

□ Bulla, Clyde Robert. *Dandelion Hill*. Illus. by Bruce Degen. Dutton, 1982, 32 pp. (k-1).
> The delightfully-told story of a cow who still wants to act like a calf. Rich with underlying lessons in kindness, understanding, the need to mature appropriately—and the fact that a "little calf" still lives in the hearts of adult member of the species!

□ Burgess, Thornton, W. *Old Mother West Wind*. Illus. by Harrison Cady. Little, Brown & Co., 1960 (1910), 140 pp. (1, 2).
> Entertaining stories of animals that behave entirely like human beings. These are favorites of a bygone day, but many people still enjoy them in spite of their seeming a little dated. There is an emphasis on "mother wit," and a strong moral tone as to the folly of pride, boasting, etc.

□ Carle, Eric. *The Rooster Who Set Out to See the World.*
   Illus. by author. Franklin Watts, 1972, 23 pp. (ps-1).
   A rooster, then two cats, three frogs, four turtles and
   five fish set off to see the world, but when night comes,
   home begins to seem better than adventure. Group by
   group, the travelers turn back, and finally the rooster
   himself goes home, enjoys his dinner and, happily
   asleep on his perch, dreams a wonderful trip around the
   world. Carle's bold, brilliantly colored illustrations are
   sure to appeal to young readers.

□ Clymer, Eleanor. *Leave Horatio Alone.* Illus. by Robert
   M. Quackenbush. Atheneum, 1974, 64 pp. (ps-3).
   An older cat wants his peace and quiet. Through an
   amusing series of events, Horatio mellows and even
   learns to play again. Humorous, especially well-written
   and delightfully illustrated. *Horatio Goes to the Country*
   offers further humorous experiences with Horatio.

□ Cole, Brock. *The King at the Door.* Illus. by author.
   Doubleday, 1979, 32 pp. (1-up).
   A clever story of a little boy who befriends an old man
   claiming to be the king. The innkeeper is skeptical—
   and unhelpful. The little boy is kind and generous and
   ultimately goes to live with the king. Underscores good
   values.

□ Dalgliesh, Alice. *The Little Wooden Farmer.* Illus. by Anita
   Lobel. Macmillan, 1930 (ps-1).
   Beloved by children since it was written over fifty years
   ago, this simple story of the little farmer and his wife
   who want "a brown cow that gives creamy milk, two
   white sheep with warm woolly coats, a fat pink pig
   with a curly tail, a rooster that will crow in the morning, a hen that will lay a large brown egg each day, a
   dog to guard my house and a cat to sit on the doorstep," continues to charm and entertain.

□ de Brunhoff, Jean. *The Story of Babar.* Illus. by author.
   Random House, 1933, 47 pp. (ps-up).
   Children continue to enjoy this fanciful story (and the
   others in the Babar series) of the mild and gracious ele-

phant Babar, his wife Celeste, their children and special friends. In *The Story of Babar,* the orphaned Babar is befriended by a rich, kindly old lady and given his opportunity for a new life in which he shares his good fortune and becomes a wise and benevolent leader. Translated from the French, the Babar stories have an interestingly "different" flavor.

☐ Delton, Judy. *Penny-Wise—Fun Foolish.* Illus. by Giulio Maestro. Crown, 1977, 44 pp. (1, 2).
Parents as well as children will appreciate this entertaining story of an ostrich who is so economical she never enjoys herself. A friend benevolently tricks her into a fun-filled outing, and she finally realizes the value of investing a little money in rewarding recreation.

☐ Erickson, Russell E. *A Toad for Tuesday.* Illus. by Lawrence Di Fiori. Lothrop, 1974, 64 pp. (k-2).
When Warton, a lovable little toad, ignores his brother Morton's advice and sets out on skis to take some beetle brittle to their Aunt Toolia, he doesn't realize that he is going to fall into the clutches of an owl who is looking for a special little tidbit to save for his birthday dinner the next Tuesday. Ingeniously imagined encounters with eccentric animal characters, warmth, humor and good underlying values characterize this and the other stories of the series. There is considerably more text (and a much more extensive vocabulary) in these books than in beginning-reader series, and they would need to be read aloud to children at the early level. Other titles include *Warton and Morton, Warton and the Castaways* and others.

☐ Ets, Marie Hall. *In the Forest.* Illus. by author. Viking, 1974, 45 pp. (ps-1).
A world of adventure takes place in a little boy's imagination as he plays in the wood. Young children can identify with the vividness of the boy's make-believe activities.

☐ Ets, Marie Hall. *Play With Me*. Illus. by author. Viking,
1944, 45 pp. (ps-1).
This endearing story involves a succession of little wild
creatures so dear to the hearts of children. A small girl
finds that if instead of pursuing the animals and insects
she longs to play with, she sits very quietly, they will
come to her.

☐ Flack, Marjorie and Kurt Wiese. *The Story About Ping*.
Illus. by Kurt Wiese. Viking, 1933, 32 pp. (ps-2).
A modern classic, this simple little story of a young
duck who lives on a boat on the Yangtze River of China, has been loved by children for more than fifty years.
When Ping, through his own doing, is left behind one
evening, he sets out in search of the "home" boat. He is
briefly caged as a prospective meal, but escapes and finally hears the familiar, "La, la" (Come, come) call of
his owner. Even though he knows he'll receive a swat
for being the last to respond, he joyfully swims home.

☐ Gág, Wanda. *Millions of Cats*. Illus. by author. Coward,
McCann, 1928, 32 pp. (ps-1).
As its longevity attests, children love this wildly impossible little story. They enjoy every minute of the old
man's bewilderment as he realizes that instead of coming home with one cat, he has somehow involved himself with millions and billions and trillions of them.

☐ Galdone, Paul. *The Little Red Hen*. Illus. by author.
Houghton Mifflin, 1973, 32 pp. (ps-1).
This is just one edition of the timeless classic that has
been enjoyed by children for generations. The moral
rightness of taking responsibility, working, and then
reaping the reward is underscored. Galdone's illustrations are especially effective as he captures the laziness
and indifference of the animals who refuse to help the
Little Red Hen work.

☐ Godden, Rumer. *The Fairy Doll*. Illus. by Adrienne
Adams. Viking, 1956, 67 pp., OP (1-4).
A charming story with a helpful real-life-related theme
(the youngest of four, "pushed around" by siblings,

lacking confidence) and some delightful fantasy. Little
Elizabeth becomes self-reliant and capable with the help
of the fairy doll, her great-grandmother and a wise
mother. The literary quality of Godden's writing is excellent.

□ Godden, Rumer. *A Kindle of Kittens*. Illus. by Lynne
Barnes. Viking, 1979, 32 pp. (k-3).
An enchanting story by a gifted writer. She-Cat, a stray
tabby, must find homes for her four lovely kittens.
How she goes about it makes fine reading. Warmth and
humor permeate each page, and illustrator Lynne
Barnes, using the town of Rye, England as a setting,
has captured the writer's tone perfectly in her delightful
pictures.

□ Goodall, John S. *Creepy Castle*. Atheneum, 1975, 60 pp.
(ps-up).
An exciting story of peril and suspense told without
words in Goodall's delicately lovely paintings. A dash-
ing young mouse and his lady fair out for a pleasant
stroll stumble upon a deserted castle. Unaware that a
villainous outlaw is lurking behind them, they seem to
be trapped when he slams a heavy door behind them
and quickly locks it. But valor and ingenuity win out
and "all's well that ends well." Goodall's illustrations
are totally captivating as always. Such wordless stories
work well in encouraging imagination and creativity.

□ Goodall, John S. *The Midnight Adventures of Kelly, Dot,
and Esmerelda*. Atheneum, 1973, 60 pp. (ps-up).
Another of Goodall's intriguing little wordless books in
which the story is clearly told in his beautiful drawings.
At midnight a toy koala bear (Kelly), a rosy-cheeked
doll (Dot), and a dainty little mouse (Esmerelda) awak-
en and embark on a perilous adventure into the land-
scape of a picture on the wall. Kelly's courage and
quick action avert disaster, and they all return safely to
their spot on the shelf. Children enjoy telling the story
which they can infer from the picture sequences.

□ Grahame, Kenneth. *The Reluctant Dragon*. Illus. by
Ernest H. Shepard. Holiday, 1953, 58 pp. (2-up).
This is the original of the story later adapted and popu-
larized by Disney, of a dragon who didn't want to
breathe fire or engage in combat. A durably entertaining tale, it uses an above-average vocabulary and a
pleasing literary style.

□ Hoban, Russell. *The Twenty-Elephant Restaurant*. Illus.
by Emily Arnold. Atheneum, 1978, 40 pp.
Older children should not be put off by the flat, picture-book size of this story. Although generously illustrated with delightful drawings, it contains more text
than the usual picture book. Its special quality is its
rather sophisticated humor. The people in the story
speak in "practical," "logical" terms about utterly zany
projects—and this in an escalating pattern that builds
throughout the book. Aside from its "fun factor," the
story introduces children to the reality that *supposedly*
logical reasoning is not always wise or true. Paradox-
ically, however, it also opens up some insights as to
adaptability and the idea that some people may choose
ways of living that are based on a logic of their own
which is out of step with the usual but not necessarily
wrong in a moral or ethical sense.

□ Johnston, Tony. *Night Noises and Other Mole and Troll
Stories*. Illus. by Cyndy Czekeres. Putnam, 1977, 64
pp. (ps-2).
Four gentle, whimsical little stories focus on the everyday activities of two loyal friends, Mole and Troll.
Whether it's trying to pull a loose tooth or being scared
by harmless night sounds that occupy their attention,
the two friends support and encourage each other with
warmth and understanding. Though similar in tone to
Arnold Lobel's Frog and Toad stories, the quality of
Johnston's writing doesn't match that of Lobel's by a
substantial margin. Nevertheless, the Mole and Troll
stories offer pleasant, easy-reading material that small
children will enjoy. Other titles in the series include
Mole and Troll Trim the Tree and *Happy Birthday Mole
and Troll*.

□ Keats, Ezra Jack. *Jennie's Hat*. Illus. by author. Harper &
Row, 1966 (k-2).
> A visual confection is created as Jennie's friends, the
> birds, transform the plain hat in which she is so disap-
> pointed into a mass of color and beauty.

□ Kipling, Rudyard. *Just-So Stories*. Black and white
illustrations by author; color illustrations by J.
McGleeson. Doubleday, 1912 (1902), 247 pp. (1, 2-
up).
> Kipling's way with language adds to the charm of
> "How the Leopard Got His Spots" and other familiar
> tales. Some stories in the collection are better than oth-
> ers; select these and *read aloud*, getting into the spirit of
> Kipling's fascinating use of words. These stories are
> part of our English-language heritage of classic works.

□ Kraus, Robert. *Leo the Late Bloomer*. Illus. by Jose
Arvego. Dutton, 1971, 30 pp. (ps-1).
> A picture-book with a short easy text that makes a very
> good point for children. Leo's father worried because
> Leo couldn't read, write, etc.—but he was just a late
> bloomer, and in his own good time he finally made it.

□ Kuskin, Karla. *James and the Rain*. Illus. by author.
Harper & Row, 1957 (ps-1).
> James goes out to play in the rain and asks a series of
> animals if they "know any excellent rainy day games."
> The text rhymes and has a counting buildup as well.

□ Lionni, Leo. *The Biggest House in the World*. Illus. by
author. Knopf, 1968, 30 pp. (ps-1).
> When a little snail tells his father he wants to have the
> biggest house in the world, his father tells him the story
> of a snail who had the same wish and who learned how
> to make his little snail house bigger and bigger and
> more and more elaborate, with dire consequences. The
> little snail learns from the story and as a result lives a
> happier life. A good point is subtly made in this color-
> fully illustrated little book.

□ Lionni, Leo. *Inch by Inch*. Illus. by author. Astor-Honor, 1960, 30 pp. (ps-1).

A little inchworm talks a robin out of eating him by offering to measure her tail. He then measures a succession of birds: the flamingo's neck, the toucan's beak, etc. When the mockingbird says he must measure her song or be eaten, he has to think of a way to escape. Colorful, imaginative illustrations.

□ Lobel, Arnold. *Frog and Toad Are Friends*. Illus. by author. Harper & Row, 1970, 64 pp. (ps-2).

The quiet, endearing atmosphere and recounting of the kind of small details children love to identify with, found in this and the other groups of stories in the Frog and Toad series, set a much-imitated standard for easy, early-reading books. Frog and Toad demonstrate the qualities of true friendship—as well as make mistakes and worry over trifles. Lobel's stories do more than laud friendship, however, The writer has an unerring ear for just the right turn of phrase and a wry, subtle wit that focuses on the frailties and foibles of human nature in the guise of his little Frog and Toad friends. Not only children, but their parents as well, thoroughly enjoy these appealing stories. Other titles include *Days with Frog and Toad, Frog and Toad Together* and *Frog and Toad All Year*.

□ Lobel, Arnold. *Mouse Soup*. Illus. by author. Harper & Row, 1977, 64 pp. (k-2).

These are stories within a story. A clever mouse talks himself out of being eaten by a weasel by telling his captor stories and then sending him on a wild goose chase while he makes his own escape.

□ MacDonald, Betty. *Mrs. Piggle-Wiggle*. Illus. by Hilary Knight. Lippincott, 1947, 118 pp. (k-3).

First-graders seem to especially enjoy Mrs. Piggle-Wiggle. A fantasy version of the somewhat rare adult who isn't at all bothered by the wide-ranging activities of children, she loves child-type fun herself—in fact, goes along with their fantasies. At the same time, she is reassuringly firm and confident, correcting their attitudes and behavior by providing highly imaginative ways of dealing with responsibility. Full of hilarity, the story (and the others in the series) make effective, practical points in a way children not only accept but enjoy. Other series titles are *Hello, Mrs. Piggle-Wiggle, Mrs. Piggle-Wiggle's Farm* and *Mrs. Piggle-Wiggle's Magic.*

☐ McCloskey, Robert. *Make Way for Ducklings.* Illus. by author. Viking, 1941, 67 pp. (k-2).
Children have enjoyed this modern classic for more than forty years. When a mother mallard and her eight little ducklings brave the dangers of city streets, it takes the expertise of a New York policeman to insure that Mother Mallard and her little flock safely keep their appointment with Father Mallard at the Public Garden Park.

☐ Milne, A. A. *Winnie the Pooh; The House at Pooh Corner.* Both illus. by Ernest H. Shepard. Dutton, 1926, 161 pp.; 1928, 180 pp. (1-3).
Milne's incomparable stories of Pooh and his friends (the real thing, not the Disney adaptation) have been taken to children's hearts for several generations. It is not a "story-line" but the conversations, the little eccentricities and habits of the books' characters that live on in the hearts of those whose childhood is long behind them. Pooh's little "hums," his fondness for honey and condensed milk—and his related plumpness; Owl and his atrocious spelling; Christopher Robin's loving and indulgent, "Silly old bear." The Pooh stories reflect a great understanding of the way children think and play, the way they like to experiment with sounds. Like so many books, however, that are loved with a passion by devoted readers, the Pooh stories aren't every child's choice. But by all means give each child the opportunity to find out whether he has a special place for Pooh and his friends in his heart.

☐ Minarik, Else Holmelund. *Little Bear's Friend.* Illus. by Maurice Sendak. Harper & Row, 1960, 64 pp. (ps-2).
Little Bear radiates an infectious joy that spreads to those around him. In the four little episodes of this book, he takes a little girl who has lost her way back to her parents, watches over a straying duckling, fixes the

broken arm of his little friend's doll, and bravely overcomes his sadness when his friend must return home at
summer's end. This book is one of a series of easy-read
books in which a warm, wise mother and benevolent,
strong father play traditional parental roles. Other titles
in the series include: *A Kiss for Little Bear, Father Bear
Comes Home* and *Little Bear's Visit.*

☐ Oakley, Graham. *The Church Mouse.* Illus. by author.
  Atheneum, 1972, 36 pp. (ps-3).
    This completely delightful story is representative of a
    particular kind of children's book in which a graphic
    artist combines his art with a story-line and turns au-
    thor. Oakley's drawings of the clever little mice that
    have taken shelter in an old English church, and their
    sturdy ally, the cat Sampson, are full of fascinating de-
    tails. The humor is clever, and the basic theme of a
    whole group of helpless little mice uniting to thwart
    (with Sampson's help) their enemies, has an unfailing
    appeal. Titles in the series include: *The Church Mice
    Adrift, The Church Mice and the Moon* and others.

☐ Peet, Bill. *The Luckiest One of All.* Illus. by author.
  Houghton Mifflin, 1982, 30 pp. (1, 2).
    Rhymed and delightfully illustrated, the story starts
    with a little boy wishing he could be a bird. The bird
    wishes it were a fish, and so it goes, through all sorts of
    creatures and contraptions—finally, the cat wishes it
    were a little boy who can do so many things! Good
    fun—and good encouragement to appreciate whatever
    one's lot may be.

☐ Piper, Watty, retold by. *The Little Engine That Could.*
  Illus. by Ruth Sanderson. Platt, Munk, 1976 (1930),
  48 pp. (ps-1).
    This is an authentic edition of the timeless classic that
    encourages stick-to-it-iveness. Children love the repeti-
    tion, sound effects and triumphant "I *thought* I could!"
    ending.

□ Potter, Beatrix. *The Tale of Peter Rabbit.* Illus. by author. Warne, 1901, 58 pp. (ps-2).

This is possibly the best known among a long list of timeless classics created by Beatrix Potter that children continue to take to their hearts and from which they learn valuable lessons. Like all the famous "animal character" stories of early childhood, they aren't really about animals at all; they are about life and people. Who can forget the clearly drawn character of the naughty, debonair Peter Rabbit—and the consequences of his ill-advised venture into Mr. MacGregor's garden. After almost ninety years, Potter's combination of stories true to the realities of human nature with her wonderful little drawings are, deservedly, more popular than ever.

□ Smith, Jim. *The Frog Band and the Onion Seller.* Illus. by author. Little, Brown, 1977, 32 pp. (k-3).

Smith, like Graham Oakley, author of the Church Mice series, is a talented artist who has become the author of children's books. Smith's cleverly characterized band of rakish performers become involved in a wildly funny, harum-scarum adventure with an onion seller who isn't quite what he seems. The colorful drawings are filled with meticulous detail, and a reader can spend minutes simply looking appreciatively at a single drawing. Enjoyable for all, such books are particularly helpful in encouraging reluctant readers. Other titles include: *The Frog Band and Durrington Dormouse* and *The Frog Band and the Owlnapper.*

□ Steig, William. *Sylvester and the Magic Pebble.* Illus. by author. Windmill, 1969 (ps-1).

There is a subtle emphasis throughout this story on the value of family, love, the supremely important things that are often taken for granted. Sylvester finds a magic "wishing" pebble, thoughtlessly wishes himself a rock, then can't touch the pebble and wish to be himself again. His grieving parents finally wander across the "rock," and his father casually picks up the pebble which is lying nearby, lays it on the rock . . . happy ending.

□ Tomlinson, Jill. *Hilda the Hen Who Wouldn't Give Up.* Illus. by Fernando Krahn. Harcourt, Brace, Jovanovich, 1967, 96 pp. (1-3).

Hilda demonstrates enterprise, courage and lasting determination, first in making it to the farm five miles away to visit her aunt who has a new brood of chicks, then in managing to sit on her own eggs against all odds. This is a hilarious book, full of slapstick humor and outrageous situations, and with sound underlying values as well.

□ Wahl, Jan. *The Pleasant Fieldmouse Storybook.* Illus. by Erik Blegvad. Prentice-Hall, 1977, 63 pp. (k-3).

Delightfully expressed stories with a unique flavor of their own. The humor is subtle, the imagery enriched. Illustrated with clever black-and-white drawings.

□ White, E. B. *Charlotte's Web.* Illus. by Garth Williams. Harper & Row, 1952, 184 pp. (k-3).

The beloved modern classic of an animal-loving little girl (Fern), a pig (Wilbur), who needed a friend, a wise and beautiful spider (Charlotte), and a rather self-centered rat (Templeton). Children have been charmed for decades by this thoroughly enjoyable story. The use of language and overall literary quality is outstanding.

□ Williams, Margery. *The Velveteen Rabbit.* Doubleday, 1922, 44 pp. (k-up).

This modern classic is a lovely fantasy about a stuffed toy rabbit that becomes real through a little boy's love. Effective simply as a story, it also conveys a valid sense of the lasting significance a special love for a childhood toy can have. Love as a life-giving force is satisfyingly affirmed.

□ Wondriska, William. *Mr. Brown and Mr. Gray.* Holt, Rinehart & Winston, OP (k-3).

A cleverly done story that contrasts the life of a contented, loving individual with that of a greedy one who can never possess enough. The King (who happens to be a horse) wants to find out what happiness is and he grants two pigs, Mr. Brown and Mr. Gray, the opportunity to have anything they want for a year. Surely then, the King thinks, they will have discovered the secret of happiness. An enjoyable, often humorous story that also emphasizes important values.

□ Zion, Gene. *Harry the Dirty Dog.* Illus. by Margaret B. Graham. Harper & Row, 1956, 32 pp. (ps-1).
    One of a series; all of the Harry stories are full of delightful humor and are excellent for reading aloud. In this story, Harry hates baths and gets so dirty that his "family" doesn't recognize him any more. Harry's subsequent adventures and the happy ending keep young listeners chuckling.

Literature: Level I
Realistic Stories—
Modern

☐ Ainsworth, Ruth. *The Ruth Ainsworth Book.* Illus. by
   Shirley Hughes. Franklin Watts, 1970, 286 pp., OP
   (ps-1).
   > Some of the thirty-six very short stories in this book are
   > fantasies, but a majority are simply about the small de-
   > tails of a child's life. There is a nice variety, a fairly sim-
   > ple vocabulary. No particular effort is made to impart
   > cardinal values, but the overall atmosphere is warm and
   > traditional.

☐ Bemelmans, Ludwig. *Madeline.* Illus. by author. Viking,
   1939, 48 pp. (k-3).
   > Clever, humorous drawings and a brief sprightly story
   > in rhyme characterize this and the other books in the
   > Madeline series of stories that have become modern
   > classics. Little Madeline and eleven other small girls live
   > in a vine-covered house in Paris under the tender care
   > of the devoted Miss Clavel. Madeline is the one to
   > whom things always seem to happen—in this book she
   > awakens in the night with appendicitis. In others of the
   > series, Madeline launches into various endeavors and
   > somehow, whatever she undertakes turns into more
   > than was expected. The stories are full of warmth and
   > kindness, as well as madcap adventures.

☐ Beskow, Elsa. *Pelle's New Suit.* Illus. by author. Harper &
   Row, 1929, 16 pp. (ps-1).
   > In this much-loved tale, the little Swedish boy Pelle
   > seeks help, step by step, in transforming the wool from
   > his lamb into a new wool suit. The quaint, colorful il-
   > lustrations are especially appealing.

□ Blades, Ann. *Mary of Mile 18*. Illus. by author. Tundra
   Books, 1971, 38 pp. (1-3).
   This simply written, beautifully illustrated little story is
   set in a homesteaders' small farming community in
   northern British Columbia. Life there is almost as rug-
   ged as it was for the pioneers of past centuries: no indoor plumbing, no electricity, no phones or television—and winters that last for seven months of the
   year. Mary, one of the Fehr family's five children, finds
   a part-wolf pup and longs to keep him in spite of the
   strictly enforced rule, "Our animals must work for us or
   give us food." How Mary finally is granted her wish
   forms the story's satisfying conclusion. The author/il-
   lustrator taught the little school at Mile 18, and her detailed "primitive" illustrations (a full-page color painting faces each page of text) convey the reality of the
   remote, yet family-settled corner of the wilderness.
   (Mile 18 is a Mennonite community according to a
   note at the end of the book, and this fact answers some
   questions that might arise as to lifestyle.)

□ Borten, Helen. *Do You Know What I Know?* Illus. by
   author. Abelard Schuman, 1970, 64 pp. (ps-2).
   Combining concrete perceptions with a playful approach, the writer helps children to become aware of
   the ways in which they learn about the world around
   them: "Red is bright, next to white/red backs down,
   next to brown/(A color's neighbor/ changes its behavior)." And, "I find out lots of things,/just by listening./I
   know/When a key is in a lock,/When a cuckoo's in a
   clock,/When a foot is on a stair,/When a fly is in the
   air/When a frog is in a log,/When a ship is in a fog." An
   enjoyable book that is excellent for encouraging sensory
   perception.

□ Carle, Eric. *Pancakes, Pancakes*. Illus. by author. Knopf,
   1970, 30 pp., OP (ps-1).
   An entertaining story that, in a playful way, also gives a
   young child some idea of the processes behind a simple
   article of food—a pancake. Jack is very hungry, but before he can have a huge pancake for breakfast he must
   obtain (from raw materials and primary sources) all the

needed ingredients. The story is accompanied by
Carle's patchwork-of-color illustrations with their fine
underlying textural detail.

□ Carlson, Natalie Savage. *The Happy Orpheline*. Illus. by
Garth Williams. Harper & Row, 1957, 96 pp. (k-2).
A charming story in a French setting, with a different
perspective. These orphan girls are very happy, consider
themselves a family, and don't *want* to be adopted. One
little orphan has a series of adventures and is *almost* unhappily adopted. Excellent underlying values throughout. This book is one of a series on the Orphelines. All
are good.

□ de Paola, Tomie. *Now One foot, Now the Other*. Illus. by
author. Putnam, 1981, 32 pp. (1, 2).
Also listed under *Handicaps and Special Problems*.
Bobby and his grandpa are close friends. When
Grandpa has a stroke, other family members think he
can't hear or understand them. Bobby senses this isn't
true and is able to help his grandfather on the road to
recovery. Bobby assumes the protecting, helping role
his grandpa used to play with him. Excellent.

□ Gordon, Shirley. *The Boy Who Wanted a Family*. Illus. by
Charles Robinson. Harper & Row, 1980, 96 pp. (1-4).
Michael wanted a home and family of his own more
than he wanted anything else in the world. But all his
life he had lived in one foster home after another.
Twice he had thought he was going to be adopted, but
both times his hopes were dashed. How Michael finally
finds a home and a happy new life is the theme of this
warm, well-told story.

□ Gundersheimer, Karen. *Happy Winter*. Illus. by author.
Harper & Row, 1982, 40 pp. (ps-1).
This is a book of children at home doing simple, homey
things: playing in the snow, dressing up, baking a cake
(the recipe is included). The text is not outstanding,
but the wonderfully detailed illustrations are absolutely
delightful, the whole atmosphere of the book warm,
cozy, and appealing.

□ Hoban, Russell. *A Birthday for Frances.* Illus. by Lillian Hoban. Harper & Row, 1968, 31 pp. (k-2).

Hoban captures children's ways of thinking and speaking in this perceptively done story involving sibling jealousy. Sisterly love triumphs in the end. This is one in the series of Frances books; all are good.

□ Keller, Beverly. *The Beetle Bush.* Illus. by Marc Simont. Coward, McCann, 1976, 64 pp. (k-2).

Arabelle Mott is convinced she is a failure—nothing she attempts turns out right. When her efforts to grow a vegetable garden produce beetles, a mole, snails and weeds, she is in despair—until suddenly inspired to view her failed garden from a different perspective. Keller understands children and writes with humor and warmth. As in her other books, the writer quietly stresses love and acceptance of the natural world and its creatures.

□ Keller, Beverly. *Fiona's Flea.* Illus. by Diane Paterson. Coward, McCann, 1981, 62 pp. (1-3).

Fiona doesn't want to go to the circus because she thinks animals don't belong in cages; and when she is bitten by a flea from a strange dog she has befriended, she wonders how she can find the flea a more comfortable life. Humorous and cleverly written, the story will elicit a sympathetic response to Fiona's way of dealing with ordinary events. The idea of reacting with kindness instead of hostility to those in need is a subtly handled theme.

□ Keller, Beverly. *Pimm's Place.* Illus. by Jacqueline Chwast. Coward, McCann, 1978, 63 pp. (1-3).

A fine story about Bradley Pimm, a quiet little boy with many fears, who wears glasses, doesn't enjoy rough and tumble or loud noises, and feels quite out of place at a large family reunion. How he finds a "quiet place" and eventually shares it with his boisterous cousins—and how he overcomes some of his fears—makes great reading. Humorous, sensitive and with a fine, imaginative use of language.

□ Lasky, Kathryn. *My Island Grandma*. Illus. by Emily McCully. Frederick Warne, 1979, 32 pp. (1, 2).

A brief, delightful story of the special times a little girl has with her grandmother. Abbey, her parents, and her grandmother spend every summer on a little island off the coast of Maine. Abbey can run over to her grandmother's cabin whenever she likes, and together they explore, sail, pick berries, stargaze, and share a close, loving relationship. An especially welcome aspect of the story is the portrayal of the grandmother as an active, resourceful, interesting person rather than as the vague, cushiony stereotypical grandmother so often found in stories.

□ McCloskey, Robert. *Time of Wonder*. Illus. by author. Viking, 1957, 63 pp. (2-up).

Beautifully illustrated by the author, the book is in a picture-book format, but with a substantial amount of text. Evocative descriptions of the natural world, of two children's experiences during summer on an offshore New England island provide the quiet story-line. This is an excellent book to use in encouraging children to observe their surroundings, the weather, etc. Good to read aloud, asking the children to picture in their minds what is being read.

□ McGinley, Phyllis. *The Most Wonderful Doll in the World*. Illus. by author. J. B. Lippincott, 1950, 61 pp. (2-up).

A little girl has an imagination that makes a doll she doesn't have "the most wonderful doll in the world," with an ever-growing list of wonderful clothes and attributes. By the end of the story she has learned the difference between dreams and reality.

□ Miles, Miska. *Aaron's Door*. Illus. by Alan E. Cober. Little, Brown & Co., 1977, 46 pp. (2-up).

Also listed under *Handicaps and Special Problems*.

A beautifully and perceptively told story in pictures and brief text. Aaron and his younger sister, Deborah, have just been adopted. Deborah is happy, ready to accept her new home and parents. Aaron, his heart filled with the bitterness of the past, can't trust, can't accept.

Aaron's emotions and the final effect of his new parents' love and acceptance of him are perceptively portrayed.

☐ Sayler, Mary H. *Why Are You Home, Dad?* Broadman, 1983 (1, 2).
A well-handled story about Kirk and Karen whose father loses his job. It expands children's awareness of the problems some children are facing today. The positive results of the family crisis are dealt with in a practical and Christian way.

☐ Scott, Ann Herbert. *On Mother's Lap.* Illus. by Glo Coalson. McGraw, Hill, 1972, 39 pp. (ps-1).
Warmly pictured and with minimal text, the story's theme is simple: there is always room for one more on Mother's lap. By using an Eskimo mother and children in the illustrations, the theme's universality is emphasized.

☐ Spier, Peter. *Crash! Bang! Boom!* Illus. by author. Doubleday, 1972, 44 pp. (ps-2).
Here is a wonderful collection of sounds. The book includes many, many of Spier's small, detailed pictures (each two-page spread shows related activities going on, with accompanying sounds named under each picture). There is a tremendous sense of action throughout, and the book would lend itself creatively to one-on-one or small-group activity with children identifying and imitating sounds, or for reading practice in decoding the written names of the sounds accurately.

☐ Spier, Peter. Two irresistible wordless books: *Peter Spier's Christmas* and *Peter Spier's Rain.* Both illus. by author. Doubleday, 1983, 38 pp.; 1982, 36 pp. (all ages).
Spier is in a class by himself with his softly colored, incredibly detailed pictures. In *Christmas* the reader follows an obviously warm, close family of two parents and three children through the beloved season: preparation and anticipation of every kind; deeds of kindness to others; the creche and the Christmas Eve church service; the gifts and the arrival of fond grandparents; the

bountiful dinner (with heads bowed first in thanks), the piled-up counters and wall-to-wall clutter—and, to end the day, the tired but warmly content husband and wife companionably cleaning up the mess, bringing order out of chaos, finally sharing a quiet moment by the fire. Even right after Christmas, Spier's book makes you want to do it all over again—and with more of the serene love that simply spills out of its pages.

In *Rain,* a young brother and sister, boots, raincoats and rainhats on, an umbrella to share between them, go walking in the rain. In the course of their wanderings, they engage in every wonderful in-the-rain activity imaginable. As always, Spier's pictures have a life of their own, creating images of innocent childhood play, loving parents, warm, sheltering homes.

□ Waybill, Marjorie. *Chinese Eyes.* Herald, 1974, 32 pp. (1, 2).

A Korean adoptee is teased by other children and called "Chinese eyes." Her confidence is restored by a wise mother's words. Deals in a subtle way with prejudice, those who are "different," etc.

□ Welber, Robert. *Frog, Frog, Frog.* Illus. by Deborah Ray. Pantheon, 1971, 31 pp. (ps-1).

On a warm summer day in the country, Christopher decides to hunt for a frog and catch it. The writer captures the joy and freedom of his outdoor adventures as he runs and leaps past flowers and trees—and finally decides he'd rather watch a frog jump freely than to catch it.

□ Yashima, Taro. *Crow Boy.* Illus. by author. Viking, 1955, 38 pp. (k-2).

An unusual picture-book story of a shy little Japanese schoolboy, nicknamed Chibi, who is unlike his schoolmates. Shunned throughout his years at school, a new teacher finally makes contact with the boy no one knows and helps others to see his unique nature and abilities.

Literature: Level I
Realistic Stories—
Historical

☐ Bulla, Clyde Robert. *The Beast of Lor.* Illus. by Ruth Sanderson. Crowell, 1977, 54 pp. (1-4).
> An imaginative story of a Celtic boy in England and of his friendship with a gentle elephant brought to Britain by an invading Roman army. An excellent possibility for use in connection with an early-grade introduction to ancient history. Well-written and interest-holding.

☐ Bulla, Clyde Robert. *Sword in the Tree.* Illus. by Paul Galdone. Harper & Row, 1956, 94 pp. (1-3).
> Shan, the son of Lord Weldon, has exciting adventures in the days of King Arthur. Robbers in the woods, brave knights, and fabled Camelot are all a part of this well-written story for early readers. Courage, determination and honesty are some of the implicit underlying values.

☐ Bulla, Clyde Robert. *A Lion to Guard Us.* Illus. by Michele Chessare. Harper & Row, 1981, 128 pp. (2-up).
> Jemmy and Meg (eight and five) depend on their eleven-year-old sister to find a way to get them all from England to the Jamestown Colony in Virginia. Their father has gone ahead to make a home for them, but now their mother has died and the callous Mistress Trippett for whom she worked has turned them out. Exciting adventure and a happy ending in this easy-read story.

☐ Bulla, Clyde Robert. *Pirate's Promise.* Illus. by Peter Burchard. Harper & Row, 1958, 87 pp. (2-up).
> Sold by his uncle as an indentured servant, Tom is forced onto a ship sailing for America. On the voyage

the ship is attacked by pirates, and Tom finds himself among the motley crew of the piratical *Sea Bird*. Through it all, Tom's spirit and courage remain strong. How he survives many dangers and finds a new life in the New World makes suspenseful reading. Easy reading level.

☐ Dalgliesh, Alice. *The Courage of Sarah Noble*. Illus. by Leonard Weisgard. Scribner's, 1954, 52 pp. (1-3).
A charming little story of eight-year-old Sarah who goes with her father into the wilderness where he has bought land for a new home. All the rest of the family (including a young baby) stay at the old home until the father can build the new house. Sarah keeps house for her father, and friendly Indians become Sarah's second family. (Based on a true story of the eighteenth century.)

☐ Mitchell, Barbara. *Tomahawks and Trombones*. Illus. by George Overlie. Carolrhoda, 1982, 56 pp. (k-2).
Some of the early settlers in America were Moravians, people from Germany who loved God and loved music. The Moravians and the native American Indians treated each other well, but some of the other settlers and the Indians began to have trouble. One year the Moravians were especially happy because they had some new trombones to play music on. They practiced for special Christmas music, but then they heard that the trouble between the Indians and settlers was so bad that even the Moravians were going to be attacked. The story, a combination of old records and some imagination as well, tells what happened that fateful Christmas day.

$\boxed{14}$ Literature: Level II
Fables, Folk Tales and Fairy Tales

☐ Colum, Padraic. *The Boy Apprenticed to An Enchanter.* Illus. by Edward Leigh. Macmillan, 1966, 150, pp., OP (4, 5).

> An imaginative, colorful fairy tale. Its imagery, settings and vocabulary are all above average, and, as in any good fairy tale, right ultimately triumphs over wrong.

☐ Craik, Dinah Maria Mulock. *The Little Lame Prince.* Watermill, 1983 (1875), 107 pp. (3-up).

> A delightful fairy tale that lauds goodness and kindness in a most appealing manner. The magic flying cloak that unfolds itself from a dark, shabby-looking little wad of cloth into a marvelous means of escape for the lonely little prince is something a child will never forget.

☐ Dawood, H. J. (retold by, from the original Arabic). *Tales from the Arabian Nights.* Illus. by Ed Young. Doubleday, 1978, 320 pp. (3-up).

> A fine retelling of the perennially popular stories, including several tales not previously found in Arabian Nights collections. Some of the stories offer more detail than is found in other generally read versions.

☐ Farjeon, Eleanor. *The Little Bookroom.* Illus. by Edward Ardizzone. Henry Z. Walck, 1956, 302 pp., OP (3-up).

> The writer herself selected for this book her favorites among the stories she has written for children. Imagination, humor, warmth and understanding infuse these tales whose characters range from kings, peasants, animals and birds to everyday children. It is unfortunate that this book, like so many of Farjeon's titles, is now out of print, but it is still widely available in libraries.

□ Krensky, Stephen. *Castles in the Air and Other Tales*. Illus. by Warren Leiberman. Atheneum, 1979, 66 pp. (3, 4).
A collection of lighthearted stories written in folk-tale form. Each story is woven around a common idiomatic phrase, with each one being given a concrete form (e.g., fish in a kettle are a central focus of the story, "A Fine Kettle of Fish"). The stories are characterized by a polished style and above-average vocabulary.

□ Lang, Andrew (collected and edited by). *Arabian Nights*. Illus. by Vera Bock. Longmans, Green, 1946 (1898), 303 pp. (3-up).
This popular old favorite, a version read by children for decades, contains all the well-known Arabian Nights tales and can be enjoyed by children of all ages.

□ MacDonald, George. *The Princess and Curdie*. Penguin, 1966 (1883), 224 pp. (3-up).
When a lovely fairy commissions Curdie, the little miner boy, to save the King and the Princess, his life changes forever. To help him in his task, Curdie is given the magic power of discerning the true character of anyone he encounters. How Curdie carries out the fairy's wishes and the part played by the use of his special gift makes a fairy story that children have loved for many decades. As in all of MacDonald's work, spiritual truth is clearly woven into this tale, and qualities of courage, loyalty and compassion are underscored.

□ Nickless, Will (illustrator). *The Book of Fables*. Frederick Warne, 1963, 160 pp., OP (3-6).
An excellent collection of fables by Aesop, La Fontaine, John Gay, Robert Dodsley, Christian Gellert, Gotthold Lessing, Claris de Florian and others. The largest number are by the prolific Aesop.

□ Perrault, Charles. *Perrault's Complete Fairy Tales*. Dodd, Mead, 1982 (1697), 184 pp. (3-up).
In this fine collection are some of the best-known fairy tales of Western literature; such stories, for example as "Puss in Boots," "Little Red Riding Hood" and "Cinderella." In addition to the unfailing charm of the

imaginative tales, Perrault's stories are full of witty comments on human nature which are a part of the subtle teaching elements of such literature.

☐ Pyle, Howard, *The Wonder Clock*. Dover, 1915 (1888), 318 pp. (3-up).
Twenty-four stories of adventure and wonder in the world of princes, princesses, talking animals and ogres. A long-lasting classic with the extensive vocabulary and elaborate writing style so characteristic of Pyle.

☐ Ruskin, John. *The King of the Golden River*. Dover, 1974 (1851), 96 pp. (3-up).
Another timeless classic. Ruskin's tale of two brutal brothers and a kind and noble younger brother is beautifully written with especially fine descriptions and an outstanding use of language.

☐ Wahlenberg, Anna. *The Diamond Bird and Other Stories*. Doubleday, OP (3, 4).
A lovely collection of fairy tales translated from the Swedish. The stories emphasize the values of kindness, industry, respect for the old, in an appealing way. Good language use and a wide range of plots and settings.

☐ Yagawa, Sumiko. *The Crane Wife*. Illus. by Suekichi Akaba. Morrow, 1981, 32 pp. (3, 4).
A classic Japanese folk tale with lovely Japanese illustrations. Greed and listening to bad advice are the downfall of the young peasant husband in the story, and he loses his gentle, beautiful "crane wife."

Literature: Level II
Myths and Legends

☐ Hawthorne, Nathaniel. *Tanglewood Tales & Wonder Book.*
Houghton Mifflin; Ohio State U. Press, 1972 (1852-
53), 476 pp. (4-up).

This combined volume comprises Hawthorne's adapta-
tions of classical myths. The events of the stories follow
the originals except in cases where the writer thought it
best to make changes or deletions. The tone is quite different from that of versions nearer the original form,
and some people object to Hawthorne's tales on that
ground. The tales are, however, American classics in
their own right and, from one viewpoint, not a bad way
at all to introduce children to some of the rather complicated characters and events which they will later encounter in more advanced study of mythology. Traditional values are strongly underscored in Hawthorne's
versions of the stories.

☐ McSpadden, J. Walker. *Robin Hood and His Merry
Outlaws.* World Publishing, 1946, 285 pp., OP (4-up).

A legendary hero for centuries, Robin Hood still captures the imagination of the children of the Star Wars
generation. This version of his story (one of a great
many) retains a traditional flavor in its use of language,
but is less demanding as to reading skills than is Howard Pyle's book on Robin Hood. It does convey the
classic atmosphere of another time, another world, a
distinctive manner of speech, all of which are of great
value in children's reading experience.

☐ Pyle, Howard. *The Merry Adventures of Robin Hood.*
   Dover, 1968 (1883), 325 pp. (4-6).
   The always-enthralling yet familiar tales—and many
   not so well-known. Pyle's language retains the flavor of
   an earlier time, making the prose especially rich and
   valuable as a literary experience. And as to the story elements: courage, idealism and heroic adventure are still
   important ingredients in good reading for children, and
   they are amply found in this favorite classic.

Literature: Level II
Fantasies

☐ Bond, Michael. *A Bear Called Paddington.* Houghton Mifflin, 1960, 128 pp. (3-7).

A little bear, Paddington, who has emigrated from "Darkest Peru," is adopted by a British family and becomes involved in a variety of humorous adventures. This is a reading-for-fun book with a good atmosphere of kindness and family warmth but not much depth. Other Paddington stories in the series also make enjoyable reading.

☐ Boston, L. M. *The Castle of Yew.* Harcourt, Brace, 1965, 57 pp., OP (3, 4).

Two boys shrink to miniature dimensions and have exciting adventures inside a clipped yew tree. This and a number of other stories by the same writer are above-average from a literary standpoint, but although there is nothing objectionable or perverse in them, traditional values are not as clearly woven into their fiber as one might wish.

☐ Carroll, Lewis (pen name of Charles L. Dodgson). *Alice in Wonderland and Through the Looking Glass.* Grossett & Dunlap, 1986 (1865; 1872), 307 pp. (3-up).

No works of children's literature have become more thoroughly absorbed into the English-speaking cultures than Lewis Carroll's classic fantasies about the little girl who enters a most confusing dream world, first by way of a rabbit hole and later through a mirror. References to the characters and events of the stories are found everywhere, and even people who have never read the books have heard of the White Rabbit, the Mad Hatter, the Cheshire Cat, the White Queen, the Walrus and the Carpenter and the rest of the cleverly drawn creations encountered by Alice. Children are able to appreciate the Alice stories at widely varying ages: some simply plunge into their topsy-turvy atmosphere and enjoy the sound of the language and the ridiculous scenes long before they are able to understand much of the subtle humor that adults so thoroughly enjoy. Other children, particularly if they are reading the books for themselves, may find the illogical, dreamlike sequences of events and the challenging language of the dialogue confusing. In the latter case, the children may enjoy the stories more when they are considerably older and more sophisticated in their reading. Often, if the stories are first read aloud by an adult who knows and appreciates them, children will thoroughly enjoy brief excursions into Wonderland.

□ Collodi, Carlo. *The Pinocchio of C. Collodi,* translated and annotated by James Teahan. Schocken, 1985 (1883), 206 pp. (3-up).

This excellent new translation is based on the premise that earlier translations have often lost the flavor of speech that Collodi (whose name was actually Carlo Lorenzini) intended the characters of his story to use. Teahan's version uses very natural, colloquial language in its dialogue, and the plentiful notations explain references to the original nineteenth-century Italian setting and culture. The classic tale of Gepetto and Pinocchio, the little wooden boy who comes to life, is the same as in earlier translations, but quite different, of course, from the shallow Disney version. It is rich in its portrayal of human nature and the inner battle between good and evil. The folly of bad companions, the dire results of lying, and a number of other basic values are graphically illustrated, along with the adventure and humor for which the story is so well-known.

□ Ford, Paul F. *Companion to Narnia*. Harper & Row, 1980, 304 pp. (3-up).
>
> Primary listing under *Reference*.
>
> A detailed guide to the "themes, characters and events" of the seven Narnia books.

□ Fritz, Jean. *Magic to Burn*. Coward, McCann, 1964, 255 pp., OP (4-up).
>
> A delightful story of the meeting and subsequent adventures of two American children, Ann and Stephen, and a four-inch high little being, a "boggart" named Blaze. The children are in England with their parents, and when they go home Blaze stows away. Ann and Stephen know that America isn't at all as Blaze thinks it is—and how will they ever get him home? To complicate matters, Blaze insists that the children tell no one else at all about him. Humor, excitement and creative imagination blend in the lively tale.

□ Godden, Rumer. *The Doll's House*. Penguin, 1976 (1947), 125 pp. (3-up).
>
> An endearing story about a doll's house and its inhabitants, with a wooden farthing doll (an old-fashioned, inexpensive little doll) as its heroine. In addition to its fine literary quality, the book underscores important values in contrasting responsibility and true worth with outward show and disloyalty.

□ Grahame, Kenneth. *The Wind in the Willows*. Scribner's, 1933 (1907), 259 pp. (3-up).
>
> Grahame's classic story both charms and teaches. In addition to richness of language and appreciation of natural beauty, the book offers a range of subtle lessons in friendship, patience, kindness, industry and loyalty. It points out, in the character of Toad, the follies of conceit, instability, and heedlessness, yet deals compassionately with his failings.

□ Heide, Florence Parry. *The Problem with Pulcifer.* Lippincott, 1983, 64 pp. (3-up).

A brief, cleverly done satire on TV addiction. Pulcifer's parents are terribly worried because he simply isn't interested in watching television—all he wants to do is read. But in his society TV watching has taken over to such an extent that classes in school all watch TV, libraries have many more audiovisual items than books, etc. Pulcifer's parents try everything to induce him to switch from reading to TV, even taking him to a psychiatrist. Children will enjoy the fun as the situation-reversal humor is developed—and perhaps be encouraged to take a more critical view of TV as well.

□ Holman, Felice. *The Cricket Winter.* Norton, 1967, 107 pp., OP (3, 4).

A whimsical, well-written little story of a boy who feels no one is listening to him, and a cricket that understands Morse code. Together, the boy and the cricket are able to improve the lives of a varied group of small animals living under the boy's sunporch, and in the process to develop some qualities of understanding and self-restraint of their own.

□ Juster, Norton. *The Phantom Toll Booth.* Random House, 1961, 255 pp. (3-6).

A light-hearted allegory full of humor that also reinforces a number of important values. Milo is a young boy who finds life boring; when he's in school, he wishes he were out, but when he's at home, he wishes he were at school. Finding a huge package in his room (it turns out to be a small-scale toll booth) he follows the enclosed directions and finds himself on a suspenseful journey through a strange and different world. The adventures of Milo and the two companions he encounters make lively reading—and will keep the reader on his or her toes catching the point of the clever humor, much of which is based on wordplay.

□ Kipling, Rudyard. *The Jungle Book.* Grossett & Dunlap, 1950 (1894), 280 pp. (3-up).

The timeless stories loved by generation after generation of children: stories of Mowgli and the wolves, Tomai of the elephants, Rikki Tikki Tavi, and others. The charm of the tales is enhanced by the rhythmic, bardic flavor of Kipling's prose. Especially good for reading aloud.

□ Krensky, Stephen. *A Big Day for Scepters.* Atheneum, 1977, 112 pp. (3-5).

A story of adventure, magic spells and the triumph of good over evil, all told with a plentiful, tongue-in-cheek humor. The good sorcerer Calandar, his friend Dirby, and young Corey set out on a quest to keep the wicked goblin Grogol from appropriating the power left hundreds of years before by the evil wizard Wroth. Well written and interest-holding.

□ Lawson, Robert. *Rabbit Hill.* Harper & Row, 1944, 127 pp. (3-up).

A modern classic with a fine literary quality. Children took this book to their hearts when it was first written forty years ago, and it continues to be popular with succeeding generations. Lively, humorous and warm, the story of Little Georgie, Uncle Analdas, Porkey and all the other Little Animals is enhanced by Lawson's irresistible drawings. (Its sequel is *The Tough Winter.*)

□ Lewis, C. S. *The Lion, the Witch and the Wardrobe.* Macmillan, 1950, 154 pp. (3-up).

In this opening book of the series known as The Chronicles of Narnia, Peter, Edmund, Susan and Lucy (brothers and sisters) enter the land of Narnia through the back of a huge old wardrobe. The children are charmed by the fauns, dwarfs and animals they meet, but soon find that Narnia is a land under a curse: it is winter the year round and the forces of evil reign.

Impelled by a desire to help the faun who has been imprisoned for helping Lucy on her first venture into Narnia, the children are caught up in a stirring adventure in which the great golden lion, Aslan, leads the forces of good in the struggle to free Narnia from the evil queen and lift the chilling curse. There is not only excitement and suspense in this and the other six books that comprise the Chronicles, but a wealth of fascinating characters, a pervasive, witty humor, and a keen insight into human nature. The latter is reflected in the unaffected naturalness of the children's dialogue. The Chronicles are not only splendid creative literature, but Christian truth is symbolized throughout as an integral part of the Narnia experience. Other Chronicles titles are: *Prince Caspian; The Voyage of the Dawn Treader; The Silver Chair; The Horse and His Boy; The Magician's Nephew; The Last Battle.*

☐ MacDonald, George. *At the Back of the North Wind* (adapted). Zondervan, 1981, 128 pp. (3-up).

MacDonald, the minister/writer so much respected by C. S. Lewis, wrote a number of stories for children. In this one, Diamond, an unusual little boy with great sensitivity to the needs of others, is encouraged by the North Wind who becomes his special friend. The poverty and illness so common at the time in which the story is set are vividly depicted, and there is a good deal of sadness throughout. For this reason, it should be used carefully, possibly in connection with British history of the last half of the nineteenth century. (This edition has been edited to delete some of the writer's discursive passages and to increase general ease of reading. Many people may wish to use an edition that contains MacDonald's original text, first published in 1871.)

□ Nesbit, Edith. *Five Children and It*. Coward, McCann, 1963 (1902), 223 pp. (4-up).

A lively family of English children of an earlier era become involved in a succession of suspenseful, imaginative adventures. In the above-titled book, for example, the children unearth a rather temperamental sand fairy that bears no resemblance whatever to conventional fairies. Written with wit and charm, Nesbit's books have been popular with children for decades. They include: *The Phoenix and the Carpet; The Enchanted Castle; The Railway Children;* and the Bastable children stories.

□ Norton, Mary. *The Borrowers*. Harcourt, Brace, World, 1953, 180 pp. (3-up).

Norton's books have that special magic that make them a delight to read. In this (and the other Borrowers titles), tiny Lilliputian-sized people survive by "borrowing" things secretly from the people of the full-sized world and ingeniously adapting them to their daily use. The stories are well-written, humorous, suspenseful, subtly conveying universal truths about human nature.

□ O'Brien, Robert C. *Mrs. Frisby and the Rats of NIMH*. Atheneum, 1971, 233 pp. (3-up).

A suspenseful fantasy about the widowed Mrs. Frisby (a mouse) and her little family; about a community of rats that are very unlike other rats; and also about parental devotion, neighborly kindness, friendship, self-respect, sacrifice, and the thinking through of moral values. Exceptionally well done, delightful to read, and full of keen, subtly made commentaries on human nature as portrayed by the little animals of the story.

□ Sewell, Anna. *Black Beauty: The Autobiography of a Horse*. Grossett & Dunlap, 1945 (1877), 301 pp. (4-up).

The reason for classifying as fantasy this story that deals with an issue (cruelty to animals) that was real and acute at the time the story was written is that it is told as though by the horse, Black Beauty, and throughout the book the animals talk to each other and think in a human manner. Apart from that, however, the book is of the realistic type as it tells the story of the lovely black horse that went from comfort and happiness to great misery before finally being restored to a loving home. Use with caution for younger children, as the very tender-hearted among them may react intensely to the cruelty shown to Black Beauty.

□ Sharp, Margery. *The Rescuers*. Little, Brown, 1959, 149 pp. (3-up).

The perilous adventures of Miss Bianca offer excitement and suspense in a delightful form. A beautiful white mouse of impeccable taste, indomitable courage and infinite resourcefulness, Miss Bianca is an appealingly drawn central figure. In *The Rescuers,* Miss Bianca, aided by a faithful helper, Bernard, and Nils, a mouse brought especially from Norway for the task, go to the rescue of a Norwegian poet imprisoned in the fearsome Black Castle. The overall literary quality, the language and settings are outstanding, the pace of the events fast-moving. Subtle humor and clever insights on human nature abound, and sound values are demonstrated. Other titles in the series include: *Miss Bianca; Miss Bianca in the Orient;* and *Miss Bianca in the Salt Mines.*

□ Tolkien, J. R. R. *The Hobbit*. Houghton, Mifflin, 1937, 317 pp. (3-up).

The exciting adventures of Bilbo Baggins, the hobbit who didn't know he had the courage, curiosity, and ability to lead, but that the wizard Gandalf was sure he possessed. Bilbo's encounters with the formidable dragon Smaug, the loathsome subterranean creature Gollum, and the many other hazards of the quest he shares with the treasure-hungry dwarves bring out the strengths that had been lying dormant as he lived his former quiet, comfortable life.

The Hobbit can be read alone as an enthralling story in itself, but it is also the important prelude to Tolkien's immensely popular Lord of the Rings trilogy and its tales of Middle Earth. Widely-read modern classics, Tolkien's fantasies are appreciated for their superb story quality, keen insight and literary excellence. Christian readers also welcome Tolkien's deeply Christian philosophy which is reflected throughout his work.

□ White, E.B. *Stuart Little*. Harper & Row, 1945, 131 pp. (3, 4).
Another modern classic, this is the famous story of the debonair little mouse born into a human family, who takes off on his own to seek his fortune and find his friend Margalo, the bird. Especially well-written, and with many charming scenes and events, the story nonetheless reflects the sense of bleakness and alienation in Stuart's life. He is unlike all his family and, though given tender care, seems able to leave without much hesitation.

Literature: Level II
Realistic Stories—Modern

☐ Benary-Isbert, Margot. *Blue Mystery.* Harcourt, Brace, Jovanovich, 1957, 190 pp. (4, 5).
> Translated from the German, this warm, eventful story has the added interest of the setting and customs of a different culture. Girls will enjoy lively, generous Annegret, her animals and friends, and the little mystery she encounters.

☐ Blue, Rose. *Seven Years from Home.* Raintree, 1976, 58 pp. (4-up).
> Eleven-year-old Mark has known since he was small that he had been adopted by parents that have always loved and cared for him. But lately he has been thinking constantly of finding his birth parents. Somehow this preoccupation is distorting everything in his life: his relationship with his parents, with his younger brother—his parents' son by birth—his attitudes, and his behavior. How Mark's thoughts and emotions take a new turn makes a story that is not only good reading, but that expands the awareness of the reader about how it sometimes feels to be adopted.

☐ Carlson, Natalie Savage. *The Empty Schoolhouse.* Harper & Row, 1965, 119 pp. (3-up).
> When St. Joseph's Catholic School is desegregated, Lullah Royall is full of happy excitement at the thought of being able to go to school with her best friend, red-haired, blue-eyed Oralee Fleury. But bomb threats, ugly phone calls, and rocks thrown through windows frighten people, black and white alike, into taking their children out of St. Joseph's. Although tensions and crises exist, the writer quietly depicts the normal course of Lullah and her family's daily life, along with the events

that work toward a happy solution of the problem. Well-drawn characterizations, particularly those of Emma, Lullah's devoted older sister, and of Lullah herself, give depth to this sensitive, well-written story.

□ Cleary, Beverly. *Henry Huggins*. Morrow, 1950, 155 pp. (3-up).

Easy-reading, hilarious events in the life of Henry Huggins, a most well-meaning young boy. Somehow, Henry's projects always seem to end up rather differently from what he had planned, with expected complications. Full of the kind of humor most kids strongly relate to, and a good choice for reluctant readers. There are a number of additional titles in the series. Cleary is also the author of the popular Ramona series and of a series about the mouse Ralph.

□ de Jong, Meindert. *The House of Sixty Fathers*. Harper & Row, 1956, 189 pp. (4-up).

The dramatic and suspenseful story of a little Chinese boy separated from his parents during the Japanese occupation of World War II. The writer not only understands children, but he is aware of the high level of courage, determination and devotedness that children can reach. Authentic in its details, warm and inspiring in its spirit, this is a splendid modern classic.

□ de Jong, Meindert. *The Wheel on the School*. Harper & Row, 1954, 298 pp. (3-up).

More than a wonderfully well-written story, de Jong's book puts readers in the heart of another time, another culture. It is, however, a world to which children of any time or place can relate, because the writer knows so well the universal qualities of childhood. The six children of a small Dutch school and their fine schoolteacher dream a dream—to bring the storks back to their little town.

Within the framework of this simple plot, a wide range of events involving suspense, personal crises, etc. take place, all seen in the light of strong traditional values. Humor, insight, models of restored or improved human relationships and growth in understanding are all offered in this outstanding story.

□ Enright, Elizabeth. *Thimble Summer*. Holt, Rinehart, Winston, 1938, 124 pp. (3-6).

One of those wonderfully written stories of children and everyday life that make the reader feel he or she can see and taste the things being written about. In this case, readers can join Garnet, Jay, Eric and the others as they play, work, adventure and dream during a long hot summer on a farm in the 1930s. Although the distinctive flavor of a specific period is present in the story, its appeal is timeless, and today's children will enjoy it just as children have been doing for almost fifty years.

□ Enright, Elizabeth. *Gone-Away Lake; Return to Gone-Away*. Harcourt, Brace, Jovanovich, 1957, 192 pp.; 1961, 191 pp. (3-6).

Adventure, imagination and delightful characters make this pair of books memorable. Julian and his cousin Portia explore the area around their summer home and make some surprising discoveries. The stories stay just (barely) this side of fantasy, and reading about the almost-abandoned little summer community of the past that the children find, of the fascinating old houses and remarkable people they encounter, will inspire many a daydream. Written in the 1950s, the stories remind adults of those peaceful—and far safer—childhood days which can no longer be taken for granted.

Along with the liveliness and interest of the stories, excellent values of kindness, fairness and helpfulness are subtly emphasized. Other enjoyable books by Elizabeth Enright no longer in print are still available in libraries.

□ Gates, Doris. *Blue Willow*. Viking, 1940, 172 pp. (3-5).

Before the disastrous "dust bowl" years turned thousands of farms into dry fields blowing away in the wind, the Larkins had had a farm in Texas. But with the farm gone, Janey and her parents have to take to the road, part of the thousands of migrant workers of the 1930s, going wherever there is farm work. Now they have settled briefly in the San Joaquin Valley of California while Janey's father works in the cotton fields. Janey has found a friend, Lupe Romero, and even a place by the river with hanging willows like the ones on Janey's precious plate, all that is left of the set-

tled, more secure life of the past. In spite of the "al-
most-too-good-to-be-true" happy ending, there is
enough reality in this well-written story to have given it
a lasting readership over the more than forty-five years
since it was written.

☐ Henry, Marguerite. *Misty of Chincoteague*. Rand,
McNally, 1947, 173 pp. (2-9).
The exciting story of a brother and sister, Paul and
Maureen, who tame two island ponies—a mare and her
colt—from Assateague, a wild island off the coast of
Virginia. For decades the horse stories of Marguerite
Henry have been avidly read by children. With few ex-
ceptions, new readers will universally enjoy this sus-
penseful tale—and be ready to start in on all the rest of
the writer's lastingly popular books.

☐ Holling, Holling Clancy. *Paddle-to-the-Sea*. Illus. by
author. Houghton Mifflin, 1957, 53 pp. (3-up).
In a little Canadian wilderness cabin north of Lake Superior, an Indian boy carves a foot-long canoe with the
figure of an Indian seated in it. Equipped with a tin
rudder behind, and a lump of lead for ballast, the little
canoe, when put in the water, will keep heading forward and will return to an upright position if upset.
Dreaming of the long water-path that leads to the sea,
the Indian boy takes the canoe to the place where melt-
ed snow will flow to the first of the Great Lakes. On its
bottom, the boy has carved these words, "PLEASE
PUT ME BACK IN WATER I AM PADDLE TO
THE SEA." In a beautifully illustrated story that has
charmed readers for over forty years, Holling tells of
the little carved Indian's journey, of the places it encounters, and of the people who help it on its way.
Many geographic details and drawings are included.

☐ Kjelgaard, Jim. *Big Red*. Holiday, 1956 (1945), 254 pp.
(4-7).
This outdoor-action story with its central theme of the
devotion between a young man and a magnificent dog
has retained its popularity since it was written forty
years ago, and is a good example of its type. Danny and
his father farm and trap on a small scale in the moun-

tains of northern New England. How Danny is given the care of his wealthy neighbor's champion Irish setter showdog, Big Red, how the dog reacts to his encounter with a marauding bear, and a variety of other suspenseful events make up the story. Courage, loyalty and integrity of purpose are some of the values that underlie its development.

□ Little, Jean. *From Anna.* Little, Brown & Co., 1973, 203 pp. (3, 4-up).

Anna Solden, the youngest of five children, wonders why all the things that seem to come so easily to her brothers and sisters are so hard for her. Awkward, uncoordinated, struggling unsuccessfully to read, she increasingly isolates herself. When her family emigrates to Canada from Germany, a doctor there discovers that she has acute vision problems; some remedies are undertaken and a new world slowly opens to Anna. This is a most perceptively written story by a writer who herself has had lifelong vision impairment. Little is particularly good at depicting the interaction between family members, and along with an interest-holding story-line, she has provided a thought-provoking background to Anna's metamorphosis.

□ Little, Jean. *Mine for Keeps.* Little, Brown & Co., 1962, 186 pp. (3, 4-up).

Sally has spent several years at a special boarding school for handicapped girls, learning skills that will help her to be independent someday in spite of her cerebral palsy. Now she is going back home to live. Wonderful though her family is, even that change seems scary; but worst of all is knowing she must go to a regular school and walk into a class full of strangers with her leg braces, her crutches, and her overwhelming fear. What happens in Sally's life—and in the lives of her family and friends—makes a warm, lively story that is not simply enjoyable to read, but that increases the reader's understanding of the needs and problems of the handicapped.

☐ Ransome, Arthur. *Swallows and Amazons*. Merrimack
   Pub., 1981 (1930), 352 pp. (4-8).
   This is the first in a much-loved series of books begun
   by Ransome over fifty years ago. The "on holiday"
   world of the four Walker children, John, Susan, Titty
   and Roger (baby Vicky is much too young to be included) is created quite simply in a realistic setting of
   the English lake country. A little sailboat, an island in
   the lake (not far from shore and the farmhouse in
   which Mrs. Walker and Vicky are comfortably installed), and permission from their father, a naval officer away at sea, to camp on the island—these are the
   down-to-earth elements from which the story is fashioned. But for the Walkers (and their many devoted
   readers) a world of imagination, adventure, unexpected
   events—and some practice in carrying responsibility
   and functioning as a team—is opened up in a way that
   makes irresistible reading. Although each book is a separate story, it is especially enjoyable to read them in sequence. *Swallowdale* follows the opening book, then in
   order: *Peter Duck; Winter Holiday; Coot Club; Pigeon
   Post; We Didn't Mean to Go to Sea; Secret Water; The Big
   Six; Missee Lee; The Picts and the Martyrs;* and *Great
   Northern*.

☐ Seredy, Kate. *The Good Master*. Viking, 1935, 196 pp.
   (3, 4-up).
   Another modern classic that has stood the test of time,
   this warm, perceptive story has been pleasing children
   for fifty years. Hungarian farm life is the setting for the
   story of Jancsi and of Kate, his headstrong little visiting
   cousin. Lively events and some important growth in
   maturity and understanding blend to form a satisfying
   whole in this well-written tale. Several other books by
   Seredy should be available in libraries, but the only one
   other than *The Good Master* now in print is *The White
   Stag*.

☐ Sobol, Donald J. *Encyclopedia Brown: Boy Detective*.
   Lodestar, 1963, 96 pp. (3, 4-up).
   Light, easy reading, full of humor and particularly popular with boys, this initial volume and the many others
   of this series of books is a good choice for encouraging

reluctant readers. Encyclopedia Brown (no one calls him by his real name, Leroy) is a ten-year-old boy who has read so much that he is a walking reference source. Encyclopedia's father is the unbelievably successful Chief of Police of Idaville, and much of his success depends on the quick, infallibly right solutions discovered by his clever son to any crime, large or small, that occurs in the community. Each chapter of the books is a "case," and the solution to each is in a section at the back of the book.

□ Streatfeild, Noel. *The Magic Summer*. Random House, 1967, 270 pp., OP (4-up).

When their father is suddenly given the opportunity to do medical research in the Far East, the Gareth children, Alex, Penny, Robin and Naomi, miss him, but know that the exciting summer holiday they and their mother are planning will help the months hurry by. Dr. Gareth, however, becomes critically ill; the children's mother must go to him at once. With no time to look for someone to take charge of them at home, their mother contacts their Great-Aunt Dymphena in Ireland (whom they have never seen and whom their mother really doesn't know) and they are off for what is to be the most unusual experience of their lives. Lively, funny, and full of event, the story moves rapidly—and along the way all four children do some growing up before the happy ending of their father's recovery and the expectation of an immediate reunion with their parents.

Literature: Level II
Realistic Stories—
Historical

☐ Anckarsvärd, Karin. *Doctor's Boy.* Harcourt, Brace, Jovanovich, 1965, 156 pp. (4-7).

> Translated from the Swedish, this appealing story set in horse and buggy days has a strong element of warm, humanitarian concern for the victims of poverty and disease. Ten-year-old Jon has already decided that he wants to be a doctor like his father, and whenever possible he rides out with him on the house calls his father makes late each day after his office hours. The writer creates an atmosphere of calm and loving concern in everything the doctor does, whether it is saving the life of a newborn child in the slums, thinking of the future needs of Jon's gifted, poverty-stricken classmate Rickard, or simply conversing with great fatherly love and interest with his young son. The story is full of lively events and portrays a warm, loving family with a consistent concern for the needs of others.

☐ Atkins, Elizabeth Howard. *Treasures of the Medranos.* Houghton Mifflin, 1957, 112 pp. (3-5).

> A romantic little story set in Old California in the days of the Spanish *rancheros*. Little Felisa Medrano unknowingly encounters a famous *bandido* (bandit) whose heart is touched by her innocent kindness. The wedding of Felisa's sister, the danger to the family's heirloom treasures, and background details of hacienda life are all part of the story.

☐ Avi. *Night Journeys,* Pantheon, 1979, 145 pp. (4-up).

> Orphaned at twelve, young Peter York is taken into the Quaker home of Justice of the Peace Everett Shinn and his family. Shinn is against violence; yet when a hunt is on for two escaped indentured children, he feels it is his

responsibility to take part in the effort to find and return the children to what amounts to a life of slavery.
The suspenseful events of the story confront Peter with
a reality quite different from his earlier views; he had
thought he would like to have a part in collecting some
of the reward money. Peter's foster father also faces a
moral crisis in this unusual, excellently written book.
The setting is Pennsylvania in the late 1760s.

□ Blaine, Marge. *Dvora's Journey*. Holt, Rinehart &
   Winston, 1970, 126 pp. (4-up).
     Life for early twentieth-century Russian Jews was be-
coming increasingly difficult. Not only were they dis-
criminated against in a variety of ways, but as the Czar
demanded more and more soldiers for his army, his
fierce Cossack troops made a point of snatching Jewish
boys for military service, even at the early age of thirteen or fourteen. For twelve-year-old Dvora's family,
this creates an imminent crisis, for her studious brother,
Saul, will soon turn fourteen and soldiers are ranging
through their part of the country with increasing fre-
quency. But Papa has a brother in America, and finally
the painful decision is made: they will join him there.
This is not a simple matter, however, for the Russian
government won't allow open emigration—particularly
if there are boys in the family. The writer creates an atmosphere of a warm, loving family, and of the turmoil
and danger of their escape to freedom.

□ Brady, Esther Wood. *Toliver's Secret*. Crown, 1976, 166
   pp. (3-5).
     Adventure and suspense during the American Revolu-
tion. When her grandfather sprains his ankle, ten-year-
old Ellen Toliver must disguise herself as a boy and carry a secret message for Washington. Things don't work
out quite as planned, and Ellen must react quickly to
dangers and mishaps. In the process of carrying
through her mission, a fearful Ellen learns that she has
more courage and sense than she thought she had.

□ Brink, Carol Ryrie. *Caddie Woodlawn*. Macmillan, 1973
(1935), 240 pp. (4-up).
A Newbery Award-winning book when it was written
in 1935, *Caddie Woodlawn* has long been a modern classic. Its story of the little red-haired tomboy who runs
and climbs with her brothers in the pioneer Wisconsin
woods and farmland of the 1860s is still enjoyed by today's young readers. Impulsive, independent and sometimes mischievous, Caddie's warmth and kindness of
heart help her to accept with grace the responsibility of
becoming a young woman and taking her part in serving the needs of others as part of wholesome growing
up.

□ Bulla, Clyde Robert. *Marco Moonlight* Harper & Row,
1976, 104 pp. (3-up).
In the early morning of his thirteenth birthday, Marco
Moonlight has dreamed of a brother. But he has no
family other than his elderly grandparents, and he lives
with them in Dorn Hall, a great manor house. On this
same day, the sinister Flint enters his life, and he finds
his dream turning to a nightmare reality. Mystery, suspense, surprise—and some clear choices between good
and evil are all a part of this exciting tale.

□ Burnett, Frances Hodgson. *The Secret Garden*. Harper &
Row, 1962 (1911), 256 pp. (4-up).
One of the best beloved of the classic children's stories.
Mary Lennox had been orphaned in India. Her father, a
British officer, and her young, beautiful mother had
died suddenly of cholera. Mary's world has crumbled
around her, and the opening sentence of the book
reads: "When Mary Lennox was sent to Misselthwaite
Manor to live with her uncle, everybody said she was
the most disagreeable looking child ever seen." A kind,
sensible young servant-girl, her brother who knows and
loves the natural world, a mysterious invalid boy hidden
away in a wing of the huge house, all have their part in
the story. Most important, however, is the secret garden
Mary finds that eventually brings remarkable changes
into all their lives. Wonderful to read aloud—or alone.
Two more fine stories by Burnett are: *Little Lord*

Fauntleroy and *The Little Princess*. Throughout all her books, the writer emphasizes kindness, fairness, courage, and a whole roster of values parents want to see developed in their children's lives.

□ Canfield, Dorothy. *Understood Betsy*. Buccaneer, 1981 (1916), 219 pp. (3-6).
An enduring story (written in 1916) of an overprotected little girl whose life and self-awareness take on new dimensions when she goes to live with Vermont farm relatives. There is a good emphasis on overcoming self-pity and needless fears, and on developing mature, compassionate ways of seeing.

□ Carr, Mary Jane. *Children of the Covered Wagon*. Harper & Row, 1957 (1934), 303 pp. (3-up).
The fictional company of pioneers that travel the Old Oregon Trail in Carr's story is very much like the real ones that trekked west in the mid-nineteenth century. Hardships and dangers abound, but the dream of fertile land in a mild and welcoming climate makes the trials bearable. And along the way there are joys to be shared and lessons to be learned by little Jerry and his "big" cousin, ten-year-old Jim. A story that has been read and enjoyed by children for fifty years.

□ Colver, Anne. *Bread and Butter Indian*. Holt, Rinehart and Winston, 1964, 96 pp. (3, 4).
A warmly satisfying story of little Barbara Baum who lived inland from the coastal area of Pennsylvania in 1793. At that time such settlements were pioneer villages, part of the movement that kept pushing the frontier farther and farther west as the years went by. When Barbara, playing down by the creek, gave her piece of sugared bread to a hungry old Indian, she didn't know that someday he would befriend her in a very real way. Family and community activities that reflect the culture of the time and place form an authentic background for the story, the main events of which are based on the true experience of the real Barbara Baum, great-great-grandmother of the writer's husband. Also based on actual family records is the adventure-filled sequel, *Bread and Butter Journey*.

☐ de Angeli, Marguerite. *The Door in the Wall.* Doubleday, 1949, 111 pp. (3-up).

> A beautifully written story set in late medieval England. A ten-year-old boy is left crippled by illness (polio?) and learns to find purpose in life. His story is told against a setting of local conflict and changing scenes. There is a splendid use of historical background, rich vocabulary, emphasis on important values.

☐ Dodge, Mary Mapes. *Hans Brinker or The Silver Skates.* Grossett & Dunlap, 1945 (1865), 314 pp. (3-6).

> Still as enthralling as ever is this classic story of the Brinker family in nineteenth-century Holland. A wonderfully interest-holding story, beautifully told, and strong in areas of Christian values: honor, compassion, patience, faith, diligence, loyalty. A head injury has reduced the once strong, loving father of the family to a mentally afflicted invalid subject to sudden, uncontrollable rages. Without the father's provision, the wife, son and daughter struggle against acute poverty, each doing what he or she can to aid their survival and care for the father and for each other. Both the Brinker children excel at ice skating, and some of the most exciting scenes of the book are built around events related to their skill on the ice. As they have for more than a hundred years, children will thrill to the courage and drama of the story and rejoice in the final resolution to the tragic circumstances the Brinkers have met with such patience and faith.

☐ Estes, Eleanor. *The Moffats.* Harcourt, Brace, Jovanovich, 1968 (1941), 290 pp. (3-up).

> Fun-filled horse-and-buggy-days adventures occur frequently in the lively Moffat family. There are Sylvie, Joey, Jane and Rufus (ranging from fifteen to five) and Mamma, struggling to make ends meet as a dressmaker because Papa died right after Rufus was born. The atmosphere of a close, caring family and a simpler age permeate this book and others in the series—as does the kind of humor that appeals to young readers.

□ Fritz, Jean. *The Cabin Faced West*. Coward, McCann, 1958, 124 pp. (3-up).

When Ann Hamilton and her family move from Gettysburg to the western frontier of the 1780s (over the Allegheny Mountains in western Pennsylvania), Ann feels that she will never be at home away from her old friends and comfortable city ways. How Hamilton Hill becomes the place Ann would rather be than anywhere else in the world is a significant part of this easy-reading story. Warm family life, a troubled, on-the-defensive neighbor boy, and a surprise visit from a famous American contribute to the eventful tale. The main characters are real people (Ann was the writer's great-great-grandmother) and some of the occurrences in the story really happened.

□ Hale, Lucretia P. *The Complete Peterkin Papers* (combines earlier volumes), 1960 (1880s), 302 pp. (3, 4).

The zany Peterkins know how to make the simplest project impossibly complicated. For more than a hundred years children have chuckled over the mixed-up activities of this fuddle-headed family: the parents, the three children whose names we are told—Agamemnon, Elizabeth Eliza and Solomon John—and the two youngest who are referred to only as "the little boys."

□ Hunt, Irene. *Trail of Apple Blossoms*. Follett, 1968, 64 pp., OP (3, 4).

A well-written story of Johnny Appleseed, the quiet, kindly man who spent almost fifty years during the first half of the nineteenth century walking the trails and roads of western Pennsylvania, Ohio and Indiana. The friend of whites and Indians, of animals and birds, Johnny (John Chapman) had a unique mission in addition to the unofficial doctoring he practiced along his way. Everywhere Johnny went, he carried and planted appleseeds, leaving a legacy of beauty and fruitfulness behind. In this particular story, Hunt emphasizes Johnny's loving, peaceable ways and his knack for soothing spirits and calming troubled waters. (Because almost all that is known about John Chapman is legendary, this story has been included with the fiction rather than being listed primarily in *Biography*.)

☐ MacDonald, George. *The Christmas Stories of George MacDonald*. David C. Cook, 1981 (3, 4).

The drama and, often, pathos of these stories of nineteenth-century children offer a glimpse of the past in a Christian context. The lovely color illustrations provide an authentic background. One story in particular, about the death of a baby, may seem too emotional or too depressing to some parents. Wise selection and reading the stories aloud will make the best use of this seasonally oriented book.

☐ Meadowcroft, Enid L. *By Wagon and Flatboat*. Harper & Row, 1938, 170 pp. (3-up).

The year is 1789 and George Washington has just been elected President of the United States. The Burd family (parents, two sons and a daughter) have decided to leave Pennsylvania and make a new start in Ohio where land is cheap and opportunity beckons. Joining forces with another family, the Burds' long journey by wagon and flatboat commences. Sickness, danger from Indian attacks, and the privations of their pioneer existence often bring fear and discouragement, but faith and courage prevail and the little settlement of Losantiville (later named Cincinnati) is finally reached. Not as strongly written as William O. Steele's stories, and without the distinctive, highly authentic atmosphere he is able to create, this is still a readable and informative story of the early westward movement in America. Good values are emphasized throughout.

☐ Meadowcroft, Enid L. *Silver for General Washington*. Harper & Row, 1967 (1944), 138 pp. (3-7).

A suspenseful story of Revolutionary War days. A young brother and sister find ways to help the struggling American cause during the disastrous winter of Valley Forge. The particular value of the book is its relation to American history and to the reinforcing of such values as loyalty, courage, compassion. The weakest aspect of the book is its use of contemporary phrasing in dialogue, and in the overall atmosphere which, while historically accurate as to facts, is too modern in the way its characters speak and act.

□ Spyri, Johanna. *Heidi.* Grossett & Dunlap, 1945 (1880), 325 pp. (4-up).

> The beloved story of the vibrant little Swiss girl who brings change and new life to those around her. So well-known that it isn't necessary to discuss the story at length, it is worth remarking that it has lost none of its unique charm over the years. Not the least of the joys of Heidi's story is the atmosphere created by the descriptions of mountain life: the goats on the steep slopes, the sparkling air, the meals of milk, bread and cheese. A lovely, timeless classic.

□ Steele, William O. *The Perilous Road.* Harcourt, Brace, Jovanovich, 1958, 191 pp. (4-up).

> Young Chris Brabson is sure he has about as fine a life as an eleven-year-old boy can have. But the Civil War is underway, and when Yankee soldiers take all the Brabsons' store of winter food, their only horse, and Chris's treasured deerskin shirt, hatred fills the boy's heart. But even worse, his parents don't share his rage. They are sorry to lose the things they badly need, but realize the need that has prompted the soldiers' raids. They feel sympathy for both sides in the conflict. How Chris tries to take matters into his own hands and harm the Union cause, and what he learns about the realities of war, make up the central theme of this effectively written story.

□ Steele, William O. *The Buffalo Knife.* Harcourt, Brace, Jovanovich, 1968 (1952), 177 pp. (3-up).

> Nine-year-old Andrew Clark and his friend Isaac Brown float with their families down the Tennessee River to a new home in what would years later become Nashville, Tennessee. Their fathers have built a big flatboat, complete with a cabin to live in and pens for pigs and chickens. A thousand miles of river, some of it full of treacherous shoals, have to be traversed, while hostile Indians lurk nearby. Authentic details of late eighteenth-century pioneer life and a high level of writing skill provide a colorful background for this well-told, often humorous tale.

□ Suhl, Yuri. *The Purim Goat*. Scholastic, 1980, 64 pp. (2-6).

> An Eastern European Jewish boy thinks of an ingenious plan to keep his pet goat from being sold to pay a debt. Humor, authentic turn-of-the-century background details, and a splendid literary quality characterize this delightful story.

□ Wilder, Laura Ingalls. *The Little House in the Big Woods*. Harper & Row, 1953 (1932), 237 pp. (3, 4).

> Set in the time before the Ingalls family moved to the prairie, this is the "how it all began" book of the warm, homey, Little House series based on the lives of the writer, her husband, and other family members. The time period of the whole series covers a number of years, beginning about 1872. Pioneering, farming and family life provide the background for these appealing, authentic stories. Fine values, faith in God and a concern for the needs of others are demonstrated throughout. The other titles in the series are as follows: *The Little House on the Prairie; Farmer Boy; On the Banks of Plum Creek; By the Shores of Silver Lake; The Long Winter; The Little Town on the Prairie; These Happy Golden Years*. Some years after these stories were published a final volume, *The First Four Years,* was added. It covers events during the first years of Laura and Almanzo's marriage.

15 Literature: Level III
Fables, Folk Tales and Fairy Tales

☐ Irving, Washington. *Rip Van Winkle, The Legend of Sleepy Hollow and Other Tales*. Smith Pub., 1980 (1819), 232 pp. (6-up).

Famous tales from the pen of one of the most noted figures of nineteenth-century American literature. Like so many other stories which have long been woven into our culture, few children today read the stories as Irving wrote them. The idea of the man, Rip Van Winkle, who slept in the woods for twenty years, woke, and went back to his little village to find everything changed may be vaguely familiar; but the delightful humor and shrewd characterizations have been missed in watered-down versions of the tale. The same is true, perhaps to an even greater extent, of the headless horseman and the whole story of Sleepy Hollow. Cartoon versions are sometimes seen at Halloween, but again such treatments bear little resemblance to the fine literature of the originals.

☐ Manniche, Lise (translated by). *How Djadja-Em-Ankh Saved the Day*. Crowell, 1977 (5-up).

The special interest of this brief tale is its background and the form in which it has been reproduced. Translated from the original hieratic script by Egyptologist Manniche, it is printed on paper made to resemble papyrus and is in a scroll form, although the sheets fold flat in sections rather than being rolled. By unfolding the sheets in one direction, the reader finds information about the Egypt of 4,500 years ago and fascinating material on Egyptian writing—they used both hieroglyphics and hieratic script. By turning the sheets the other way, the reader can follow the little folk tale that comes to us from the ancient world.

□ *Tales from the Arabian Nights.* Illus. by Brian Wildsmith.
Henry Z. Walck, Inc., 1962, 281 pp., OP (5-up).
First published by the Oxford University Press, this
version uses sophisticated language in a traditional
"wonder tales" style. This in itself lends a special atmosphere to the stories, giving the diction an exotic flavor
that suits the descriptions of jewels, luxurious fabrics
and magical events with which the tales abound, and
which Wildsmith's illustrations so beautifully depict.

Literature: Level III
Myths and Legends

□ Bierhorst, John. *Black Rainbow: Legends of the Incas and
Myths of Ancient Peru.* Farrar, Straus, Giroux, 1976, 131
pp. (adv. 6-up).
A well-written collection of stories, with a scholarly but
readable essay on the background of the Incas, their
"arts, theology, history, literature, and mythology."

□ Gottlieb, Gerald (retold by). *The Adventures of Ulysses.*
Random House, 1959, 170 pp., OP (5-up).
One of the excellent old Landmark Books, this version
of the Odyssey offers an exciting, smoothly-reading story in contemporary language. Fine as a story that will
be enjoyed simply for its adventurous excitement, but
that also acquaints the reader with famous literary characters and events.

□ Hamilton, Edith. *Mythology.* New American Library,
1971 (1942), 335 pp. (6-up).
A splendid collection of Greek, Roman and Norse
mythology. The distinctive flavor of the different original writers has been preserved by Hamilton, a widely
known classicist. Excellent in its story quality and valuable in providing in one volume a broad introduction
to the mythology of that part of the ancient world in
which Western civilization has its roots.

□ Kingsley, Charles. *The Heroes.* Macmillan, 1954 (1856), 193 pp. (5-up).
> Stirringly retold stories from Greek mythology, exciting hero tales of Perseus, Theseus and Jason. Aside from the important literary background provided in studying the mythology of the ancient world, such reading offers much in its color, imagery and food for imagination.

□ Lang, Andrew. *Tales of Troy and Greece.* Faber & Faber, 1978 (1907) (5-up).
> Lang's classic retelling of the Homeric Greek epic of Odysseus and other important Greek myths. The writer has adapted the stories and included background information on setting, ancient Greek and Trojan culture, etc. The adventures are heroic, and the language is in harmony with the content, embodying some of the flavor of Homer's work and of other early mythologists.

□ Picard, Barbara Leonie (retold by). *The Iliad of Homer; The Odyssey of Homer.* Oxford University Press, 1960, 210 pp.; 1952, OP (5-up).
> Picard recounts the stories of the Iliad and the Odyssey in a lively, dramatic style. Opening new worlds of the imagination to readers, the books also provide a background on the world of ancient Greece which is invaluable for students in later secondary and college studies.

□ Pyle, Howard. *The Story of King Arthur and His Knights.* Scribner's, 1933 (1903), 312 pp. (5-up).
> The famous saga of the legendary King Arthur, with all its romance, idealism, knightly valor and pomp and ceremony. Pyle uses a demanding vocabulary and a phrasing that has a similarity to the language of the King James Version of the Bible. The language suits the imagery and drama of the story and, incidentally, provides excellent practice for the advanced reader in dealing with English in an older form than that used today.

□ Sutcliff, Rosemary. *The Light Beyond the Forest; The Sword and the Circle.* Dutton, 1980, 144 pp.; 1981, 256 pp. (5, 6-up).
> Retellings in Sutcliff's gifted prose of some of the Arthurian legends. The first book is the story of the quest

for the Holy Grail. Written later, but with events that precede those of the Grail quest, *The Sword* deals with the coming to power of Arthur and with adventures of the storied Knights of the Round Table. With their glowing idealism, their gallant heroes who fight for right and honor—and often for the deliverance of fair maidens—the stories are a fresh delight to read, even for those already somewhat familiar with the legends.

□ Westwood, Jennifer. *Stories of Charlemagne.* S. G. Phillips, 1976, 153 pp. (5, 6).
Legends about the great Charlemagne retold from the old French epics, the *chansons de geste* (songs of deeds). As with the stories of the great English hero King Arthur, these are literature rather than history, but they accurately reflect the way in which the people of the twelfth and thirteenth centuries thought about the eighth-century heroes whose exploits they celebrate.

Literature: Level III
Fantasies

□ Alexander, Lloyd. *The Book of Three.* Holt, Rinehart & Winston, 1964, 217 pp. (5, 6-up).
Alexander has written a tale of high adventure in a mythical kingdom with a Welsh flavor, in the days of enchanters, armored warriors and perilous quests. Taran, Assistant Pig-Keeper to a very special ceremonial pig, longs to become a hero, and when Prydain is threatened by evil forces, he takes up the challenge on the side of right. Alexander combines humor and exciting action with a fine literary style in all of his work, including the books that follow *The Book of Three* and, with it, comprise The Prydain Chronicles: *The Black Cauldron; The Castle of Llyr; Taran Wanderer; The High King.*

□ Bacon, Martha. *Moth Manor.* Little, Brown, 1978, 148 pp. (4-6).
A haunted dollhouse, New England antiques and a Gothic flavor are some of the ingredients of this fantasy/reality story. Love, aesthetic sensitivity and an appreciation of tradition triumph over crassness, bitterness and deceit. There is a good sprinkling of humor, and the quality of the writing is high.

□ Bond, Nancy. *A String in the Harp.* Atheneum, 1976, 370 pp. (6-up).
A long, interest-holding story that combines several important elements: the individual growth and adjusting that keep the Morgan family from disintegrating after the sudden death of Mrs. Morgan; the vivid sense of a particular part of Wales, both as it is in its natural setting and in its mythic past; and the use of fantasy to make reality more understandable.

□ Goudge, Elizabeth. *The Little White Horse.* Avon, 1946, 219 pp. (4-6).
This is the kind of fantasy/reality combination that Goudge does so splendidly. Orphaned Maria Merryweather is sent to live with an elderly cousin of her father on his estate, Moonacre Manor. Strange, unexplained things start to occur as soon as she arrives, and Maria's unusual adventures in her new home are beautifully and suspensefully told. One of the lovely things about any book of Goudge's is the warmth and coziness, the intriguing little details she describes so appealingly. And underlying all of Goudge's writing is her strongly Christian sense of values.

□ Lawhead, Stephen R. The Dragon King Trilogy: *In the Hall of the Dragon King; The Warlords of Nin; The Sword and the Flame.* Crossway, 1982, 351 pp.; 1983, 367 pp.; 1984, 313 pp. (5-up).
From the start of the first book of the trilogy, in which the young acolyte Quentin confronts fear and the power of evil, the reader is caught up in Lawhead's colorful and action-filled fantasy saga. Imaginative settings and well-drawn characterizations are given a deeper significance as the clear contest develops between the follow-

ers of the "old gods" and those to whom the "Most High" has been revealed. During the years of Quentin's life covered by the stories, his own spiritual pilgrimage is charted, climaxing in an ultimate challenge at the close of the final volume.

Advanced readers who enjoy Lawhead's richly imagined fantasies may want to go on to the recently-released first volume of his new Pendragon Cycle, *Taliesin* (Crossway, 1987, 452 pp.), which takes place in the legendary worlds of survivors of the lost Atlantis and of Arthurian Britain. (Note: *Taliesin* is written on a considerably more complex and adult level than are the books of the Dragon King Trilogy.)

□ Lawhead, Stephen R. *Dream Thief*. Crossway, 1983, 410 pp. (6-up).

From the space station Gotham, to a deserted subterranean city on Mars, to a sinister control center in a remote corner of India, dream research scientist Dr. Spencer Reston races against time to find the evil force threatening to control the minds of all mankind. Rich in imagination and suspenseful action, this long, complex science fiction novel with its underlying Christian worldview is not a children's book, but will be appreciated by advanced young readers who find the realm of science fiction fantasy especially appealing.

□ L'Engle, Madeleine. A trilogy: *A Wrinkle in Time; A Wind in the Door; A Swiftly Tilting Planet*. Dell, 1976 (1962), 192 pp.; 1974 (1973), 208 pp.; 1978, 278 pp. (5-up).

These imaginative stories are sometimes spoken of as "science fiction," but they actually have little in common with that genre. They may be more accurately classified as fantasy in which events (and the people involved) transcend the usual limits of time and space. In the framework of well-crafted story plots, subtle forces that are larger than any single set of events are consistently felt. In the first book of the three, Meg, her little brother, and her friend Calvin embark on a perilous quest to free her father from his captivity in another world. The conflict between good and evil is implicit, not only in this opening book, but throughout the trilogy. L'Engle writes excellent prose on a level of complexity that demands some mind-and-imagination stretching, always a rewarding experience in reading.

□ Ormondroyd, Edward. *Time at the Top.* Parnassus Press, 1963, 176 pp. (4-6).

A lively, well-written fantasy about a girl of 1960 who goes back in time to 1881. The strange-looking old woman on the street whom Susan has helped tells her she will give Susan "only three" as a reward. By the time Susan realizes that the "three" are three trips into the past, she is already deeply involved in the lives of the lovely family who live in the tall Victorian house that stands where Susan's apartment building will someday be built. A fast-moving plot with both humor and fairy-tale qualities brings the reader to a surprising and satisfying happy ending.

□ Siegel, Robert. *Alpha Centauri.* Crossway, 1980, 255 pp. (5-up).

A visiting professorship brings Becky's father to London from Massachusetts, and he invites his daughter to come along. Reveling in being surrounded by reminders of people and events of the past, Becky is unaware that soon she will be plunged into dangerous adventures in the Britain of thousands of years ago. On a visit to rural Surrey, a ride on an unusual horse takes Becky through the "Eye of the Fog" and into the distant past to a village of kind and gracious centaurs whose very existence is being threatened by the evil Rock Movers. Becky is called upon to act with faith, courage and love as she becomes a key figure in the centaurs' survival. More than simply a well-told fantasy, *Alpha Centauri* is enriched by Siegel's strong spiritual values, poetic use of language, and compellingly vivid descriptions.

□ Siegel, Robert. *Whalesong.* Crossway, 1981, 143 pp. (5-up).

Siegel's lyrical fantasy of the young whale Hrūna combines beauty of language and setting with interest-holding action and Christian truth in allegorical form. To say that *Whalesong* is the story of Hrūna's coming of age and of his Lonely Cruise—an obligatory rite of passage—gives little idea of the book's scope. The ocean environment, the close bonds among the pod (group) of humpbacked whales, the threat to the continued existence of their species by high-tech commercial whale-killing, the fascinating patterns of the whales' lives and journeyings—all are part of this fine book. Recommended for older children, *Whalesong* would also make an excellent read-aloud choice for many third- and fourth-graders as well.

☐ Swift, Jonathan. *Gulliver's Travels*. Grossett & Dunlap, 1947 (1726), 331 pp. (5, 6-up).

Swift's story of the seafaring Lemuel Gulliver is a masterpiece of adult satire, but the wonderfully and playfully imagined worlds of the tiny Lilliputians, the immense Brobdingnagians, the eccentric Laputans, and the dignified Houyhnhnms so captured the imaginations of children that *Gulliver's Travels* has been a children's classic for generations, while at the same time it continues to be studied in college literature classes. Some children will especially enjoy hearing the stories read aloud; other advanced readers will want to delve into its fascinating pages for themselves.

☐ Tolkien, J. R. R. *Farmer Giles of Ham*. Houghton Mifflin, 1978 (1949), 63 pp. (5-up).

In this insightful, somewhat satiric story, a reluctant hero eventually becomes wealthy and powerful and is finally made king. The story includes hilarious encounters with a devious and calculating dragon and a pompous king. Giles is not quite the alienated antihero of modern fiction, but certainly an antihero nonetheless. Look for splendid settings, outstanding humor and *challenging* vocabulary.

☐ Tolkien, J. R. R. The Lord of the Rings trilogy: *The Fellowship of the Ring; The Two Towers; The Return of the King*. Houghton Mifflin, 1967 (1954-55), 423 pp.; 352 pp.; 440 pp. (5-up).

Some children may be ready to follow their reading of *The Hobbit* with the trilogy, but it is at just the time when some very book-oriented children seem quite capable of going on to these beautifully written fantasies with their strongly Christian underlayment that a real division of interest arises among children: some of them simply do not continue to enjoy fantasy as much, particularly when it is written in the challenging vocabulary and demanding sentence structure of The Lord of the Rings. Since some of these children will later be ready for the trilogy (and others will never care for it), it is wiser simply to make the books available but not to press the issue.

□ Tyler, J. E. A. *The New Tolkien Companion*. St. Martin's Press, 1979, 649 pp. (5-up).
Primary listing under *Reference*.
This comprehensive handbook for honorary citizens of Middle Earth can become a welcome part of the Lord of the Rings reading experience.

□ Verne, Jules. *From the Earth to the Moon*. Dodd, Mead, 1962 (1874), 308 pp. (6-up).
An exciting and suspenseful story of space travel—written in 1865. Youngsters interested in today's space shuttles and interplanetary travel will be especially intrigued by Verne's detailed descriptions of his fictional space ship and how it works and the trip to the moon. There is no way to explain the amazing foresight Verne showed, for although technical details differ, of course, he clearly had an almost prophetic vision of coming breakthroughs in space travel, submarines, etc. For example, in this particular story, written more than 120 years ago, it is the United States that is launching the moon-flight—and from southern Florida!

□ Verne, Jules. *Twenty Thousand Leagues Under the Sea*. Scribner's, 1960 (1874), 403 pp.
The ever-fascinating story of the submarine *Nautilus*, Professor Aronnax and his two companions as they roamed the undersea world while held in the power of the mysterious Captain Nemo. Suspenseful, imaginative and prophetic of the powerful submarines which did not exist at the time, Verne wrote the story over 110

years ago. Readers will also want to continue the story in its sequel, *The Mysterious Island*. Other Verne titles to look for are: *Journey to the Center of the Earth; Master of the World; Voyage to the Moon.*

Literature: Level III
Realistic Stories— Modern

☐ Branscum, Robbie. *For Love of Jody.* Lothrop, Lee & Shepard, 1979, 111 pp. (5-up).

Frankie struggles with her own contradictory feelings about her ten-year-old sister Jody, who is retarded. Her mother is expecting another baby and doesn't know the anxiety Frankie feels; she and her dad have not told her mother about the kittens and chicks Jody has squeezed to death in her attempts to hold and love them. A down-to-earth story of an Arkansas farm family who find good answers to their problems and grow closer in the process.

☐ Branscum, Robbie. *To the Tune of a Hickory Stick.* Doubleday, 1978, 119 pp. (4-7).

A heartwarming story of a courageous hill girl who keeps herself and her brother going in the midst of cruelly hard circumstances. A temporarily empty country schoolhouse and a kind schoolteacher also figure prominently in the story. Some of the story's wonderfully realistic details are a bit on the earthy side, but in a perfectly wholesome way.

□ Brown, Fletch. *Street Boy.* Moody Press, 1980, 152 pp. (5-up).

> Primary listing under *Bible Stories and Spiritual Teaching.*

> Jaime Jorka uses his sharp wits, retentive memory, and fast-running legs on the streets of Manila as he steals, begs and scrounges to survive. "Home" is a crowded hovel in Tondo, a teeming mass of squatters' shacks. Jaime is desperately anxious to find a better life, to get out of Tondo; and though he begins to dream of ways he can use his intelligence to organize a gang of thieves, to somehow get money and a comfortable life, he faces the bleak fact that a way out could be only a hopeless dream. Invited to a Christian camp for street boys, he finally makes a skeptical what-have-I-got-to-lose decision to go—and finds not only an unheard-of routine of eating three meals a day, of games, music and study, but also encounters an unselfish love and concern that he initially resists as too unreal to believe. Brown has not only created in Jaime a very appealing youngster, but he writes with a good ear for the talk of the varied characters of his story and a good eye for the seamy surroundings of Tondo. A well-done, credible story of a street boy who finds faith and a new life. (A sequel, *Street Boy Returns,* continues Jaime's story.)

□ Burnford, Sheila. *The Incredible Journey.* Bantam, 1977 (1960), 145 pp. (5-up).

> A warm and wonderful story of a family's pets (two dogs and a Siamese cat) as they make their way home across wild forest land, escape hazards of many kinds but fall victim to others, become separated from each other, narrowly miss death—but never lose the inner compulsion to reach home and the people who love them. A beautifully and perceptively written story.

□ Donahue, Marilyn C. *To Catch a Golden Ring.* David C. Cook, 1980 (5, 6).

> Angie and her best friend, Con, start building a dream of the future—which includes getting away from the depressing tackiness of Bundy Street. A tragic accident seems, at first, to put an end forever to their hopes, but Angie and Con learn that there is more than one way

for dreams to become reality. A warm and captivating
story that emphasizes personal growth, loyalty and
courage. There is also a spiritual emphasis that is woven
naturally into the fabric of the story.

□ Du Bois, William Pène. *The Alligator Case*. Harper &
Row, 1965, 63 pp. (5, 6).
Not only a highly entertaining and humorous story, but
excellent for developing an awareness of style and specialized use of language in writing. Du Bois parodies
the writing style of the "private eye" detective story
(clipped, factual language, etc.) in this tale of a young
boy who pretends he is a detective. His adventures are
hilarious as he sleuths, bumbles and catches the crimi-
nals more by luck than by skill.

□ Farley, Walter. *The Black Stallion*. Random House, 1944,
192 pp. (5-up).
The first in the series of fast action, boy-and-horse
Black Stallion stories that have been so popular for the
past forty years. A shipwreck at sea, a half-drowned boy
clinging to the rope of a magnificent black stallion as it
swims toward a small, uninhabited island—these are
some of the ingredients of Farley's suspenseful tale. It is
far from being great literature, but its simple, fast-moving style holds the interest of reluctant readers and provides easy "just-for-fun" reading even for youngsters
who also enjoy more challenging material.

□ Hámori, László. *Dangerous Journey*. Harcourt, Brace,
World, 1962, 190 pp. (4-7).
Authentic children's stories of life in Iron Curtain
countries are not easily found, but in this case the writer himself was born in Hungary and knows his material
from personal experience. When the grandmother with
whom Latsi has been living dies, the twelve-year-old
boy flees from Budapest, hoping to reach Vienna and
then to contact his parents who had escaped earlier to
Sweden. His adventures are exciting and suspenseful,
and even when he finally reaches Vienna, the only person he finds who speaks Hungarian is an unscrupulous
Communist agent. The story is not only good reading,

but it emphasizes the value of freedom (and the plight of those in Communist-dominated countries) far more effectively than any number of lectures on the topic would do.

□ Hámori, László. *Flight to the Promised Land.* Harcourt, Brace, World, 1963, 189 pp., OP (5-up).

In 1948 a group of devout Jews in remote Yemen decide that since Israel is now a nation, they should return to the Promised Land. Shalom, a bright and questioning twelve-year-old, and his family are among the immigrants. Hámori tells the story of their hard and dangerous trek, and of Shalom's experiences as he moves from a culture that has changed hardly at all since the Middle Ages, to the bustling life of an Israeli Kibbutz, a culture anxious to take advantage of as much modern technology as it can afford. The writer has based his unusual story on that of the real Shalom Mizracki who later became a pilot for El Al Airlines.

□ Haugaard, Erik Christian. *Chase Me, Catch Nobody.* Houghton Mifflin, 1980, 209 pp. (adv. 6-up).

The year is 1937, and thirteen-year-old Erik goes with other boys from his school in Denmark on a short tour of Germany. The serious theme of the book is Erik's awakening to the nature of Nazism and the persecution of the Jews. But there is also a suspenseful adventure story as Erik consents to deliver a mysterious package for a man in a ragged gray raincoat and ends up fleeing across Germany from the Gestapo, with a little Jewish girl in tow. The story is pervaded by a witty, perceptive humor that is sometimes hilarious as Erik and his schoolmates interact with each other, with the two very different teachers who accompany them, and as they encounter German boys in the Hitler Youth organization. As is true of all Haugaard's books, the literary quality of the writing is outstanding.

Note: Early in the story, before Erik leaves on his trip, the boy's father, a parent who seems to have little idea of how to relate to his teenage son, asks Erik (much to the boy's disgust) some crass questions about what kind of relationships he's had thus far with girls.

There is nothing shocking or in any way like the constant suggestiveness of most TV programming in the father and son's conversation, but some parents may want to give it a quick preview.

□ Haugaard, Erik Christian. *The Little Fishes*. Houghton, Mifflin, 1967, 214 pp. (5-up).
This is a moving story about twelve-year-old Guido (and the two other children he helps), orphaned by war and poverty, surviving on his own in the Naples, Italy, of 1943. It is, in another sense, the story of all the children everywhere who must try to live on the streets, children for whom the adult world is simply not making provision. Guido sometimes has to steal to eat, but he knows it is stealing and neither steals nor begs if there is any alternative. In spite of the wretchedness of his life, Guido remains strong in spirit, caring, and compassionate. A fine, deeply real book that will enlarge children's understanding and compassion.

□ Henderson, Lois T. *A Candle in the Dark*. David C. Cook, 1982 (5, 6).
A particularly well-done story of an early-teen girl, blind from birth. Chris leaves her residential school for the blind to live at home with her devoted mother and an ideally wise, kind and helpful new stepfather—and attend public school. How Chris grows, learns, matures and gains both friends and new insights on herself is the substance of the story told in a Christian setting that seems natural and unforced.

□ Hergé. A series: The Tintin books. Little, Brown & Co. (4-7).
Published in twenty-nine countries (and twenty-eight languages), this series of picture-story books has a large following of devoted readers. The format is similar to that of a comic book, but the dialogue involves more reading than do most comic books. Tintin, the intrepid boy-reporter, his companion Captain Haddock, and their friend Professor Calculus become embroiled in one hair-raising adventure after another in every corner of the globe. In one story they may be in Egypt, in another Peru, etc. The colorful drawings reflect the me-

ticulous research of the writer/cartoonist as they show authentic details of places, objects and activities in the stories' varied settings. In addition to nonstop action, the dialogue and events are full of the sort of humor that particularly appeals to children (and to a good many adults as well). Especially helpful in providing palatable reading practice for reluctant readers.

□ Holm, Anne. *I Am David* (Alternate title: *North to Freedom)*. Harcourt, Brace, World, 1965, 190 pp. (4-6).

First published in Denmark twenty years ago, the English translation of Holm's moving and suspenseful story was warmly received. David, whose only memories are of his miserable existence in a Communist prison camp, is suddenly allowed to escape, with only a few cryptic directions and the advice to make his way to Denmark. David's experiences hold the reader's attention from start to finish, but the most notable aspect of the book is the delineation of David's character. Molded by his circumstances in which deprivation and fear were completely dominant, David had also been powerfully influenced by a fellow-prisoner, a remarkable man who has died before the story opens. The writer has imagined what the responses of a boy with such a background, combined with the guidance of his former mentor, might be, and the result is unusual and thought-provoking. (The reason given for David's release, and the crucial encounter which reveals to him his identity, tend to strain the reader's credulity, but do not at all negate the value of the story.)

□ Holman, Felice. *Slake's Limbo*. Scribner's, 1974, 117 pp. (5-up).

At thirteen, Aremis Slake has become accustomed to neglect of every kind, to ridicule, oppression and fear. One of today's rootless children without nurturing care, he considers himself unbelievably fortunate to find a small, underground refuge behind the wall of a subway tunnel. There is reality, pathos and a good deal of humor in this unusual story. The writer expects sensitivity and perception from her readers—who are rewarded with a sense of having gained an increased awareness of another aspect of the human condition (and enjoyed a fast-moving, thoroughly interesting story in the process).

□ Holman, Felice. *The Wild Children*. Scribner's, 1983, 151 pp. (5-up).

It is the early 1920s in Russia, and everywhere is an awareness that people are disappearing. The secret police come without warning, usually at night, and a whole family, or an individual, is gone without a trace. When twelve-year-old Alex, accustomed to a comfortable, secure life, awakens to find his parents, sister and grandmother gone, he finally realizes that it is only because he was asleep in the little hidden storage room that could only be reached through his parents' room that he wasn't taken also. Sheltered briefly and in secret by his schoolteacher, he slips out of town and makes the difficult trek to Moscow to find his uncle—only to learn that the uncle, too, has been "taken" only a month before. Without food or shelter, he is befriended by one of the bands of wild children that are everywhere: displaced children surviving on their own and avoiding the unbearable misery and deprivation of the government's prison-like "children's homes" into which the authorities try to lock them away. Freezing, starving, dying of illnesses, at least they have a degree of freedom on their own. This splendidly written, quietly stated story follows Alex and his new friends as they struggle to survive and finally as they pursue a desperate bid for real, permanent freedom.

□ O'Hara, Mary. *My Friend Flicka*. Harper & Row, 1973 (1941), 272 pp. (6-up).

A modern classic since it was written almost forty-five years ago, O'Hara's story of a boy and his horse has considerably more depth and fully developed characterization than many such stories. Ten-year-old Ken, dreamy and absent-minded, is constantly at odds with his strong, competent rancher father. Ken longs for a colt of his own; his father insists he must first demonstrate more efficiency and maturity. Ken's mother finally convinces her husband that perhaps a reversal of the process might work: having his own colt might be just the incentive Ken needs to keep his daydreaming under control. The story of how Ken responds to being given his colt, Flicka, is the central theme of the book, but there is much more than that involved: the relationships within the family—Ken and his brother, the husband and wife, the parents and sons—the ever-changing cycle of activities on the ranch, all are explored perceptively. Finally, the natural world of the book's setting in the wildness and beauty of Wyoming is an ever-present element throughout this long, appealing story.

□ Ottley, Reginald. A trilogy: *Boy Alone; The Roan Colt; Rain Comes to Yamboorah*. Harcourt, Brace, Jovanovich, 1965, 191 pp.; 1967, 159 pp.; 1967, 159 pp. (5-up).
Set in the remote Outback of Australia, this unusual trilogy vividly conveys the flavor of life on a remote cattle station, one that does not have a resident family unit. The central figure is the young "wood-and-water-joey," a boy in his early teens. Lonely and vulnerable, the boy at the same time has a stubborn resiliency and an instinctive reaching out for shared closeness which is reflected in a variety of subtly drawn relationships with some of the people—and animals—of the station. The stories are full of action and event, but the nature of the people and place, and the adjustment of the boy to the conditions of his life are of primary interest. Realism without sordidness characterizes these fine books. (The stories are based on real experiences and people from the 1930s, but except for some increased technological conveniences, much remains the same in Outback life today.)

□ Pollock, Penny. *Keeping It Secret*. G. P. Putnam's, 1982, 112 pp. (4-6).
Sixth-grader Mary Lou (Wisconsin) Spangler dreads starting school in the new town to which her family has just moved. Tense and prickly because she is so conscious of the hearing aid she has recently had to start wearing, she hides the aid under her hair and resolves no one will know of her handicap. Because of her own emotional turmoil (and some hearing problems the aid can't fully cope with) Wisconsin goes around with the

proverbial chip on her shoulder, rejecting the efforts of her classmates to reach out to her, and becoming more and more miserable. The writer does a good job of portraying the emotions and language of a troubled youngster and shows how, with the help of wise, loving parents and a helpful teacher, Wisconsin's kind of problem can be worked through successfully.

□ Robinson, Joan G. *The Dark House of the Sea Witch.* Coward, McCann & Geoghegan, 1979, 128 pp. (5, 6). Realistic without being sordid, the story handles two important themes well in the framework of a fast-moving plot. Theme one portrays the older sister holding an inner jealousy of her younger brother, unable to admit her feeling to herself. During the course of the story, she matures measurably and recognizes some of the problem, modifying her attitudes accordingly. Theme two focuses on a woman living in a rather remote house; she is strange-looking and poorly dressed, thus spoken ill of, even referred to as a "witch." Yet in a crisis she rescues the children and proves to be a responsible, worthwhile person—simply an eccentric, nonconforming artist. The story is interest-holding and very well-done from a literary standpoint.

□ St. John, Patricia M. *Where the River Begins.* Moody Press, 1980, 128 pp. (4-6). Ten-year-old Francis is a very troubled boy. His family has disintegrated, and the rough gang he has recently joined won't let him end his association with them, even though he very badly wants out. In his desperation, he turns to the Glennys, a kindly farm family who had befriended him in an earlier misadventure. The Glennys are not only kind, but they have a living faith in God, and as Francis temporarily shares their home he comes to know the source of the love and goodness in their lives. St. John does a splendid job of writing a thoroughly realistic contemporary story with a beautifully natural Christian message and nothing forced or preachy in the book.

□ St. John, Patricia. *Star of Light*. Moody Press, 1953, 256 pp. (5, 6).

Hamid lives in a tiny mountain village in the valley below the Riff Mountains of Morocco. His widowed mother, with no source of income, has no choice but to marry the harsh Si Mohamed. When it becomes evident that Hamid's little sister, Kinza, is blind, his stepfather first rents, then plans to sell her to a callous old beggar (a little blind child appeals to the pity of passersby and increases their giving). Desperate to save her child, Hamid's mother entrusts Kinza to him and sends them on a risky quest. This is the story of what happens as Hamid carries out his mission. The writer spent some years in Morocco and brings great authenticity to the depiction of people, places and events in her story.

□ St. John, Patricia M. Three books: *Rainbow Garden; The Secret at Pheasant Cottage; The Tanglewood's Secret*. Moody Press, 1960, 255 pp.; 1978, 160 pp.; 1948, 147 pp. (4-6).

Three stories of preteens who mature in their relationships with others and who learn and grow spiritually as they struggle through family crises. As in St. John's other books, there is a refreshing appreciation of the beauties of the natural world, along with lively plot developments. The specifically Christian emphasis is well-integrated with the development of the stories.

□ Serraillier, Ian. *The Silver Sword*. S. G. Phillips, 1959, 187 pp. (6-9).

Three children, Ruth, Edeb, and Bronia, are thrown on their own in the turmoil of Warsaw during World War II. Fearful that they may never see their parents (snatched away by the Germans) again, the children learn after several years of hazardous survival that their father escaped the Germans and was going to try to reach Switzerland. Sustained by a moving faith and courage, the little family (the two older ones are now in their midteens) and Jan, a streetwise, light-fingered casualty of the tragic times, set out for Switzerland. They are in danger from Russian as well as German troops, and both their faith and courage are taxed to the limit before they win through to a satisfying reunion and a new life.

□ Series: Starring You! A Making Choices Book. David C. Cook, 1982 (5, 6).

Several books by various writers comprise this series. The reader is asked to pretend he or she is the central character of each adventure—and at the end of every page or two there is a choice to be made. If the reader chooses the No. 1 course of action, he or she is asked to turn to a certain page for the next step in the story. Choice No. 2 means turning to a different next step. The stories are short, light, but even include some reinforcing of worthwhile values. Just plain fun reading— and a real inducement for the reluctant reader. Some of the series titles are: *The Cereal Box Adventures* and *Flight Into the Unknown,* by Barbara Bartholomew; *Professor Q's Mysterious Machine,* by Donna Fletcher Crow; and *The President's Stuck in the Mud* by Stephen A. Bly.

□ Stolz, Mary. *Cider Days.* Harper & Row, 1978, 130 pp. (5, 6).

When Polly's best friend moves to California, Polly hopes that newly-arrived Consuela will become her friend, someone with whom she can share long talks and companionable horseback rides. But Consuela is painfully shy, very silent, and misses her native Mexico desperately—Vermont seems just too different, too far from all she has known and loved. But Consuela's artist-mother turns to Polly's family for friendship and advice, and gradually Consuela warms to the Lewises' strong, serene family life. Woven into the story are realistic episodes of family and school life and some subtly made points about the difference between worthwhile activities and the unwholesome preoccupation of some of Polly's schoolmates whose parents pay no attention to what their children are doing. A good, contemporary story in which some growing up is done and some lessons in living are learned.

□ Stolz, Mary. *A Dog on Barkham Street.* Harper & Row, 1960, 184 pp. (4, 5).

A keen understanding of children and the way they think underlies this lively, humorous story of Edward

Frost as he struggles with his own irresponsibility, his fear of a neighborhood bully, and his longing for a dog of his own. The writer manages to suggest valuable ways of dealing with the struggles of preteen life, all in the framework of an interest-holding, enjoyable story.

□ Streatfeild, Noel. *When the Sirens Wailed.* Random House, 1976, 176 pp. (4-6).
Three London children from an impoverished working-class family are sent to the country during World War II to escape the bombing. Holding out against being separated, they are taken in by a crusty but kindly retired colonel and the comfortable country couple who work for him. The colonel is determined to help the children as to their manners and speech, but after some difficulties in adjustment, the children's lives are going quite smoothly when the old colonel dies. The ensuing crisis and its resolution are an important part of the story's development. Lively action, well-handled humor, and a strong element of family devotion all play prominent parts in this appealing story.

□ Thiele, Colin. *Fight Against Albatross Two.* Harper & Row, 1976, 192 pp. (5, 6).
With a small Australian fishing town as its setting, this thoroughly researched story gives a well-balanced view of conflicting ecology-oil industry interests. A likeable brother and sister, their friends and fellow townspeople are effectively characterized, as are the men who direct and man the giant off-shore oil rig that has just been installed. Enjoyable simply for its story interest and its appealing characters, the book also expands the reader's knowledge both of a faraway part of today's world and of an industrial activity that affects all of us everywhere.

□ Willard, Barbara. *The Gardener's Grandchildren.* McGraw-Hill, 1979, 143 pp. (6-up).
Willard creates a small, beautifully imagined world in this story of a little island off the west coast of Scotland—an island that has been turned into an unbelievably beautiful garden. It is a garden held and cared for in trust by Ella and Rob's grandfather. On one level, there is mystery, suspense, and echoes of the past; on a second level, it is the sensitively developed account of

Ella's growing up and of the interrelationships among the main characters that impresses the reader most lastingly.

Literature: Level III
Realistic Stories— Historical

□ Alcott, Louisa M. *Little Women*. Little, Brown & Co., 1968 (1868), 444 pp. (5-up).

It is quite probable that no other children's novel has been as dearly loved by as many girls as has this wonderful old classic. The elements of the story are simple enough: a gentle, scholarly, minister-father (away serving as a chaplain in the Civil War during the first half of the book); a warm, strong mother dedicated to her family but also concerned about the needs of others; four teenaged daughters; a wealthy, crochety neighbor and his handsome, fun-loving grandson. The girls are each very different from the other, with their individual personalities and resultant interaction an important part of the development of the story. The reader immediately becomes involved with this lively, very human family, and the lessons in character, the compassionate but firm view of life and human failings so clearly expressed by the writer, are just as applicable today as they were more than a hundred years ago. (Movie versions, unfortunately, fail to capture the true atmosphere of the story and the nature of its characters, giving viewers a poor idea of what the book has to offer.)

Of the eight children's novels Alcott wrote, the three most outstanding are *Little Women, Eight Cousins,* and *An Old Fashioned Girl*. And thoroughly enjoyable to read are the others: *Little Men* and *Jo's Boys* which follow *Little Women; Rose in Bloom,* the sequel to *Eight Cousins;* and two unrelated stories, *Jack and Jill* and *Under the Lilacs*. We are listing Alcott's books in the

grade 5-up section (where, technically, they belong),
but many of them should be tried out in reading aloud
to younger children. As in the case of most of the classics written some time ago, it is very important to introduce children to the different language and atmosphere of these books at as early an age as possible—
but never in a way that creates in the listener a dislike
of the story. The parent or teacher should feel his or
her way and be guided by the particular preferences of
the child.

☐ Alexander, Lloyd. *The Marvelous Misadventures of
Sebastian*. Dutton, 1970, 204 pp. (4-8).

A fictional Germanic country is the setting for this
eighteenth-century story that stays largely in the realm
of the "possible," but has touches of fantasy. Sebastian,
the young Fourth Fiddle in the establishment of Baron
Purn-Hessel, seems to have a remarkable affinity for disaster. Dismissed from his musician's post because of a
luckless accident, Sebastian sets out to seek a new position. A fine set of adventures follow, and before he
knows it, Sebastian is involved in helping the determined Princess Isabel avoid an unwanted marriage to
the tyrannical Regent, Count Grinssorg. As in all of
Alexander's books, the humor is abundant and witty,
the language level excellent, and the underlying values
sound.

☐ Avery, Gillian. *A Likely Lad*. Holt, Rinehart and
Winston, 1971, 222 pp., OP (5-7).

Young Willy Overs' favorite things are school and
books, but his self-made father has other plans for his
elder son. Willy is to leave school at thirteen and start
on the bottom rung of the corporate ladder of a large
insurance company. There was nothing unusual about
this sort of arrangement in the Victorian era in which
the story is set, but the prospect fills Willy with gloom.
Warmth and delightful humor permeate this lively story
in which the bookish Willy takes matters into his own
hands in a surprising way and stands up not only for
himself but for an elderly woman who has befriended
him. In the process, Willy learns how much he and his
family mean to each other, and his father sees education
in a new light.

□ Blackmore, Richard D. *Lorna Doone*. Buccaneer Books, 1981 (1869), 345 pp. (6-up).

An old favorite classic, the romantic and suspenseful story of Lorna, a ward of the fierce and sinister Doones, and of John Ridd, the strong, gentle man who loves her. John and Lorna's dramatic story is told against a background of seventeenth-century rural England. Vivid descriptions, appealing characterizations, mystery, humor and stirring action have kept this story popular for over a hundred years. (With its great length and challenging language level, this is a book for advanced readers.)

□ Blos, Joan W. *A Gathering of Days*. Scribner's, 1979, 144 pp. (6-8).

An unusual and beautifully done fictional journal of a New England girl in her thirteenth and fourteenth years. The writer has set the time in about 1830, and although she has simply imagined her material in its specific details, she has captured the speech and thought of the time quite effectively.

□ Bronte, Charlotte. *Jane Eyre*. Grossett & Dunlap, 1983 (1847), 552 pp. (6-up).

Orphaned, penniless, and friendless, Charlotte Bronte's famous heroine, the shy, intense, far from beautiful Jane Eyre, endures enough childhood misfortune to thoroughly crush a weaker spirit. Jane, however, weathers the difficult early years, quite unaware of the drama, tragedy—and great joy—that will come to her as the result of a change in the direction of her life. At eighteen, Jane comes to Thornfield Hall as governess to the ward of the abrupt, darkly brooding Mr. Rochester. Suspense builds as Jane becomes aware of mystery and danger. But many twists and turns of the plot are yet to come before the final resolution. This literary classic will be best appreciated by advanced readers.

□ Cervantes, Miguel de (adapted from the Motteaux translation by Leighton Barrett). *The Adventures of Don Quixote de la Mancha*. Knopf, 1939, 307 pp., OP (6-up).

> Cervantes's story, first published in 1605, has been read ever since, and this abridged version recounts Don Quixote's humorous adventures in a lively, interest-holding style that makes the material accessible to young readers.

□ Cervantes, Miguel de (translated and abridged by Dominick Daly). *The Adventures of Don Quixote*. Macmillan, 1957, 256 pp., OP (5, 6-up).

> Another modern translation of Cervantes's classic story that moves quickly and brings out the tale's delightful humor. Children love the ridiculous and should thoroughly enjoy the bumbling, self-deluded Don Quixote.

□ Chamberlain, Barbara. *Ride the West Wind*. David C. Cook, 1979 (5, 6).

> This fictionalized account of one of the worst voyages experienced by seventeenth-century colonists seeking a new life in America realistically portrays some of the hardships they endured. The colonists in this case are Quakers, and thirteen-year-old Nathan Cowell is the book's central figure. His growing awareness of his people's faith in God and their charitable, forgiving spirit is a strong element in the story. From a literary point of view, the writing is far from outstanding. The use of language is particularly uneven, with intermittent attempts made to have the characters use something approaching the speech of the seventeenth century, while at other times contemporary terminology is used. It is worth reading, however, because it is based on an actual voyage and offers insights on an important group of American colonists.

□ Defoe, Daniel. *Robinson Crusoe*. Scribner's, 1957 (1719), 368 pp. (5-up).

> This is another of the famous old classics that everyone knows *about*, but that so often is not really known because it is not being read through in its original form. After running away to sea, Crusoe is wrecked and

spends the next twenty-four years on an uninhabited island near South America. One of the charms of island
survival stories is the amazing ingenuity demonstrated
by the individual or group trying to stay alive, and Crusoe is no exception. But even inventiveness and hard
work can't entirely prevent loneliness. Reading the Bible brings encouragement and fresh determination, and
later Crusoe rescues a young native, Friday, who becomes his helper and companion. They continue to
have a variety of adventures and are finally rescued from
their isolation. A wonderful reading experience both for
its enthralling story and its capacity-stretching language.
(For advanced readers, or read aloud.)

□ Dengler, Sandy. *The Melon Hound* and other titles in the
Pioneer Family Adventure series. Moody Press, 1980,
127 pp. (5-7).
This series offers unpretentious stories of a pioneer
family, with the primary focus on thirteen-year-old
Daniel. Plenty of action and suspense, solid values, a
good natural atmosphere with the Christian element
well integrated into the flow of the story. Light leisure
reading.

□ Dickens, Charles. *Oliver Twist*. Dodd Mead, 1941 (1837-
38), 541 pp. (6-up).
The famous classic story of Oliver, a foundling, who
arouses the wrath of those in charge of the orphanage
by asking for more gruel. Apprenticed to a miserly and
harsh undertaker, Oliver soon runs away, only to come
under the power of Fagin, the devious criminal who
trains children in thievery and profits from their loot.
As always, the "real thing" as written by the author is
an infinitely more enriching experience than film versions, watered-down condensations, or selected excerpts. Skilled, advanced readers with a love for language, setting and characterization are ready for
Dickens by or before sixth grade, but such reading
should be a joy, not a hated task. Parents and teachers
need to feel their way on this. Other works of Dickens
that the kind of young readers mentioned above may
particularly enjoy are: *David Copperfield; Great Expecta-
tions; A Tale of Two Cities;* and *Our Mutual Friend.*

□ Dickinson, Peter. *The Dancing Bear*. Little, Brown & Co., 1973, 256 pp. (6-up).

It is the year 558, and savage tribes from the east continue to attack what remains of the once rich and powerful Roman Empire. The old Byzantine Empire still endures, but it too is under attack. A Hun raid on a powerful household in Byzantium (later called Constantinople, now Istanbul) leaves few survivors: a slave boy, Silvester, a tame bear, and a professional holy man. The daughter of the house has been taken by the raiders. Silvester and the bear, accompanied by the eccentric saint, set forth on a perilous journey north, hoping to rescue the captive girl. Incited by false accusations of the powerful man who wants to inherit the estate of the girl's father, Silvester is pursued by agents of the Empire. Rich, colorful and imaginative, the story moves powerfully from start to finish, strongly creating the picture of another world and its conflicting cultures, and vividly recounting the adventures of its central characters.

□ Drewery, Mary. *Devil in Print*. David McKay, 1966, 216 pp., OP (5-up).

An exciting story of William Tyndale's translating of the Bible into English at a time when this was considered rank heresy, worthy of death. Young Thomas Warlingham and his family are the fictional characters the writer has used to add story content. Thomas's father has been unjustly accused of treasonous activity not connected with Tyndale's work, but they all must flee England, and do so together. How the translation goes on, and the way a change in royal policy comes about that allows the Bible to be freely read in English, are the central themes of this fine story.

□ Forbes, Esther. *Johnny Tremain*. Houghton Mifflin, 1943, 305 pp. (6-up).

When Johnny's hand is badly burned, he realizes he can no longer continue training to be a silversmith. With courage and determination he puts the past behind him and involves himself in the fight for the freedom of the American colonies. Popular for forty years, Forbes's book has long been a modern classic.

□ Fritz, Jean. *Early Thunder*. Coward, McCann &
  Geoghegan, 1967, 255 pp. (6-up).
   Fourteen-year-old Daniel West, living in Salem, Massachusetts, is from a Tory family and considers himself a
   staunch Tory as well. But all around him the unrest and
   the resentment against arbitrary English sanctions
   against the colony grow stronger. Dan finally has to
   face the issues as he sees them and make a choice. The
   story provides good historical background on the
   months immediately preceding the outbreak of the
   American Revolution. The way the characters speak,
   and some of the attitudes expressed have been somewhat shaped to modern readers' abilities and tastes; but
   on the whole the book is worth reading not only as an
   interesting tale, but also for the historical material and
   the account of the process of personal decision-making
   through which Daniel struggles.

□ Fritz, Jean. *Brady*. Coward, McCann, 1960, 223 pp.
  (5-up).
   Young Brady Minton hasn't really given any thought to
   the issue of slavery. But even in 1836 it has become a
   serious (and bitterly controversial) topic for many.
   When Brady accidentally sees some runaway slaves being hidden near his home, his habit of talking without
   thinking causes him to blurt out what he has seen. Fortunately he is talking to his family and some visiting relatives who are sympathetic to the work of the Underground Railway. But Brady soon realizes that his
   habitual inability to keep a secret has caused his father
   to distrust his reliability. How Brady comes to his own
   conclusions about slavery and demonstrates his new
   maturity are the underlying theme of this suspenseful
   and well-thought-through story.

□ Harnett, Cynthia. *The Writing on the Hearth*. Viking,
  1973, 320 pp. (6-up).
   A carefully researched story of fifteenth-century England in the years just preceding the period of the Wars
   of the Roses. Young Stephen is plunged into events that
   are linked to political plotting and suspected involvement with witchcraft and sorcery. In the midst of peril
   and confusion, Stephen thinks deeply about discerning

good from evil and learns to follow his conscience even when he fears the consequences. Suspenseful and well written.

□ Haugaard, Erik Christian. *Hakon of Rogen's Saga; A Slave's Tale.* Houghton, Mifflin, 1963, 132 pp.; 1965, 217 pp. (6-up).

These two books form one complete story, though each can be read independently of the other. The harsh life common to Norway at the end of the Viking period is portrayed with both honesty and understanding. Hakon and Helga, the two young people who are the stories' central figures, reach a hard-won maturity under hazardous, difficult circumstances. The atmosphere and historical background have a highly authentic flavor, and the writer possesses the art of telling an exciting story in a manner that does not romanticize the often violent and brutal Viking culture, but that makes appropriate reading for older elementary students.

□ Haugaard, Erik Christian. *A Messenger for Parliament; Cromwell's Boy.* Houghton, Mifflin, 1976, 218 pp.; 1978, 214 pp. (6-up).

This pair of stories can be read separately or in sequence. Oliver's mother dies when he is eleven, leaving him to the dubious mercies of his weak-willed, drunken father. In a desperate effort to survive, Oliver joins a ragged group of children camped in a war-ravaged cathedral. Set against the background of the English civil wars, the stories follow Oliver as he becomes a part of the people surrounding Cromwell, first as a messenger boy, later with even greater responsibilities. The historical background is excellent, the writing is perceptive and enthralling, and the author has used solid realism without dwelling on depravity or sordidness.

□ Hawse, Alberta. *Vinegar Boy.* Moody Press, 1970 (5-up).

The writer has created an appealing and credible set of fictional characters and events and related them to the crucifixion of Christ. Abandoned as a baby, and known simply as "Boy" or "Vinegar Boy," the child with the large, disfiguring red birthmark on his face has been raised in the Roman garrison. For three years (since he was eight) one of his duties has been to take the sponge and the bags of vinegar and wine to Golgotha's hill when there is a crucifixion scheduled. For some time the boy has been planning to seek Jesus out and ask him to miraculously remove the birthmark that has brought him so much scorn and distaste. The day comes; the boy joyfully prepares to set forth, only to be stopped at the last minute—he must carry vinegar to Golgotha, and Jesus of Nazareth is one of the three being executed. Hawse has written a dramatic, well-crafted story that focuses on the tragedy and triumph of the cross, and that also keeps the reader involved with the lives of Vinegar Boy and those around him.

□ Henderson, Lois T. *Touch of the Golden Scepter*. David C. Cook, 1981, 144 pp. (5, 6).

A pleasingly done fictionalized story of Queen Esther, worked into the framework given in the Biblical account. Henderson's highly romanticized account is intended as pleasant reading matter for young girls and fulfills that purpose admirably. Obviously it doesn't try to seriously recreate the atmosphere of ancient Persia or to realistically portray the character of its King.

□ Henry, Marguerite. *Justin Morgan Had a Horse*. Rand, McNally, 1954, 170 pp. (4-6).

This well-written story of the first Morgan horse has become a modern classic. Set near the end of the eighteenth century in Vermont, it is not at all romanticized and reflects a conscious attempt at realism. This may be a little overdone for some tastes, as a majority of the story's characters seem markedly lacking in sentiment or idealism. The hero, however, has a deep devotion to the plucky little horse as well as demonstrating the worthwhileness of other important values. The cultural patterns of the time have an authentic ring as portrayed in the story, and their very hard realities may be a good balance to the high adventure and drama of most stories of the late eighteenth century.

□ Hewes, Agnes Danforth. *With the Will to Go.* Longmans, Green, 1960, 244 pp., OP (5-up).

Near the end of the sixteenth century the Dutch are making every effort to wrest some of the Indies trade from Portugal. Young Pieter Gerritsz is right-hand man to his uncle Noel, a prominent Amsterdam grain merchant and owner of freight ships. When Noel decides to have a new kind of freighter built, one that can carry more cargo and supplies, he doesn't know that at a crucial moment Pieter will be able to use the new ship in a suspenseful adventure that becomes part of history in the making and starts a new era in trade and expansion to the New World.

□ London, Jack. *The Call of the Wild.* Macmillan, 1963 (1903), 128 pp. (6-up).

London's classic story of a heroic, larger-than-life dog. It is gripping, suspenseful, and in the telling of this dramatic tale, the writer voices an intense, primitive philosophy of life. It is idealistic as to courage, devotion, loyalty, but not in other respects. A fine choice to read aloud.

□ Mayne, William. *Max's Dream.* Greenwillow, 1978, 88 pp. (5-up).

An unusual, beautifully written story that will linger in the memory. Narrated in the 1890s country speech of her little English village, Katie tells of the crippled boy Max whom she helped to care for, of his compelling dream and the unraveling of the mystery surrounding his past. Subtle, imaginative and outstanding in its literary qualities and in its perceptively developed theme of selfless love, this is a story to read aloud, to savor, to reflect upon.

□ Montgomery, Lucy Maud. *Anne of Green Gables.* Grosset & Dunlap, 1970 (1908), 299 pp. (5-up).

One of the most widely known and best loved girls' stories of all time, *Anne of Green Gables* is set on Canada's beautiful Prince Edward Island. It is there that orphaned, red-haired Anne Shirley comes to live with an elderly brother and sister, Matthew and Marilla Cuthbert. By turns a bookish dreamer and an impulsive spit-fire, Anne is essentially an appealing child with a desperate need to love and be loved. How she not only finds a place in more than one heart, but learns to know herself better, is the underlying theme of Montgomery's eventful, often humorous story. Five more Anne stories added to the first comprise the series: *Anne of Avonlea; Anne of the Island; Anne of Windy Poplars; Anne's House of Dreams; Anne of Ingleside*. A briefer series starting with *Emily of New Moon* is not as widely known and goes in and out of print, but is worth looking for. The other two titles are *Emily Climbs* and *Emily's Quest*.

□ Muir, John. *Stickeen*. Houghton Mifflin, 1937 (1909), 81 pp., OP (4-6).

An unusual dog story by the mountain man/naturalist of Yosemite fame. Unlike most dog stories, particularly those written some years ago, this one is not even slightly sentimental and is out of the ordinary both in the nature and actions of the dog and in the amazing experience Muir recounts of the perilous walk on the glacier. A good biographical preface on Muir is included.

□ O'Dell, Scott. *Island of the Blue Dolphins*. Houghton, Mifflin, 1960, 184 pp. (5-up).

This is the widely-praised modern classic that tells the story of a courageous Indian girl, Karana, who spent eighteen years alone on an island off the coast of California. Frequently in danger, dependent on her own efforts for physical survival, and without the comfort of even one other human being's presence, Karana not only lives but grows in strength and serenity. A lovely story, enhanced by its close relationship to the natural world of plants, animals, sea and sky.

□ O'Dell, Scott. *The Hawk That Dare Not Hunt by Day*. Houghton, Mifflin, 1975, 222 pp. (6-up).

A gripping story of Tom Barton, a young seaman who helped smuggle William Tyndale's Bibles into England. Forces of intrigue from all over Europe gather to prevent Tyndale from accomplishing his mission of putting

God's Word into English and getting it into the hands of anyone who wants to read it. Religious and political turmoil are on every hand, and Tom's involvement with Tyndale becomes acutely dangerous. A well-written story with a splendid historical background.

□ O'Dell, Scott. *The King's Fifth*. Houghton, Mifflin, 1966, 264 pp. (6-up).

A story of the Spanish conquistadors and the lust for gold which distorted their values and bred disaster. Esteban Sandoval, a young map-maker, loses his joy of adventure as he, too, falls under the spell of the shining metal. But as he experiences great hardship and suffers at the hands of ruthless men, he finds a new perspective and newly ordered values.

□ Porter, Jane. *Scottish Chiefs*. Scribner's, 1982 (1809), 520 pp. (6-up).

Written in 1809, this romantic tale of William Wallace, Scottish hero during the ten years that spanned the end of the thirteenth century and the start of the fourteenth, was a favorite children's classic for more than a hundred years. Generations of children thrilled to the story's idealism, patriotism and drama, to "escapes through mysterious underground passages, movable pillars, secret doors . . . wardrobes replete with disguises." Like the stories of her literary superior, Sir Walter Scott, Porter's melodramatic and highly romanticized tale is long, the vocabulary and sentence structure challenging. But advanced readers with a taste for historical novels will still find much to enjoy and learn in the stirring adventures of Wallace and his friends.

□ Prokop, Phyllis S. *The Sword and the Sundial*. David C. Cook, 1981 (5, 6).

King Ahaz failed as a ruler and as a father because he refused to be faithful to God. But his young son Hezekiah, the central figure of the book, loved God and was determined to be true to Him. Like so many Biblical characters, Hezekiah's life had more than enough drama to make an exciting story. The writer has based this account on Scripture, adding only events and characters about which the Bible is silent. Prokop has done a good job in researching and including colorful details of daily life and customs, and in bringing the Biblical characters to life.

□ Pyle, Howard. *Men of Iron*. Harper & Row, 1891, 330 pp. (6-up).
   Adventure, conflict and romance in early fifteenth-century England. Myles Falworth's family have lost home and fortune with the dethroning of Richard II and accession of Henry IV. As he grows into manhood, it is Myles' responsibility to make his own way and to try to restore the fortunes of his family. A long-time classic that is still well worth reading.

□ Pyle, Howard. *Otto of the Silver Hand*. Dover, 1967 (1883), 136 pp. (4-6).
   A story set in the Germany of feudal barons. The time period covers several years preceding and just following the accession of Count Rudolph of Hapsburg as German emperor. In the context of an eventful story, the reader becomes aware of the harshness of life (both in castle and cottage) in feudal times. The contrasting life in the monastery where Otto is cared for after receiving a cruel injury may perhaps be idealized, but the point is well made as to violence and harshness, vs. love, justice, peace. As always, Pyle uses a superior vocabulary and a stately literary style.

□ Pyle, Howard. Compiled by Merle Johnson. *Howard Pyle's Book of Pirates*. Harper & Row, 1921, 246 pp. (5-up).
   Johnson has selected a colorful group of Pyle's writings and paintings of pirates. Some of these originally appeared as short stories in magazines; others are excerpts from his books. The exciting material is enhanced by Pyle's elegant writing style.

□ Rawlings, Marjorie Kinnan. *The Yearling*. Scribner's, 1985 (1938), 400 pp. (5-up).
   Rawlings's justly-praised classic about Jody, a twelve-year-old farm boy, and his love for a pet deer is, of course, about a great deal more than that. Its portrayals of the 1860s back-country of northern Florida, of the

people who lived there and wrested a living from its untamed land, reflect a clear-eyed realism without cynicism. Jody's childhood ends with the death of the deer, but as he has endured heartbreak and what seems, briefly, to be betrayal, has faced the basic issues of hunger and survival, he has also grown up and is ready to deal responsibly with his life. The descriptions of the natural world, and the penetrating insights into human nature add to the pleasure and value of reading this Pulitzer-Prize-winning book.

□ Rawls, Wilson. *Where the Red Fern Grows*. Bantam, 1974 (1961), 256 pp. (6-up).
An authentic story of a boy in the Oklahoma Ozarks in the early part of this century. Billy wanted a pair of coon hounds more than anything on earth, but there was simply no money to buy them. How Billy's dream became reality, and what his dogs meant in his life are the theme of this well-written book. A thought-provoking background element is the way that the trapping of wildlife and related activities are viewed by the kind, God-fearing people of the story. Excellent to spark some serious discussions.

□ Scott, Sir Walter. *Ivanhoe*. Dodd, Mead, 1979 (1820), 499 pp. (6-up).
One of the most lastingly popular of Scott's classic novels, *Ivanhoe* is set in the period following the Norman Conquest. Full of drama, intrigue, romance and pageantry, the story follows the fortunes of Wilfred, Knight of Ivanhoe. Leading feminine characters are the lovely Rowena, and the vivid and charming Jewess, Rebecca. Like all of Scott's work, *Ivanhoe* is long, written in an era when short sentences and brief books were exclusively related to beginning readers. The language is challenging, and it is important for children to be able to read such books with pleasure. Advanced readers with a taste for the wonderful atmosphere of the romantic classics will find great enjoyment in *Ivanhoe* and in some of the other novels of Scott, such as *Rob Roy, Quentin Durward, Kenilworth* and *The Black Dwarf*.

□ Speare, Elizabeth G. *The Bronze Bow*. Houghton Mifflin, 1961, 272 pp. (5, 6).

> The story is set in Palestine at the time of Christ. In the context of a suspenseful plot, the need to learn to love rather than hate is emphasized (the hatred of the Jews for the Romans, the scorn of many Romans for the Jews, for example). The characters are well-drawn and historical and cultural background details are effective.

□ Stevenson, Robert Louis. *The Black Arrow*. Airmont, 1964 (1888), 274 pp. (5-up).

> An enthralling classic full of peril and suspense. In the turmoil of one of the Wars of the Roses, young Dick Shelton finds himself pursued first by one side and then by the other. It is with an outlaw band who with their dreaded black arrows are avenging wrongs done to them that Dick finds refuge. His subsequent adventures and final attainment of knighthood make thrilling reading.

□ Stevenson, Robert Louis. *Kidnapped*. Grossett & Dunlap, 1948 (1886), 340 pp. (5-up).

> Stevenson's classic adventure story (set in the mid-eighteenth century) of David Balfour and his friend Alan Breck, a fleeing Jacobite leader. Planning to cheat David of his rightful inheritance, David's uncle has him kidnapped and taken to sea by a dishonest ship's captain. At sea, David and Alan meet and become comrades. Sea battles, perilous chases across the Scottish hills, and a mysterious murder are some of the suspenseful events that follow.
>
> In the adventure-filled sequel, *David Balfour* (Scribner's, OP), David and Alan Breck continue to have hazardous escapes. David also meets the lovely Catriona, whose scoundrel father does not look kindly on the young Scotsman. All is eventually well, but not before the overcoming of many seemingly insurmountable difficulties.

□ Stevenson, Robert Louis. *Treasure Island*. Scribner's, 1981 (1881), 273 pp. (5-up).

> One of the world's best-known books for children, Stevenson's story of pirates and high adventure continues

to be a favorite. Many of today's young people, however, are familiar only with movie, TV, or abridged substitutes for the original story itself, which creates its own wonderful atmosphere of colorful characters, sinister meetings, faraway places and suspense-filled moments.

□ Stockton, Frank R. *The Lady or the Tiger and Other Stories.* Scribner's, 1914 (1884), 201 pp. (5-up).
Stockton's classic short stories are a bit hard to classify in the 1980s. They are clearly dated; yet they are still highly readable, with their mild satiric commentary on human nature, sophisticated (in the manner of another era) humor, and occasional excursions from the realistic to the fantastic. Included in this collection is the writer's most lastingly famous work, "The Lady or the Tiger," a story that, once read, is never quite forgotten. For advanced readers.

□ Sutcliff, Rosemary. *Blood Feud.* Dutton, 1977, 144 pp. (6-up).
Kidnapped from England, the orphaned seventeen-year-old Jestyn is taken to the slave market in Dublin. There he is bought by a young Viking, Thurmond, who becomes Jestyn's friend. Later Thurmond gives Jestyn his freedom, but they stay together on an adventurous trek that ranges from Denmark, through a wild area that will later become part of Russia, and on to Constantinople in the heart of the Byzantine empire. What occurs on this strange journey and how Jestyn finally realizes his own destiny—which is quite different from the restless warrior life into which he has been drawn—makes splendid reading and offers new insights on a little-mentioned part of history.

□ Terhune, Albert Payson. *Lad: A Dog.* Dutton, 1967 (1919), 286 pp. (5-up).
This and a number of other Terhune titles comprise the stories of the wonderful collies of Sunnybank. The tales are exciting and eventful, but they are written in a dated and sometimes highly sentimentalized manner. They are, however, inoffensive leisure reading for lovers of dog stories.

□ Twain, Mark (pen name of Samuel Clemens). *The Adventures of Tom Sawyer.* Dodd, Mead, 1958 (1876), 307 pp. (6-up).

A perennial classic, the story of boyhood in a small, nineteenth-century Missouri town. Tom and the fence-painting episode, his embarrassed fondness for Becky Thatcher, and a number of the other story elements are firmly interwoven into the fabric of American culture. *Tom Sawyer* provides a good introduction to the work of one of the prominent figures in American literature, and reading it aloud encourages discussion and analysis of Twain's humor and insight, as well as his attitudes toward the cultural patterns of his day and toward the church and Christianity.

□ Twain, Mark. *The Prince and the Pauper.* Harper & Row, 1909 (1882), 296 pp. (5-up).

Twain's famous classic about young Prince Edward and Tom Canty, his beggar-boy look-alike. In writing this exciting and imaginative story of the two boys' exchange of roles, Twain was not only weaving an entertaining tale, but also showing how cruel and inhumane some of the laws and customs of the midsixteenth century were. A challenging level of language usage is maintained, and the historical material incorporated into the background relates effectively to the study of sixteenth-century English history.

□ Verne, Jules. *A Long Vacation.* Holt, Rinehart, Winston, 1961 (1888), 224 pp., OP (6-up).

Shipwrecked on an uninhabited island near the southern part of South America, fourteen schoolboys struggle to survive. All students from the same school in New Zealand, the boys had expected to spend six weeks on a vacation cruise, boarding the privately-owned schooner the night before the trip is to start. While all the adults are still ashore and the boys are asleep, the ship is loosened from its moorings, drifts to sea, and the perilous adventure is underway. Although far from being a sophisticated work of serious literature such as Golding's modern boys-on-an-island book, *Lord of the Flies,* Verne does include personality conflicts and problems of self-government along with the usual ship-wreck-island elements of exploration, ingenuity, peril and the unwelcome arrival of ruthless strangers.

□ Verne, Jules. *Michael Strogoff: A Courier of the Czar.* Scribner's, 1927 (1876), 397 pp. (6-up).
An exciting adventure story set in nineteenth-century Russia, in which a heroic young man, Michael Strogoff, journeys through thousands of dangerous miles to save Western Siberia from disaster at the hands of the savage Tartars.

□ Walsh, Jill Paton. *Children of the Fox.* Farrar, Straus & Giroux, 1978, 114 pp. (5, 6).
Three stories of courage and adventure set in the fifth-century Grecian world. Although the young people of the stories are fictional, the historical events are not, and of course the Athenian general Themistokles, the Spartan leader Pausanias, and others mentioned are people from history. Well-written and entertaining as well as offering excellent historical background.

□ Wiggin, Kate Douglas. *Rebecca of Sunnybrook Farm.* Houghton, Mifflin, 1925 (1903), 355 pp. (5, 6-up).
Written in 1903, this lively story of a young girl's passage from childhood to early young womanhood holds up despite its age. Excellent values of patience, sacrifice, aspiration, etc. are underscored, but in a fresh and far from stuffy manner. Humor and happy solutions offer a good balance to the more serious side of this story that has been a favorite with girls since its first appearance.

□ Willard, Barbara. *The Lark and the Laurel.* Harcourt, Brace and World, 1970, 207 pp. (6-up).
The first of a series (The Forest Novels), *Lark* introduces Cecily Jolland and Lewis Mallory, both with troubled, mystery-shadowed childhoods. The political use of children (usually through arranged betrothals and marriages) among the highborn, the helplessness of both women and children to avoid exploitation are underlying themes, but the story is suspenseful and excit-

ing in its own right. Set in England at the time of the accession to the throne of Henry VII, the first Tudor king (1485), the book includes good historical background and details of late fifteenth-century life in a rural environment.

□ Wyss, Johann David. *The Swiss Family Robinson*. Sharon Publications, 1981 (1814), 432 pp. (5, 6-up).

The much-loved classic story of a Swiss family shipwrecked at sea who find refuge on an island and create for themselves a home and way of life. Difficulties, adventures, ingenious inventions, and surprising discoveries abound. This is another of the classics that has been trivialized in mass media forms. In its true form, the language and attitudes of the past are clearly reflected, and there is an explicitly godly tone. This is a splendid book to read aloud over a period of weeks.

16 Literature: *Poetry and Rhymes*

☐ Brewton, Sara and John E. and J. B. Blackburn (compiled by). *Of Quarks, Quasars and Other Quirks: Quizzical Poems for the Supersonic Age*. Crowell, 1977, 114 pp. (5-up).
> A collection of short poems by a variety of poets, focusing on topics particulary related to space-age phenomena/technology. Many of the poems are humorous, some ironic, some designed to question or criticize.

☐ Cole, William (selected by). *Poem Stew*. Lippincott, 1981, 96 pp. (all ages).
> A wonderful collection of rhymes about food—clever, funny, great to listen to and learn.

☐ de Gasztold, Carmen Bernos. *Prayers from the Ark*. Viking, 1962, 71 pp. (all ages).
> Perceptive and imaginative poems that capture the distinctives of a number of animals and birds, and use them to express a variety of ways in which the human spirit can offer itself, *its* distinctives, to God.

☐ Ferris, Helen (selected by). *Favorite Poems Old and New*. Doubleday, 1957, 598 pp. (all ages).
> More than seven hundred poems for children attractively presented in a pleasingly chunky anthology. This is a well-selected collection, and a delight to browse through.

☐ Frost, Robert. *You Come Too*. Holt, Rinehart and Winston, 1959, 94, pp. (6-up).
> The poet chose this selection of his work to be read to and by young people. Frost's life included frequent contact with children, and he especially enjoyed making this collection of his poems that were their favorites.

□ Jarrell, Randall. *The Bat Poet*. Illus. by Maurice Sendak. Macmillan, 1964, 42 pp. (3-up).

>Poet Jarrell talks about the making of poems, the lack of audience for poetry in today's world, the varied response to it, and does it all in a story about a bat who is also a poet. Several delightful poems are included as part of the story. A very special book—try reading it aloud, watch for individual response.

□ Knapp, John, II. *Pillar of Pepper*. David C. Cook, 1982, (ps-4).

>Clever, bouncy nursery rhymes arranged overall in a Genesis-to-Revelation order. Used in conjunction with Bible stories, the rhymes should reinforce children's familiarity with Bible characters and their experiences. But also read them just for fun and for their pleasing sounds. Attractive illustrations, many in color.

□ Lear, Edward. *The Complete Nonsense Book*. Dodd, Mead, 1912, 430 pp.

>All of Lear's delightful rhymes, limericks, poems ("The Owl and the Pussy Cat," "The Jumblies," and "The Quangle Wangle's Hat" are probably the best known) and nonsense alphabets. Nothing else takes the place of this classic collection of fun with language.

□ O'Neill, Mary. *Hailstones and Halibut Bones*. Doubleday, 1961, 59 pp. (all ages).

>Twleve poems about colors. The form and style of the poetry itself are not outstanding, but the metaphors used enhance sensory perception and encourage new ways of seeing. "And in the fall/When the leaves are turning/Orange is the smell/Of a bonfire burning."

□ Opie, Iona and Peter (chosen and edited by). *The Oxford Book of Children's Verse*. Oxford University Press, 1973, 407 pp. (all ages).

>This is a splendid collection of children's verse, the sort of book that becomes a family treasure. The Opies, whose lifework has been the gathering and evaluating of the literature of childhood, have chosen poems of wide-ranging appeal from the fourteenth century

through the contemporary era. The verses are arranged chronologically and a wonderful Authors and Sources section at the end of the book provides brief biographical information about the poets and discusses the circumstances surrounding the poem's writing.

This collection should not be confused with their book on nursery rhymes, which we list next.

□ Opie, Iona and Peter (chosen and edited by). *The Oxford Nursery Rhyme Book.* Oxford University Press, 1955, 223 pp. (all ages).

The definitive volume of nursery rhymes, this book is a fine companion to the Opies' book of children's poetry (see above). The eight hundred rhymes in the collection represent years of loving research on the Opies' part. The 150 most familiar rhymes are included, along with others less well-known. All of these are a part of our English language heritage, but aside from their literary and cultural value, recent research indicates that children who listen to and learn nursery rhymes enjoy being read to more and learn to read more easily. The pleasing rhythms and wide variety of sound patterns lay a helpful foundation for later facility with written language.

□ Plotz, Helen (edited by). *The Gift Outright: America to Her Poets.* Greenwillow, 1977, 204 pp. (all ages).

Plotz has assembled a fine collection of poems about America by noted poets from the seventeenth century to the contemporary era. In addition to their literary value, many of these poems relate interestingly to American history and to the lives of famous Americans.

□ Stevenson, Robert Louis. *A Child's Garden of Verses.* Illus. by Alice and Martin Provensen. Simon & Schuster, 1951 (1885), 76 pp. (ps-up).

This beloved children's classic is still able to charm its readers. No child should be denied the opportunity to open his or her heart to, "I have a little shadow/ Who goes in and out with me/ And what can be the use of him/ Is more than I can see"—and all the other perceptive verses that reflect so timelessly and enjoyably the world of childhood. Because of the book's lasting popularity, there are many different editions, produced by a number of publishers. Three of the many are illustrated by popular children's artists Tasha Tudor (Macmillan), Jessie Willcox Smith (Scribner's), and Brian Wildsmith (Oxford University Press).

⟦17⟧ Mathematics

☐ Apfel, Necia H. *It's All Relative*. Lothrop, Lee & Shepard, 1981, 144 pp. (5-up).
   See listing under *Science* for description of this book on Einstein's theory of relativity.

☐ Bendick, Jeanne. *Archimedes and the Door of Science* (Immortals of Science Series). Franklin Watts, 1962, 143 pp., OP (5, 6-up).
   Born in 287 B.C., the Greek mathematician Archimedes is considered by many to be the single most important person in the history of mathematics. The things he discovered are basic to much of all later mathematical knowledge. The writer tells interestingly, in clear, simple terms, of some of Archimedes' work and of the later knowledge based on what he first discovered. Along with discussions of mathematical concepts is background information on Archimedes' life and the culture of his time.

☐ Charosh, Mannis. *Mathematical Games for One or Two*. Harper & Row, 1972, 33 pp. (1-5).
   Enjoyable games for math-oriented students. Some can be played alone, others with a second player. The materials needed are readily available: toothpicks, cards, checkers, bottle caps—and even these can easily be substituted with other small items at hand. Each game starts with a very simple version, then works into succeedingly more complex versions of the same concept.

□ Charosh, Mannis. *Number Ideas Through Pictures*. Harper & Row, 1974, 40 pp. (1-5).

Approaching numbers through play will give many children a feel for some of the inventive possibilities in mathematics. Using small objects (or drawing them), then following the patterns in the book, children are introduced to the concepts of odd and even numbers, combinations of these, consecutive numbers, square and triangular numbers, etc.

□ Dilson, Jesse. *The Abacus: A Pocket Computer*. St. Martin's Press, 1968, 143 pp. (5-8).

For centuries people have used the abacus for computing. Widely used in Asia, a skilled user can operate an abacus with lightning speed—even winning contests against computers, impossible as this seems. The writer explains the principle on which the abacus is based, discusses its history, talks about its continuing use in Asia and in Soviet schools—and even gives directions for making one.

□ Donner, Michael. *Calculator Games*. Western Publishers, 1977, 48 pp. (3-up).

While most educators and parents recognize the importance of students' being able to compute manually on the basis of learned mathematical principles, it is also true that pocket calculators are an ever-present part of today's life, and a child needs to learn how to operate one, to feel at home with it, and to be able to do successful computations of practical problems. This lighthearted book offers a wide variety of fun and fact, and in addition to its skill-developing qualities also includes questions that help to encourage curiosity and experimentation. (Note: Parents and teachers should be aware that one of the games—Pokulator—is related to poker and uses some of its terminology, etc.)

□ Froman, Robert. *Less Than Nothing Is Really Something*. Harper & Row, 1973, 33 pp. (1-5).

A beginning-level introduction to negative numbers. The concepts of adding, subtracting, multiplying or dividing using both negative and positive numbers often causes students difficulty at some point in their math study. A clear grasp of some of the facts that are explained simply in this book can be very helpful. (For example, − 2 is one more than − 3, etc.) The number line, with its graphic representation of the fact that moving to the right from the central dividing point between the positive and negative numbers represents one more at each step, while moving to the left from the same point reverses the process, helps visually to reinforce the concept.

□ Gardner, Martin. *Mathematical Puzzles*. Harper & Row, 1961, 114 pp. (6-up).

A plentiful supply of old and new puzzles divided into categories: arithmetic, money, speed, probability and six other groupings. Each section is headed with a discussion of the nature and importance of the kind of mathematics to be used in solving the puzzles in that particular group. Gardner explains each solution in detail and makes suggestions as to further paths that can be pursued with this type of problem. The writer obviously enjoys mathematics—and wants his readers to share the fun.

□ Gies, Joseph and Frances. *Leonard of Pisa and the New Mathematics of the Middle Ages*. Crowell, 1969, 127 pp. (6-up).

Italy was one of the prominent European powers during the Middle Ages, and both the scholars and traders of its wealthy, bustling cities had frequent contacts with their counterparts in the Moslem world. Thus it was that at the beginning of the thirteenth century a brilliant young mathematician, Leonard Fibonacci, of the city of Pisa, had learned of the Hindu-Arabic system of numerals and eventually wrote a book on this system which was, in time, to revolutionize mathematics. It is true that small numbers of European scholars here and there had known of the Hindu-Arabic numeration, but knowledge of it was not being developed or used in the West. (It is these Arabic numerals that we use today and on which whole areas of modern scientific inquiry rely.) The Gieses' book includes fascinating material on the two spheres of influence of the Mediterranean and European medieval world: the nominally Christian and

the Moslem. This is a scholarly and also a lively account
of the life and work of a key figure in mathematics who
is little known or written about. Excellent for advanced
students and for parents and teachers.

□ James, Elizabeth and Carol Barkin. *What Do You Mean by
"Average"?* Lothrop, Lee and Shepard, 1978, 60 pp. (5,
6-up).
   A clear, thoroughly demonstrated treatment of how to
   turn raw data into meaningful figures: mean averages,
   medians, modes; and how to determine *which* of these
   methods to use. Presented in story form (a high school
   election campaign), the mathematical facts are seen in a
   practical, interest-holding form.

□ Knight, David C. *Isaac Newton: Mastermind of Modern
Science.* Franklin Watts, 1961, 153 pp., OP (6-up).
   See listings under *Biography* and *Science*.

□ Linn, Charles F. *Probability.* Harper and Row, 1972, 40
pp. (4-6).
   Examples of probability estimates are shown. The concept is illustrated, then a number of sample problems/
   experiments in probability are given.

□ Madison, Arnold, and David L. Drotar. *Pocket
Calculators: How to Use and Enjoy Them.* Nelson, 1978,
144 pp. (6-up).
   A serious and detailed treatment of the subject. The authors believe that while almost every home has one or
   more calculators, many people don't really know how
   to make full use of them or understand the principles
   on which they operate. A fuller knowledge should lead
   to more pleasure and benefit from the use of a calculator, and this book provides a good basic education in
   the calculator: how to use it and what to use it for. The
   book also includes some puzzles, games and tricks that
   can be done with a pocket calculator.

□ Riedel, Manfred. *Winning with Numbers*. Prentice-Hall, 1978, 64 pp. (5-9).

A longer, more detailed and sophisticated approach to the subject of statistics than that of Srivastava's *Statistics* (listed below), Riedel's book is designed to be used with older children. Statistics is defined as a method of gathering facts, and a brief background on its development is given. Then, using sample situations, Riedel has fictional junior high age kids going through a variety of procedures to gather statistics and draw conclusions. In some cases, they realize they have used invalid samplings and discuss how the process could be done in such a way as to make the results valid. Methods of reporting statistics and ways to avoid being deceived by improperly handled statistics are also discussed.

□ Sitomer, Mindel and Harry. *Zero Is Not Nothing*. Harper & Row, 1978, 34 pp. (1-3).

The basic mathematics of the zero is explained clearly. Its importance and historical background are discussed, then practical applications of its use are detailed. In addition to its crucial function as a place holder, the zero is also used in a variety of other important ways. Clear illustrations illumine the concepts throughout.

□ Srivastava, Jane Jonas. *Computers*. Harper & Row, 1972, 32 pp. (1-4).

In easy-to-understand language, the writer explains what a computer is and how it works. Computer language, flow-charts and typical computer tasks, are discussed in a lively, informative manner.

□ Srivastava, Jane Jonas. *Statistics*. Harper & Row, 1973, 31 pp. (1-5).

An amusingly illustrated introduction to the world of statistics. Today's children are going to be inundated with statistical "evidence" throughout their lives, in the form of consumer advertising, political campaigning, requests for money, exposé articles and more. In addition to explaining what statistics are, the writer suggests that each time one reads a statistic he or she ask some thoughtful questions to help decide whether the statistic can be trusted.

□ Stonaker, Frances Benson. *Famous Mathematicians.*
Harper & Row, 1966, 118 pp. (4-9).
The stories of eleven famous mathematicians down
through the ages. Each account, written in a lively, popular style, is of necessity only a summary of the person's
life and work. The material does offer good general information and serves as an introduction for the reader
who wants to dig more deeply into a specific mathematician's achievements. For the student who does not expect to concentrate especially on math, it provides the
basic identification of important mathematicians that is
so beneficial to a well-rounded education.

□ Trivett, Daphne and John. *Time for Clocks.* Crowell,
1979, 33 pp. (1-3).
An in-depth treatment of time-telling. Includes use of
2-place addition, many complex concepts. Two possible
uses are (1) as a primary text to teach time-telling to
advanced first- or second-graders or (2) as individual-
ized material for grade 2 or 3 students to expand their
concept of time-telling, to offer review and reinforcement.

□ Wyler, Rose and Gerald Ames. *It's All Done with
Numbers.* Doubleday, 1979, 128 pp. (5, 6-up).
"Magic" tricks involving prediction, mind-reading and
lightning calculation are actually all done with numbers.
This interesting book explains the processes used and
gives instructions for a large number and variety of the
seemingly baffling tricks of the "mental magician." In
addition to an ability to remember and repeat the steps
of each process (not unduly difficult), the success of
performing as a mental magician depends upon the dramatic flair and showmanship of the performer. Some
suggested "patter" to accompany the tricks is given.

18 Miscellaneous

☐ Charlip, Remy and Jerry Joyner. *Thirteen*. Parents' Magazine Press, 1975, 40 pp. (3-up to all ages).
A unique picture-book that unfolds thirteen different sequential picture stories in thirteen double-page spreads. The particular value of this book, in addition to sheer enjoyment, is the advanced level of mental and visual "sorting out" it involves and the subtle humor waiting to be appreciated, the stimulus to the imagination it offers.

☐ Fixx, James F. *Solve It: A Perplexing Profusion of Puzzles*. Doubleday, 1978, 94 pp. (5, 6-up).
A wide variety of puzzles/problems in several categories: logic, spatial relationships, language usage, mathematical reasoning, etc. Most of the problems call for leaps of logical thought. These are puzzles for students of above-average intelligence—a welcome supplement for specific students.

☐ Murphy, Jim. *Weird and Wacky Inventions*. Crown, 1978, (5, 6-up).
A real find for the youngster who thinks it would be great to be an inventor. Murphy has delved into patent records and come up with dozens of inventions (from various time periods) that never quite "got off the ground." The method of presentation adds to the fun: A drawing of an invention is shown and the reader is invited to answer a multiple-choice question as to what the object is intended to be/do. The next page gives the answer and sometimes also shows and describes one or two other inventions that had a similar purpose.

□ Press, Hans Jürgen. *The Adventures of the Black Hand Gang*. Prentice-Hall, 1977, 128 pp. (3-6).

> More of a picture-puzzle collection than a literary experience, this lighthearted book is for fun—and for sharpening visual observation skills. A little group of four friends have become skilled in the art of detection and find themselves involved in a rollicking, wholly improbable adventure. Each page of the story asks a question at the bottom that is related to a clue to be found in a detail-filled illustration on the facing page. Entertaining to read, and requires a keen focus on visual details.

□ Schwartz, Alvin. *Unriddling: All Sorts of Riddles to Puzzle Your Guessery*. Illus. by Susan Truesdell. Lippincott, 1983, 128 pp. (4-up).

> Folklorist Schwartz has drawn this collection of riddles from American folklore. People used to say, he tells the reader, that there was a special part of the brain, called the "guessery," that solved riddles. Riddling and unriddling (solving the riddle) were said to stretch the mind and be good for it. Be that as it may, riddles have entertained people (and exercised their brains) for thousands of years, and continue to do so. Schwartz offers dozens of riddles, divided into eighteen different categories. Great fun and plenty of challenges for readers' "guesseries."

19 Music

☐ Bakeless, Katherine Little. *Story Lives of Great Composers*. Lippincott, 1940, 264 pp., OP (4-up).

Informative, lively narrative accounts of the life and work of Rachmaninoff, Richard Strauss, Stravinsky, Massenet, Dvořak and Scarlatti. The quality of the writing is not exceptional from a literary standpoint, but it is competent and readable.

☐ Berger, Melvin. *The Story of Folk Music*. S. G. Phillips, 1976, 127 pp. (6-up).

A survey-style discussion of folk music: its characteristics, history and contemporary development. Prominent collectors of folk music as well as well-known performers are noted. The writer seems to have focused largely on performers known for their strong (sometimes radical) social protest, while generally ignoring less controversial folk-singers. The book, however, offers the kind of overview that can lead readers to doing further research and developing their own skills and interest in specific areas of folk music.

☐ Berger, Melvin. *The Trumpet Book*. Lothrop, Lee & Shepard, 1978, 128 pp. (3-7).

A brisk, survey-style treatment of the trumpet: a little of its known history, its development, and the principle on which it works, how it is made, and the kinds of trumpets and "trumpet family" instruments made. Noted trumpeters are briefly discussed, as are the kinds of music played on the trumpet. The last chapter, "You and the Trumpet," gives suggestions as to trumpet care and professional possibilities. A glossary of terms concludes the book.

□ Boni, Margaret, and Norman Lloyd (selected and edited by). *Fireside Book of Favorite American Songs* and *Fireside Book of Folk Songs*. Simon and Schuster, 1963, 360 pp.; 1966, 323 pp. (all ages).

> Splendid collections of the songs of our musical heritage, songs people have sung for decades—sometimes centuries—at work, play, worship. Such songs should be part of children's heritage as well. These are colorful, appealing books which include piano and guitar arrangements for the songs.

□ Bulla, Clyde Robert. *The Ring and the Fire*. Crowell, 1962, 135 pp., OP (4-up).

> The versatile Bulla tells the stories that make up Wagner's opera cycle, *The Ring of the Nibelung*. The operas are based on stories from Norse and German mythology, mysterious and dramatic. Bulla retells the stories as they are used in the operas and includes the theme music for each one.

□ Bulla, Clyde Robert. *Stories of Favorite Operas*. Crowell, 1959, 277 pp., OP (4-up).

> In a lively, interest-holding manner Bulla has retold the stories on which twenty-three well-known operas are based. The works of Mozart, Rossini, Richard Strauss and others are represented. Notes related to the first productions of the operas and to biographical data on the composers are helpfully included.

□ Elliott, Donald. *Alligators and Music*. Illus. by Clinton Arrowood. Gambit, 1976, 50 pp. (all ages).

> A whimsical book that nevertheless does some serious informing. It is an introduction to the symphony orchestra, picturing and describing each instrument and its particular function, then addressing the qualities of the orchestra as a whole. All the instruments are shown as being held or played by elegantly dressed alligators. The book abounds with delightful touches (seats in the concert hall designed to accommodate the physical shape of alligators, for example) and subtle humor. A fine supplement in music study.

□ Garson, Eugenia, and Herbert Haufrecht (compiled and edited by). *The Laura Ingalls Wilder Songbook.* Harper & Row, 1968, 160 pp. (all ages).

A beautifully done book containing sixty-two of the songs and hymns sung by the Ingalls family. A splendid companion to the Little House books, each song is annotated with the book's title and the page number on which it appears in a given story. Arranged for voice, piano and guitar.

□ Glazer, Tom. *Do Your Ears Hang Low?* Doubleday, 1980, 110 pp. (all ages).

Fifty "fun" songs with finger play suggestions included. Piano arrangements and guitar chords shown.

□ Greene, Richard C. *The King of Instruments.* Carolrhoda Books, 1982, 32 pp. (k-up).

The writer offers a simple introduction to the pipe organ that is easily accessible to the very young reader (or look-and-listener). The brief text is accompanied by a wealth of photographs. The basic principles on which a pipe organ works, and some typical arrangements of pipes, swell-boxes and other components are shown. Green doesn't attempt to go into the history of the pipe organ and does not focus on specific important organs or discuss the actual music in any detail. The book's purpose is simply to acquaint children with basic facts about the components and technical aspects of pipe organs and it does this very clearly.

□ Hatch, Eric. *The Little Book of Bells.* Duell, Sloane & Pierce, 1964, 85 pp., OP (4-up).

This is one of two books on the same general topic written separately by a pair of men who had worked together on the Independence Day bell project. The second book is *The Sound of Bells,* by Eric Sloane (Doubleday). The books are full of a variety of information and anecdotes about bells. Both bring in a variety of fascinating details and include many tie-ins with historic events and other lands. Both make enjoyable, informative reading.

☐ Hawkinson, John, and Martha Faulhaber. *Music and Instruments for Children to Make* and *Rhythms, Music and Instruments to Make*. Albert Whitman & Co., 1969, 47 pp.; 1970, 95 pp., OP (ps-2; 3-up).

> Hawkinson, an arts and crafts specialist, and Faulhaber, a teacher/musician, combined to put together two books on helping children to be intimately involved in music-making, creating their own pipes, drums, rhythm sticks and other percussion instruments. Detailed instructions and illustrations are used throughout.

☐ Hill, Elizabeth Starr. *Bells*. Illus. by Shelly Sachs. Holt, Rinehart & Winston, 1970, 48 pp., OP (3-up).

> A brief, pleasing and artistic introduction to bells: their general history, development, variety, and some especially famous bells. Thoroughly researched, both as to text and illustrations, children will find much of interest in this little book.

☐ Hosier, John. *The Sorcerer's Apprentice and Other Stories*. Oxford University Press, 1960, 64 pp., OP (4-up).

> Five lively, effectively-told stories, each of which is associated with a well-known suite of music such as the *William Tell* overture and the suite mentioned in the book's title.

☐ Ingman, Nicholas. *What Instrument Shall I Play?* Taplinger, 1976, 128 pp. (6-up).

> Not only a valuable source of information for the young person trying to decide on an instrument in which to specialize, Ingman's book may be used most often as a detailed reference on the composition and nature of an orchestra and its individual instruments. The history of each instrument, its development and modern use, famous players and representative music for the instrument are all discussed. Obviously the treatment must be brief, but the writer manages to pack in a surprising amount in the space allotted to each instrument.

□ Langstaff, Nancy and John. *Jim Along, Josie.* Harcourt, Brace, Jovanovich, 1970, 127 pp. (all ages).

>The Langstaffs (both are musicians and teachers) have assembled a fine collection of folk songs, singing games and action songs that have a wide appeal for children. A helpful preface and notes on using the guitar with the songs are included, and for some of the songs optional percussion accompaniments are given.

□ Lasker, David. *The Boy Who Loved Music.* Illus. by Joe Lasker. Viking, 1979 (2-5).

>The story of Haydn. See listing under *Biography.*

□ Ritchie, Jean. *From Fair to Fair: Folk Songs of the British Isles.* Henry Z. Walck, Inc., 1966, 93 pp., OP (all ages).

>Noted folk-singer Jean Ritchie has collected sixteen of Britain's traditional folk songs and presents them here with a brief explanatory story and relevant photograph accompanying each. To tie the presentation together, she has invented a wandering minstrel, Jock, who goes from fair to fair, sharing in each locality's distinctive music. Piano and guitar arrangements are included.

□ Ritchie, Jean. *Jean Ritchie's Swapping Song Book.* Henry Z. Walck, Inc., 1964, 93 pp., OP (all ages).

>Ritchie herself grew up in the Southern Appalachian mountains of Kentucky, singing the folk songs she later began to share with the world. More than a performer, Ritchie is a recognized authority on our old folk songs, many of them brought from England, Scotland and Ireland by pioneer settlers. Music (including piano and guitar arrangements), lovely photographs, and short textual introductions to each song combine to make an exceptionally appealing book.

□ Seeger, Ruth Crawford. *American Folk Songs for Children.* Doubleday, 1980, 192 pp. (all ages).

>Especially designed as a book for children, parents and teachers, this collection of ninety-four folk (traditional) songs includes somewhat more text than the usual songbook. The writer tells how the book came into be-

ing, why folk music is so valuable to use with children, gives hints on how to sing the songs, how to use them at home and at school, suggestions as to accompaniment (fine, but not necessary, says the author), and comments on the value of the humor in such songs.

□ Stevens, Byrna. *Ben Franklin's Glass Armonica.* Illus. by Priscilla Kiedrowski. Carolrhoda Books, 1983, 48 pp. (k-3).

Designed for easy reading in the primary grades, this book provides surprising and interesting information about still another invention of the versatile Benjamin Franklin. Using an idea that apparently originated in China, Franklin, an accomplished and enthusiastic musician, elaborated on it and came up with something he called an armonica—glass bowls of varying sizes that were played with the fingers while being rotated by a foot pedal. A delightful bit of musical trivia, and another sidelight on the remarkable Mr. Franklin.

□ Tolkien, J. R. R. and Swann, Donald. *The Road Goes Ever On: A Song Cycle.* Houghton, Mifflin, 1978, 75 pp. (4-up).

With Tolkien's assistance, Swann set the words of songs sung in The Lord of the Rings trilogy (and one from *The Adventures of Tom Bombadil*) to music. The pages are decorated with Elvish script, and a section of notes and translations of Elvish terms concludes the handsomely done book.

□ Winn, Marie (collected and edited by). *The Fireside Book of Children's Songs,* and *The Fireside Book of Fun and Game Songs.* Simon and Schuster, 1966, 192 pp.; 1974, 224 pp. (all ages).

Wonderful collections of all kinds of singable songs: ballads, game and action songs, silly songs, lullabies, rounds. Sprightly illustrations brighten the pages, and the piano and guitar arrangements are simply done and excellent as accompaniment.

20 Outdoor Activities
Other Than Group Games

☐ Bachert, Russel E. *Hundreds of Ideas for Outdoor Education*. Interstate Printers and Publisher, 1979, 152 pp. (all ages).

Primary listing under *Teaching Resources*.

The book contains brief "idea generators" related to exploring the outdoor world.

☐ Coombs, Charles. *Be a Winner in Tennis*. Morrow, 1975, 128 pp. (5-9).

Coombs offers detailed suggestions for becoming a proficient tennis player. He starts with a brief history of the game, details the layout of a court and the basic rules, discusses rackets, and on through techniques and strategies. The same author has also written a number of other books on a variety of outdoor activities.

☐ Dickmeyer, Lowell and Annette Jo Chappell. *Tennis Is for Me*. Lerner, 1978, 46 pp. (k-4).

One of the Lerner series titles that introduce young people to the basics of specific sports or activities. Twelve-year-old Sandy tells of her beginning steps in learning to play tennis, and photographs of each step accompany the text. Look for other titles in this series on football, baseball, soccer, skateboarding and more.

☐ Freeman, Tony. *Beginning Backpacking*. Children's Press, 1980, 48 pp. (3-up).

This "starter" book on backpacking goes into considerably more detail than does the other introductory book we list below, and is written on a more advanced reading level (though it is far from difficult). Equipment and supplies are discussed in some detail, and the book is illustrated throughout with color photographs.

☐ Gavett, Bruce and Conrad Brown. *Skiing for Beginners*. Scribner's, 1971, 57 pp. (4-up).

> A clear, step-by-step instruction manual for the beginning downhill skier. Each step is thoroughly illustrated with pictures of children actually doing each procedure, accompanying each picture by telling in their own words what they are doing. Written by a ski school director (Gavett) whose whole family are totally immersed in skiing, and a ski instructor turned editor (Brown), the book gives thorough coverage to the method used in most of our ski schools, the American Ski Technique. The book can be used either as an effective self-teacher, or an indispensable complement to ski-school lessons.

☐ Gerston, Rich. *Just Open the Door*. Interstate Printers and Publisher, 1982, 112 pp. (all ages).

> Primary listing under *Teaching Resources*.
>
> Lesson plans and activities that tie outdoor/environmental experiences to classroom curriculum.

☐ Hawkinson, John. Two books: *Our Wonderful Wayside* (OP); *Let Me Take You on a Trail*. Albert Whitman & Co., 1966, 40 pp.; 1972, 48 pp. (4-up).

> Things to look for, make, and do out in nature. The wayside book is less applicable to the dry areas of the southwestern United States, but its concepts—finding treasures in the natural growth that springs up outside built-up areas between roads and fences or roads and woods—would hold true in many areas, even though specific plants and animals would vary. The trail activities are applicable in most fairly wild areas. In both books, children are encouraged to see what is around them, to investigate and collect, to make usable items from simple materials. (Parents/teachers should be careful to inform themselves and their students of any existing laws prohibiting collecting, either of specific items or in specific areas.)

☐ Hogrogian, Nonny. *Handmade Secret Hiding Places*. Overlook Press, 1975 (all ages).

> Primary listing under *Crafts, Hobbies and Domestic Arts*.
>
> Ideas for making a number of different little hideaways in a hurry. A small, delightful book.

□ Krementz, Jill. *A Very Young Rider.* Knopf, 1977, 125 pp. (4-up).

> Another in Krementz's series on children who have mastered specific physical skills, this book focuses on ten-year-old Vivi Malloy, a serious rider with long-range Olympic ambitions. The daily reality of Vivi's life is recorded (with dozens of photographs and an easy-reading text): her care of her pony, Ready Penny, her classes in riding and jumping, her appearances in competition. A relevant, helpful book both for the child who wants to become a skilled rider, and for the many other readers whose world is enlarged by learning about the skills and interests of others.

□ McManus, Patrick F. *Kid Camping from Aaaaiii! to Zip.* Lothrop, Lee & Shepard, 1979, 125 pp. (3-8).

> With expertise and abundant humor McManus talks to kids about camping. As he so perceptively points out, there is only one requirement for kid camping: being a kid. Even when an adult has started his camping early in life and has camped frequently ever since, the adult shouldn't expect ever to recapture the unique kid-camping experience. But he *can* remember. It is with this memory-filled consciousness, along with current interviews with his own four daughters, that the writer plunges into this highly entertaining—and highly practical—handbook. Briskly organized as alphabetically as the title implies, the book digs right in to such topics as bears, beds, beverages, blisters (to name just a few of the B's). Helpful and hilarious.

□ Ogilvie, Robert S. *Basic Ice Skating Skills.* Lippincott, 1968, 176 pp. (6-up).

> In use for almost twenty years, this Official Handbook of the United States Figure Skating Association is still popular with ice skaters, whether skating simply for recreation or to develop competitive skills. Starting out with answers to preliminary questions (at what age should a child be started?, for example), moving on to equipment and then into techniques, the book thoroughly covers all areas of figure skating and illustrates each point with photographs and diagrams. (The text

explains that the term *figure skating* covers everything not falling into the ice hockey or speed skating categories.)

☐ Swan, Malcolm D., ed. *Tips and Tricks in Outdoor Education*. Interstate Printers and Publisher, 1978 (all ages).

Primary listing under *Teaching Resources*.

A fine source book for outdoor activities. Its eighteen chapters focus on different areas: animal studies, weather, plants, and many more.

☐ Thomas, Art. *Backpacking Is for Me*. Lerner, 1980, 48 pp. (3-up).

A brief introduction to backpacking, with the same format as the other books in this series. (Easy reading for early graders.) Worded as though told by the young preteen camper, the account describes his first backpacking trip with a young-adult brother. Photographs throughout illustrate the text. The book serves more to interest and involve the young potential backpacker than to tell him all he needs to know. Young beginners should, of course, always be with older, experienced campers.

☐ Washington, Rosemary G. *Cross-Country Skiing Is for Me*. Lerner, 1982, 48 pp. (2-up).

A good introduction to cross-country skiing, written in simple, direct language as though by the girl (about a twelve-year-old) pictured throughout. Necessary equipment and clothing are discussed, as are the various basic techniques. Most youngsters will need some personal instruction in addition to this book. (The details of the forward kick needed to propel the skier on, the stance of the body and weight distribution aren't as completely clear, for example, as the instructions in Gavett and Brown's downhill ski book, *Skiing for Beginners*.) Overall, a useful book that would make a helpful complement to hands-on instruction in cross-country techniques.

21 Physical Education and Organized Games

☐ Bentley, William B. *Indoor and Outdoor Games*. Pitman Learning, 1966 (k-6).

> A collection of almost two hundred indoor and outdoor games for children in grades 1 to 6. They are grouped in three sections: K-2; 3, 4; 5, 6, then subdivided into their indoor or outdoor categories.
>
> All of the games involve active group participation and have been personally tested by the writer, a physical education teacher and camp athletic counselor.

☐ Block, Susan Dimond. *Me and I'm Great: Physical Education for Children Three Through Eight*. Burgess, 1977 (adult use for ps-3).

> An excellent comprehensive manual for use in providing a physical education program for children ages three to eight. The writer shows the *how* and *why* of physical education for the young child, and points out that coordination, flexibility and physical skills don't just "come naturally" to children—they need appropriate instruction. The programs detailed by Block use homemade equipment and a minimal amount of supplies.

☐ Capon, Jack. Perceptual Motor Development Series (5 booklets). Pitman Learning, 1975 (adult use for ps-3).

> Activities in these useful booklets are presented in the order in which a child could be expected to master each skill. Such guidelines can be particularly important in home teaching or in classrooms where no perceptual motor development standards are included in the educational program. In such cases, parents or teachers might not be aware of an individual child's special problems unless they had activity guidelines like the ones presented in this series, through which informal assessments of the child's skills could be made.

□ Carr, Wendy. *Fit for Kids.* Addison-Wesley (adult).

The program overview states: "*Fit for Kids* is an exer-
cise-to-music program designed to increase physical fit-
ness through the improvement of circulatory function,
strength, flexibility, body awareness and general movement ability." Guidelines are given for each of four
grade levels: K-1, 2-3, 4-5 and 6-7. Instructions, tim-
ing, background information are all clearly set forth,
and over seven hundred photographs of children have
been used to illustrate the exercise patterns.

□ Radlauer, Ed and Ruth. *Some Basics About Women's
Gymnastics.* Children's Press, 1980, 32 pp. (4-up).

A very brief overview of the topic. Background information on gymnastics is noted and general facts given
about the various kinds of skills involved and how these
are developed. Illustrated with color photographs. The
focus is informational rather than "how-to" since gymnastics is an activity that relies heavily on skilled coach-
ing and hands-on instruction.

22 Reference and Research/ Study Skills

☐ Cassandre. *Life When Jesus Was a Boy*. Judson Press, 1981, 48 pp. (3-up).

Based on extensive research into life in Jesus' time, this narrative of the things Jesus was likely to have encountered reflects the customs, foods and routines of day-to-day life, and the religious and political situation in early first-century Palestine. Generously illustrated (including detailed descriptions of many specific objects) and clearly told.

☐ Dicks, Brian (consultant). *The Children's World Atlas*. Celestial Arts, 1981, 128 pp. (4-6).

See listing under *Geography* for description of this book.

☐ Ford, Paul F. *Companion to Narnia*. Harper & Row, 1980, 450 pp. (4-up).

A detailed guide to "the themes, characters, and events" of the seven Narnia books. Entries are arranged in alphabetical order, cross-referenced and annotated. Maps and illustrations add to the guidebook's usefulness.

☐ Fritz, Jean. *George Washington's Breakfast*. Illus. by Paul Galdone. Coward, McCann, 1969, 47 pp. (2-up).

A contemporary "George" with the same birthday as the "father of our country" decides to find out what our first President ate for breakfast. The story of his research (which involves his whole family) and what he learned is not only entertainingly written, but opens new doors for young children as to how to go about researching a topic.

☐ Greenfeld, Howard. *Books: From Writer to Reader.*
   Crown, 1976, 211 pp. (6-up).
> Most of us take books for granted, and few people oth-
> er than those in publishing have any idea of the process
> involved in the creation of a book. Drawing on his
> years of experience in publishing, Greenfeld has written
> a clear, readable "how-it's-done" account of this pro-
> cess. He starts with the writer, then the literary agent
> and on through each successive step, finally following
> the completed book to the stores where it is made avail-
> able to the reader. Generously illustrated, the book also
> includes a glossary of publishing terms.

☐ Grum, Bernard. *The Timetables of History: A Horizontal
   Linkage of People and Events.* Simon and Schuster, 1982
   (4-up).
> A unique broad-spectrum view of history in which the
> reader can scan horizontally across the book's category
> columns (History, Politics; Literature, Theatre; Reli-
> gion, Philosophy, Learning; Visual Arts; Music; Sci-
> ence, Technology, Growth; Daily Life) and see events
> of significance (or merely of whimsical interest) which
> occurred in different aspects of culture and in different
> parts of the world during the same time period. The
> book is not only most helpful for reference, but is also a
> pleasure to browse through. The coverage begins with
> the year 5000 B.C., and up to 1000 B.C. events are
> grouped in 500-year periods—not too much was going
> on as to detailed, recorded change and development at
> that time. From 1000 B.C. to 500 B.C., the time period
> is reduced to 100-year sections, then to fifty-year spans
> up to 500 A.D., and from 501 A.D. on, a separate verti-
> cal time slot is allowed for each year. The entries run
> through 1978.

☐ *The Illustrated Bible Dictionary.* Tyndale House, 1980 (all
   ages).
> An excellent reference source on Biblical terms, objects,
> people and places. Lavishly illustrated with photo-
> graphs, drawings and diagrams, most in full-color, this
> three-volume set provides a wealth of carefully re-
> searched and clearly stated information.

☐ Laird, Stan. *Hands-On Grammar: An Instant Resource.*
Pitman Learning, 1978 (5, 6-up).

> In forty-four clear, concise pages Laird has managed to
> list the essential rules of grammar. Not intended in any
> way as a substitute for a more complete handbook or
> grammar text, this little book serves as a fast, accessible
> reference source. In many cases, particularly when a
> teacher or parent has had a good grounding in English
> grammar, the briefly stated rule in Laird's book will
> serve to remind the reader of material he has once
> known but somewhat forgotten. In many other cases,
> the reader will be made aware that he or she needs to
> study more extensively about a particular rule of gram-
> mar, and Laird's book is a good starting-point to lead
> him or her to more complete coverage in a standard
> grammar/usage handbook such as the *Harbrace College
> Handbook* or other similar books. While an advanced
> or older student might find the book helpful, its prima-
> ry purpose is to function as outlined above for the par-
> ent or teacher.

☐ Mickelsen, Berkeley and Alvera. *The Family Bible
Encyclopedia.* David C. Cook, 1978 (all ages).

> A good "starter" encyclopedia that children can use
> themselves. The entry words are in large boldface type
> followed by the phonetic pronunciation when needed.
> Illustrations are generally drawings in two-color or full-
> color, with a few two-color photographs. Information
> is clearly and concisely presented in simple language
> and reflects traditional evangelical thought.

☐ *Nelson's Bible Encyclopedia for the Family.* Nelson, 1982
(all ages).

> Grouped under twenty main categories, information
> about the Bible itself, the culture of Bible lands, and
> many more areas are clearly presented. There is a wealth
> of beautiful illustrations: countless photographs, draw-
> ings and maps, almost all in full-color. The entries are
> both readable and carefully researched.

□ *NIV Pictorial Bible,* Zondervan (4-up).

> See the note on this edition of the *New International Version* of the Bible as listed under *Bible Stories and Spiritual Teaching.*

□ Parker, Bertha Morris. *The New Golden Dictionary.* Western Publishing Co., 1972, 120 pp. (ps-1).

> An excellent bridge from the picture-book world to the academic world in which the organizing of material and ideas is so important. The definitions are clear and readable; the illustrations (over two thousand) are so pleasing that a child pores over this colorful dictionary for sheer enjoyment.

□ Preksto, Peter W., Jr. *Basic Library Skills.* Creative Education, 1979 (4-up).

> A concise (twenty-nine pages), clear outline of library skills, including a description of the Dewey Decimal System and a list of some of the most widely used reference books. Intended for students (starting at about grade 4) to read for themselves, but would be a helpful teacher/parent reference when helping a child learn library skills.

□ Tunis, Edwin. *Colonial Living.* Harper and Row, 1976, 160 pp. (5-up).

> Primary listing under *History.*
>
> Good source of information as to artifacts, customs and daily routines in America during the period from about 1564-1770.

□ Tunis, Edwin. *Frontier Living.* Harper & Row, 1976, 168 pp. (4-up).

> Primary listing under *History.*
>
> Tunis records a wealth of detail on the cultural history of frontier Americans in the era of westward expansion. Excellent illustrations amplify the text.

□ Tunis, Edwin. *Indians.* Harper & Row, 1979, 157 pp. (4-up).

    Primary listing under *History.*

    Helpful reference source as to the tools, weapons and houses used by American Indians before the arrival of the white man.

□ Tunis, Edwin. *Oars, Sails and Steam: A Picture Book of Ships.* Harper & Row, 1977, 77 pp. (5-up).

    Primary listing under *Science and Technology.*

    Fine information and detailed drawings of ships from the earliest known to those of modern times. As always, Tunis includes relevant historical/cultural details.

□ Tunis, Edwin. *The Tavern at the Ferry.* Harper & Row, 1973, 109 pp. (4-up).

    Primary listing under *History.*

    Loosely using a particular location by the Delaware River and succeeding generations of the Baker family as focal points, Tunis writes in great detail about the cultural history of the colonists in the central seaboard area for the hundred years from 1687 on. Tunis's excellent, detailed drawings aid in the vivid depiction of objects used in daily life.

□ Tunis, Edwin. *Wheels: A Pictorial History.* Harper & Row, 1977, 96 pp. (5-up).

    Primary listing under *Science and Technology.*

    A chronologically arranged presentation of wheeled vehicles (except for those that run on rails or tracks) from the earliest known to those of modern times. Tunis always relates the things people use to relevant historical and cultural patterns of the time. Fine, detailed drawings accompanied by explanatory text.

□ Tunis, Edwin. *The Young United States: 1783-1830.*
   Harper & Row, 1976, 160 pp. (6-up).
>
> Primary listing under *History.*
>
> Details of social/cultural developments during the
> first fifty years of the new nation. Tunis focuses on a
> wealth of activities and objects involved in daily living
> and gives them added illumination with his fine draw-
> ings.

□ Tyler, J. E. A. *The New Tolkien Companion.* St. Martin's
   Press, 1979, 649 pp. (4-up).
>
> An invaluable handbook for lovers of Middle Earth and
> all that Tolkien wrote about its history and people. This
> large concordance to the books includes much of the
> High History of the Elven peoples. Among other
> things, it provides a detailed guide to the Elvish writing
> system and offers maps, helpful charts and genealogical
> tables.

□ Urdang, Laurence. *The Timetables of American History.*
   Simon and Schuster, 1981, 470 pp. (4-up).
>
> Inspired by an earlier book (see separate listing), *The
> Timetables of History* (Simon and Schuster), this useful
> reference book is organized in columnar form under
> four categories: History and Politics; The Arts; Science
> and Technology; and Miscellaneous. Each category has
> a column headed "America" and one headed "Else-
> where." Each year is listed vertically in the left margin.
> Thus one can follow across the page for the year 1818,
> for example, and find listed seven significant political
> events (three in America and four elsewhere), nine im-
> portant happenings in the arts (three in America and
> six elsewhere), five events in science and technology,
> etc. The idea behind this horizontal approach is to
> broaden students' concepts of history and to encourage
> them to see patterns and interrelationships of events.

Dictionaries: children's intermediate

All of the following are worthwhile children's dictionaries. These
are dictionaries that are intermediate in scope between early childhood picture dictionaries and regular college or desk editions. In-

termediate dictionaries offer simpler language in their definitions, larger type, more illustrations and less of the linguistic information, puzzling abbreviations, and so forth than do college editions. They also, of course, offer considerably fewer entries. The dictionaries are listed in alphabetical order of publisher.

□ *Webster's New World Dictionary for Young Readers.* Collins, 1979, 880 pp.

□ *Children's Dictionary: An American Heritage Dictionary.* Houghton Mifflin, 1979, 864 pp.

□ *Macmillan Dictionary for Children.* Macmillan, 1982, 784 pp.

□ *Webster's Elementary Dictionary.* Merriam Webster, 1981, 582 pp.

Parents, teachers and advanced or older students will want to have good adult dictionaries at hand. Of the college or desk editions, the following are recommended: *American Heritage* (Houghton Mifflin); *Random House* (Random House); *Webster's Collegiate* (Merriam Webster); *Webster's New World* (Collins). It is very important to check the title and publisher; many inferior dictionaries, for example, use the name "Webster" in their titles—in itself, no guarantee of scholarship.

As many other good reference books as possible are valuable to have in the home. *World Book Encyclopedia* (World Book) is recommended for children; the *Encyclopedia Britannica* is still the best compilation of its kind for adults, although in many cases *World Book* can be used by all ages.

The list of desirable reference books could be almost endless. A good thesaurus, a variety of atlases, an up-to-date almanac, specialized dictionaries in the fields of music, medicine, the classics—the possibilities are as varied as the reader's interests. There are excellent geographical and biographical dictionaries, invaluable guides to American and English literature, field guides to plants, wildlife, rocks and minerals—and more. Many people find a large reference book on familiar quotations helpful, and for the person with a "back to the roots" interest in the English language, the multivolume *Oxford English Dictionary* (frequently referred to as the OED) is indispensable. Fortunately for the majority of people whose financial resources aren't unlimited, the OED is published in a two-volume compact edition (micro-reduced printing) and comes complete with a magnifying glass.

Having, and using, a wealth of good reference material in the home is one of the most effective ways of establishing invaluable research skills—and encouraging wide-ranging interests—in the lives of children.

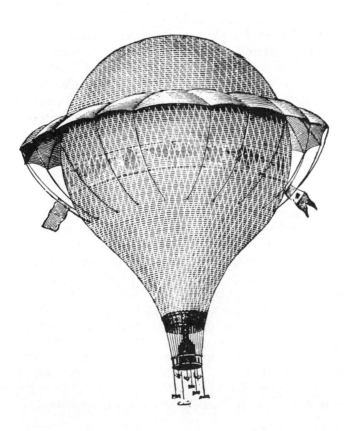

23 Science and Technology

☐ Apfel, Necia H. *It's All Relative: Einstein's Theory of Relativity*. Lothrop, Lee & Shepard, 1981, 144 pp. (5-up).

As writer Apfel states in her preface, "A knowledge of advanced physics and math is necessary to comprehend Einstein's theory fully, but even without such a background it is possible to understand its basic principles and its effect upon the world of science." Apfel goes on to point out that some knowledge of this theory is essential for the mathematicians and physicists of today and tomorrow, and that if elementary school students begin to grasp some of its concepts, it will be easier for those who do go on to higher levels of math and science to comprehend the ideas that seem so different from what we are accustomed to. In clear, understandable language, and with the constant use of analogies, examples and diagrams, Apfel explains Einstein's theory and its simpler implications. Even in the "basic" form, many students (and many adults) will feel unable to really grasp the complex theory. But for others with the necessary kind of aptitude for abstract mathematical thought, the book offers an important opportunity for them to begin to familiarize themselves with the concepts on which advanced math and physics are based.

☐ Bendick, Jeanne. *Archimedes and the Door of Science*. Franklin Watts, 1962, 143 pp., OP (5, 6-up).
See entries under *Biography* and *Mathematics*.

□ Berger, Melvin. *Quasars, Pulsars and Black Holes in Space.* G. P. Putnam's Sons, 1977, 64 pp. (5, 6-up).

An excellent simplified treatment of a complex subject. The book is entirely secular, but its content causes the Christian reader to see its scientific data in relation to an omnipotent God. As with all astronomical material, the realities are mind-boggling. This book could be used as supplementary reading for a science unit on astronomy, or it could be used as a short study unit in itself.

□ Borland, Hal. *The Golden Circle.* Crowell, 1977, 53 pp. (5-up).

Observations on nature in each month of the year by writer-naturalist Hal Borland, accompanied by stunning full-color paintings by Anne Ophelia Dowden. The pattern of the seasons follows the climate of the American northeast, but even for readers in the South, the far West, or for those in other lands it makes lovely, informative reading.

□ Branley, Franklyn M. *Halley: Comet 1986.* Dutton, 1983, 86 pp. (5-up).

Every seventy-six years, approximately, the orbit of Halley's Comet brings it close enough to the sun and to earth's orbit to be visible to us. In this 1983 book, Branley discusses the then-imminent 1985-86 appearance of the comet, and gives information on its past appearances, on what a comet actually is, on other famous comets, and on possible international events related to the observation of Halley's Comet during 1985 and 1986. Photographs and diagrams are used generously throughout.

□ Brown, Marion Marsh. *Homeward the Arrow's Flight.* Abingdon, 1980, 175 pp. (5, 6-up).

Primary listing under *Biography.*

This excellent biography relates to medical science in the 1880s. It is the story of the first American Indian woman doctor in history.

□ Clapp, Patricia. *Dr. Elizabeth*. Dutton, 1974, 156 pp.,
OP (6-up).
Primary listing under *Biography*.
Medicine in America and England in the latter half
of the nineteenth century as seen in the experience of
Elizabeth Blackwell who became the first woman doctor
since the time of the ancient world.

□ Cobb, Vicki. *Lots of Rot*. Lippincott, 1981, 40 pp. (1-3).
The writer provides information for the inquiring
young scientist on what causes rot. Simple, clearly described projects result in the discovery of facts about
bacteria, mold and mildew.

□ Cole, Joanna. *Cars and How They Go*. Crowell, 1983, 32
pp. (2-6).
Clear, simplified drawings and a concise text explain the
basic "how's" of a car's working parts. Valuable information for all—and a wonderful way to add to the
budding engineer's or mechanic's store of knowledge.

□ Cooper, Gale, M.D. *Inside Animals*. Little, Brown & Co.,
1978, 32 pp. (all ages).
The strength of this book is in its detailed drawings of
animal interiors. The book proceeds through the animal
forms, starting with the cell, amoeba, paramecium,
through to (and including) the mammals. A concluding
section is on "Special Parts of Special Animals" (neck of
giraffe, silk gland of spider and other such distinctive
body parts). The text is in very simple, scientific form,
and the book offers virtually no language benefits (except to demonstrate the value of precision and cogency
in scientific writing—and perhaps to add a few zoologi-
cal terms to a student's vocabulary).

□ Cottrell, Ron. *The Remarkable Spaceship Earth*. Accent,
1982, 64 pp. (6-up).
Space-engineer Cottrell (a participant in the development of the Saturn V Apollo moon rocket) has put together an effective, written-for-the-layman presentation
of some of the remarkable aspects of earth's design. The
approach is factual, brief and low-key, including the results of scientific studies calculating the mathematical

probability that on a *chance* basis, over eons of time, a planet could evolve that was capable of supporting life. The unavoidable conclusion is made: earth was purposefully designed. Relevant photographic illustrations complement the text.

□ Cousins, Margaret. *The Story of Thomas Alva Edison.* Random House, 1981, 160 pp. (5-9).
Primary listing under *Biography*.
The life and work of the Wizard of Menlo Park make enthralling reading. Edison, inventor of the incandescent light bulb, the phonograph, the motion picture and many other devices, is a prominent example of the unpredictable and inexplicable gift of genius that characterizes so many of the world's innovators and discoverers. Coupled with Edison's genius, however, was an almost obsessive preoccupation with his work, and once he started on an idea he would repeat experiments, make tests, seek for better solutions literally thousands of times if necessary. From the explosion of interest the nine-year-old Edison experienced as he read his first science book, to his death at eighty-four while still working avidly on projects, his life was an ongoing experience of a curious, restless, analytical mind seeking answers to, and practical applications of, scientific truths.

□ d'Aulaire, Ingri and Edgar Parin. *Benjamin Franklin.* Doubleday, 1950, 48 pp. (2-4).
Primary listing under *Biography*.
An excellent introductory biography to use in connection with Franklin's scientific experiments and discoveries.

□ Epstein, Sam and Beryl. *Dr. Beaumont and the Man with a Hole in His Stomach.* Coward, McCann and Geoghegan, 1978, 57 pp. (4-6).
Most important discoveries in medical science have come because a dedicated doctor or scientific researcher was trying to find ways to improve health care, to save lives, to spare people various kinds of pain or impairment. But all the essential facts about how the stomach digests food were learned in the 1820s by a rather cal-

lous doctor with a less than admirable character and a great desire for fame, who took advantage of a freak accident that befell a young French Canadian voyageur. The Epsteins tell the bizarre story of Dr. Beaumont's research with an underlying humor, but with a clear account of the scientific data involved. A fascinating commentary on human nature, and on the state of medical research in the America of 160 years ago.

☐ Goldin, Augusta. *The Shape of Water*. Doubleday, 1979 (1-3).

In this science book for young children, a simplified explanation shows the way in which molecular behavior and structure determine the form of matter. Goldin writes frequently on science topics for children, and a number of her books are in the Let's Read and Find Out Science Book series (Harper & Row). Representative titles are: *Ducks Don't Get Wet; Straight Hair, Curly Hair;* and *Spider Silk*. A criticism of Goldin's work is that she writes in "educationist" style, using excessively short, choppy sentences, monotonous sentence structure (no varying of subject-verb order), and limited vocabulary. Apart from these shortcomings, the books are quite informative and suggest simple experiments that demonstrate various scientific principles.

☐ Heller, Ruth. *The Reason for a Flower*. Grossett & Dunlap, 1976, 24 pp., OP (k-2).

A vividly colorful introduction to the seed-forming function of flowers. The brief, rhymed text accompanies dramatic illustrations in this fashion: "Birds and bees and these, and these [butterflies, moths, a hummingbird, bat, are pictured] sip nectar from the flowers." Pollination is briefly described and pictured, then: "The reason for a flower is to manufacture . . . SEEDS that have a cover of one kind or another." A beautiful array of seeds is shown, and the following pages show ways that seeds are distributed in nature, some of the wide varieties of plants there are, all coming from seeds, and finally some of the things we use that come from plants: paper, coffee, bread, cotton fabric and more. A delightful, purposeful book.

□ Jones, E. G. *Television Magic*. Viking, 1978, 61 pp. (4-6 and up; adv. 2, 3).

An attractively presented look at how television works, how specific effects are created, how programs are produced. Dozens of full-color photographs, drawings and diagrams complement the clear, concise text. TV is a significant part of contemporary life and one more area about which many young people will want to be informed.

□ Judson, Clara Ingram. *Soldier Doctor*. Scribner's, 1942, 151 pp. (4-9).

Primary listing under *Biography*.

As an army doctor, Gorgas (who was later to become the U.S. Surgeon-General) was determined to conquer yellow fever, which was one of the world's most dreaded diseases before its eradication in the early part of the twentieth century. Gorgas had long been interested in combating this disease, but no one yet had the key—the fact that a particular kind of mosquito transmitted it. A Yellow Fever Board was established by the United States government and worked in Havana, Cuba. Dr. Walter Reed, Dr. Carlos J. Finlay and others, including Gorgas, were involved, and once Reed and Finlay had established beyond a doubt that the mosquito theory was true, Gorgas directed the successful implementation of the eradication program. This is excellent supplementary reading in relation to medical science, public health, and "the making of a doctor."

□ Kiefer, Irene. *Global Jigsaw Puzzle*. Atheneum, 1978, 79 pp. (adv. 6-up).

A clearly presented account of the comparatively new geological concept of continental drift and plate tectonics. This is important background information for earth science students. Although the main subject content provides the chief value of the book, another aspect is of special interest to Christians. While the writer is obviously a believer in the "big bang" theory of the existence of our planet, she clearly states that our knowledge of the why's and how's of the natural world is limited and constantly being revised. The whole matter of continental drift has only been thoroughly studied since World War II and has already turned much of the former basis for geological studies upside down.

□ Knight, David C. *Isaac Newton: Mastermind of Modern Science* (Immortals of Science Series). Franklin Watts, 1961, 153 pp., OP (6-up).
Primary listing under *Biography*.
Sir Isaac Newton (1642-1727), mathematician and physicist, is considered by many the greatest scientist of all time. Best known in general as the discoverer of the law of universal gravitation, he also discovered other vitally important laws of physics and mathematics. Even for the student who does not plan to focus intensively on science, a good general knowledge of this important scientist's life and work is of real value.

□ Lerner, Sharon. *I Found a Leaf.* Lerner, 1967, 36 pp. (1-up).
An excellent introduction to close observation of leaves, identification of trees by their leaves, brief descriptions of outstanding characteristics of the trees. Well-written and illustrated.

□ Mandell, Muriel. *Physics Experiments for Children.* Dover, 1968, 96 pp. (4-6).
Dozens of simple but effective experiments using readily available materials. Scientific facts about air, water, mechanical energy, heat, sound, light, magnetism and electricity are demonstrated by experiments for which clear step-by-step instructions are given.

□ May, Julian. *Sea Otter.* Creative Educational Society, 1972, 40 pp. (3-up).
An excellent, biologically accurate introduction to this charming—and endangered—sea mammal. Well-thought and using an effective vocabulary, this book is one of an excellent series on endangered animals. Other titles are: *Cactus Fox; Cascade Cougar; Eagles of the Valley; Glacier Grizzly; Prairie Pronghorn;* and *Sea Lion Island.*

□ Newton, James. *A Forest Is Reborn*. Crowell, 1982, 32 pp. (3, 4).

> The aftermath of a forest fire seems to be total devastation, but after a while the forest will return. Newton tells of the natural progression in which nature reclaims the fire-ravaged land. First come small, sun-loving plants; gradually new trees spring up from seeds unharmed by the fire. Each phase of the renewal is illustrated with beautiful drawings, including detailed sketches of germinating seeds, leaves of specific plants, forest animals and a variety of trees.

□ Provensen, Alice and Martin. *The Glorious Flight*. Viking, 1983, 39 pp. (k-2).

> The 1984 Caldecott Medal winner, this picture-book story is based on a significant piece of aviation history that has been largely forgotten. In 1901 Louis Bleriot, a settled family man with a wife and five children, became enthralled with the idea of flight. Eight years (and eleven airplanes) later, he became the first man to fly across the English Channel. The Provensens have told this story in beautifully chosen words, with a subtle, charming humor, and with page after page of wonderfully authentic illustrations, detailed and, in the case of the airplane scenes, shimmering with light and creating a sense of buoyancy and movement through the air.

□ Provenzo, Eugene and Asterie. *Rediscovering Astronomy*. Oak Tree, 1980, 128 pp. (5-up).

> The Provenzos discuss the people responsible for the development of astronomy through the ages. Included are detailed instructions for building a sundial, water lens, rotating quadrant, sextant and two types of telescope.

□ Provenzo, Eugene and Asterie. *Rediscovering Photography*. Oak Tree, 1980, 128 pp. (5-up).

> A book about the basic inventions (and their inventors) that have made modern photography possible. Complete instructions and diagrams are given for making various kinds of basic cameras, many with materials of-

ten found around the home. Instructions are also included for making sunprints and negative and positive photographic prints.

□ Quackenbush, Robert. *Ahoy! Ahoy! Are You There? A Story of Alexander Graham Bell.* Prentice-Hall, 1981, 36 pp. (1-4).
Primary listing under *Biography.*
This is a brief, lively introduction to Bell and the principles on which he was able to invent the telephone. Good supplementary reading when the subject of sound transmission is encountered in a regular science curriculum.

□ Quackenbush, Robert. *Here a Plant, There a Plant, Everywhere a Plant Plant! A Story of Luther Burbank.* Prentice-Hall, 1982, 35 pp. (2-5).
Primary listing under *Biography.*
An entertaining introduction to the work of the man who developed many new varieties of fruits, vegetables and flowers, including the Burbank potato and the Shasta daisy.

□ Russell, Solveig Paulson. *What's Under the Sea?* Abingdon, 1982, 48 pp. (2-4).
The writer explores the underwater realm of the sea, discussing currents and tides, the different depths of water and the types of sea life found in each one. Plants and minerals are noted, as well as the search for oil and and the work of oceanographers. A number of attractive drawings illustrate the text, and an index and brief glossary are also included.

□ Samson, John G. *The Pond.* Knopf, 1979, 134 pp. (5, 6-up).
This is an exceptionally well-done account of all the varieties of life in and near a 100-yard by 300-yard pond in a small piece (about three hundred acres) of upstate New York woodland.
The book is organized by seasons, and the wildlife activities and descriptions are fascinating to any reader interested in the natural world. Regrettably, as with

most of the really outstanding books on nature, this one reflects a non-Christian view of the origins of life. But the *facts* of our remarkable natural world reinforce the existence of the creating mind of God; the *opinions* of those who write about nature are just that—opinions. The wise parent or teacher has no fear of honest discussion or questions and when such issues arise, as in a book like this, deals intelligently with the matter.

□ Scheffer, Victor B. *The Seeing Eye*. Scribner's, 1971, 47 pp. (5, 6-up).
    Primary listing under *Art*.
    More effective observation of the natural world is encouraged. Scheffer increases the reader's awareness of the aesthetic qualities in the things naturalists study.

□ Selsam, Millicent E. *How Animals Live Together* (revised edition). Morrow, 1979, 95 pp. (5-up).
    A fact-filled (and fascinating) study of how the life of animals is organized in relation to one another. Pecking order, social groups among mammals, insect societies are just a few of the topics discussed. An excellent supplement for a science unit on animal life. Only facts are discussed; there is no attempt to promote theories of evolution.

□ Selsam, Millicent E. *The Plants We Eat*. Morrow, 1981, 128 pp. (4-up).
    The writer gives the history and characteristics of virtually all of the vegetables and fruits that are part of our food supply today. Excellent black-and-white photographs illustrate the text.

□ Shuttlesworth, Dorothy. *Animal Camouflage*. Natural History Press, 1959, 111 pp., OP (5-up).
    An informative, beautifully illustrated study of the many ways animals are camouflaged in nature to help them blend in with their environment. The facts are discussed without any attempt to tie them to evolutionary theory.

□ Shuttlesworth, Dorothy. *The Doubleday First Guide to Rocks.* Doubleday, 1963, 30 pp., OP (1-3).

Even young children can learn to recognize different kinds of rocks. This brief book is a helpful introduction to the subject. The three basic groupings into which rocks are categorized are identified and discussed, then commonly-found examples of each of the three forms— igneous ("fire-formed"), sedimentary ("made-over") and metamorphic ("changed")—are described and pictured.

□ Simon, Seymour. *Science in a Vacant Lot.* Viking, 1970, 64 pp. (3-6).

Even in an urban setting there is often a nearby vacant lot or a neglected part of a backyard where observations of nature can be made. Each chapter of the book focuses on different natural phenomena: rocks, soil, insects, plants and trees. Each discussion is a good general introduction to its subject and also describes specific activities and experiments that will help a child learn more about and enjoy more of the natural world. The suggestions are all applicable to country settings as well. A good book for either class-related or independent nature study.

□ Sootin, Harry. *Robert Boyle: Founder of Modern Chemistry* (Immortals of Science Series). Franklin Watts, 1962, 133 pp., OP (6-up).

Also listed under *Biography* and *History.*

From boyhood on, Robert Boyle (1627-1691) was fascinated by the natural world and its orderly laws which were slowly being discovered. Although he was born into a very wealthy family, Boyle had no interest in a life of luxury or self-amusement. Instead, he began to spend his time both in studying and experimenting on his own, and in listening to a group of educated, intelligent men, all eagerly interested in forwarding the progress of science. Boyle's chief interest was in chemistry and physics, and he made a number of significant advances, particularly in the field of chemistry. An important scientific concept in relation to gases is still identified today as Boyle's Law. Sootin's biography is a

well-written account of Boyle's life and work, with a
high level of human interest as well as much specific
discussion of his experiments and discoveries.

□ Stone, A. Harris. *Science Projects That Make Sense.*
McCall, 1971, 47 pp., OP (3, 4).
This is excellent primary material in training sensory
perception. It moves in the field of everyday objects and
actions. Students are asked, for example, to decide
whether it is easier, by "feel" to identify from outside,
the objects in a paper or a cloth bag. An important feature of the book: *No answers* are given. A competent,
knowledgeable instructor would need to lead the young
experimenters to the scientific concepts that *explain* the
data they would observe in the experiments. Very helpful in training students in observation, data gathering,
relating data to basic scientific concepts.

□ Tunis, Edwin. *Chipmunks on the Doorstep.* Harper &
Row, 1971, 69 pp. (5-8).
A close-up view of every aspect of the lives of chipmunks through the full cycle of the seasons. The writer
made his observations while sitting patiently in his own
backyard, noting behavior and making drawings. In addition, he read extensively on the subject. The result is
an informative, enjoyable book, enlivened with action,
humor, and dozens of wonderful color drawings of
chipmunks in every conceivable activity. Not only well
worth reading for itself, but a splendid example of what
can be learned about any nearby wild creature through
careful observation and interested study.

□ Tunis, Edwin. *Oars, Sails and Steam: A Picture Book of
Ships.* Harper & Row, 1977, 77 pp. (5-up).
Not a picture-book in the usual sense of the word, this
is a wonderful gallery of ships from the earliest known
to those of modern times. The detailed drawings are accompanied by informative text, diagrams and a glossary
of nautical terms. As always, Tunis brings his extensive
historical knowledge (and his lively sense of humor) to
bear on his subject matter. Delightful to browse
through, splendid for reading and reference.

□ Tunis, Edwin. *Wheels: A Pictorial History.* Harper & Row, 1977, 96 pp. (5-up).

A chronologically arranged account of representative kinds of wheeled vehicles (not including those that run on rails or tracks) from the earliest known to those of the midtwentieth century. As in his other fine books, cultural history is always woven into his interesting and frequently humorous text. His clear, lively, meticulously accurate drawings enliven every page. Readers who enjoy history and historical stories should be particularly happy to find illustrations of the vehicles they often read about, but seldom see pictured in any detail or with any accompanying explanations.

□ Urquhart, Jennifer C. *Animals That Travel.* National Geographic, 1982, 32 pp. (ps-2).

A beautiful picture-book on animal migration. Over twenty different animals and birds are mentioned in the brief large-print text. Not intended as an in-depth treatment, the book provides a good introduction to the idea of animals that change their location periodically.

□ Walther, Tom. *A Spider Might.* Scribner's, 1978, 144 pp. (3-7).

A very special kind of book on spiders. It contains a great deal of clearly stated and scientifically accurate facts about many kinds of spiders, but it is handled in a form that also encourages imagination and brings the life of the spider into a more comfortable relationship with the reader. For example: "If one day while climbing in and swinging through trees, you saw Miss Muffet below eating curds and whey, would you swing down and give her a scare? Though you wouldn't or certainly shouldn't, a spider might." The writer then goes on to tell briefly about the real Dr. Muffet who studied and wrote about spiders in the late 1500s. A book that is both scholastically excellent and a delight to read.

☐ Wexler, Jerome. *Secrets of the Venus's Flytrap*. Dodd, Mead, 1981, 64 pp. (4-up).

　　Primary listing under *Horticulture*.

　　Wexler's clear, detailed photography and concise text provide an excellent botanical study of this carnivorous plant. One of the most fascinating sections focuses on the pollination process and the development of the seeds.

☐ Wilson, Dorothy Clarke. *Ten Fingers for God*. Nelson, 1982, 288 pp. (6-up).

　　Primary listing under *Biography*.

　　The story of Dr. Paul Brand and his remarkable pioneering work in restorative surgery and rehabilitation of the victims of leprosy. While the book is written for the layperson, Wilson does go into a substantial amount of medical description and detail. Exciting reading for those interested in the medical field—and for those who are inspired by people who care and dare and accomplish great things. Reading aloud some of the episodes most directly related to Brand's medical work would be one good way to use the book with children's science curriculum.

☐ Wilson, Mike. *Jet Journey*. Viking, 1978, 59 pp. (4-6 and up; adv. 2, 3).

　　Another of the Viking series on technology, lavishly and colorfully illustrated, concisely worded. This one offers an introduction to the world of modern flying: an airport layout, a recognition chart for various planes, a "how-it-works" section on jet engines, a typical passenger plane layout—even instructions for making a model of a Concorde.

A series of illustrated books about applied science

☐ See Inside series. Franklin Watts, all 1978, 1979, 29 pp. (4-up).

☐ Beal, George. *See Inside a TV Studio*

☐ Kerrod, Robin. *See Inside a Space Station*

□ Rutland, Jonathan. *See Inside a Submarine*

□ Rutland, Jonathan. *See Inside an Oil Rig Tanker*
>These brief captioned-picture surveys are colorful and attractive, appropriate as supplementary materials which focus on the readily observable characteristics and functions of their respective subjects. Once introduced, for example, to the unique world of the submarine, an interested student could be directed to more in-depth reading on the topic.

²⁴ Special Days and Seasons

☐ Cole, Ann. *A Pumpkin in a Pear Tree*. Little, Brown & Co., 1976, 112 pp. (all ages).
   Creative ideas for twelve months of holiday celebration: handicraft, games and special recipes.

☐ Cosman, Madeleine Pelner. *Medieval Holidays and Festivals*. Scribner's, 1981, 128 pp. (6-up).
   This interesting and unusual book invites its readers to create their own festive events based on the way each holiday was observed in medieval times. Cosman offers a special celebration for each month, discussing its background and how it was observed. The concluding chapters give directions for making festal banners and costumes and recipes for medieval dishes. With all of this information, the reader can recreate the music, decorations, costumes and food of medieval celebrations. The book is embellished with art prints of the period.

☐ Cuyler, Margery. *The All-Around Christmas Book*. Holt, Rinehart & Winston, 1982, 96 pp. (all ages).
   Why is mistletoe associated with Christmas? How do people in other countries observe Christmas? These and a number of other questions are interestingly answered in this homey little collection of Christmas customs, traditions, crafts and recipes.

☐ Dalgliesh, Alice. *The Thanksgiving Story*. Scribner's, 1954, 32 pp. (1-3).
   Primary listing under *History*.
   A well-written story of the first Thanksgiving from the perspective of a fictional family involved in the celebration.

□ Jordan, Nina R. *Holiday Handicrafts*. Harper & Row, 1938, 245 pp. (4-6).

    A book of simple crafts to make for each of more than a dozen holidays throughout the year. A concluding section focuses on gifts, birthdays and hats and masks.

□ Liniam, Gail. *Celebrate Christmas*. Broadman (all ages).

    Day-to-day Christmas activities for December 1-25: Scripture verses, Bible stories, suggestions for family worship, meaningful and enjoyable Christmas activities.

□ Purdy, Susan. *Christmas Cooking Around the World*. Franklin Watts, 1983, 96 pp. (4-up).

    Primary listing under *Crafts, Hobbies and Domestic Arts*.

□ Sarnoff, Jane. *Light the Candles! Beat the Drums! A Book of Holidays*. Scribner's, 1979, 32 pp. (all ages).

    A month-by-month listing of commemorative days and holidays with a brief explanation of the history and celebration of each day.

□ *The Saturday Evening Post Christmas Book for Children*. Curtis Publishing, 1981, 112 pp. (all ages).

    This nostalgic collection includes some of the special moments treasured by children's parents and grandparents. Classic illustrations from the *Post*, favorite stories (including the Gospel of Luke account of Jesus' birth), poems, carols, recipes, crafts and puzzles all help to provide traditional Christmas memory-makers.

□ Soilien, Sandra. *Keeping Christmas*. Augsburg (all ages).

    A fine collection of Bible readings, music, activities and projects for celebrating the twelve days of Christmas (December 25-January 5). The book is not large, but there are enough ideas for several Christmases.

25 Supplemental Teaching Resources

May be used for all ages

☐ Allison, Linda. *Trash Artists Workshop*. Pitman Learning.
Primary listing under *Crafts and Hobbies*.
  A worthwhile collection of things to make from
throwaway materials. Many of the objects made are
more useful and creative than those in some craft
books.

☐ Bachert, Russel E., Jr. *Hundreds of Ideas for Outdoor
Education*. Interstate Printers and Publisher, 1979,
152 pp.
  Bachert offers (each one very briefly) many ideas to explore in the outdoor world. These are not grouped or
organized, and are without "how-to's" of any kind. As
"idea-generators" they could be very useful, but the
reader should not expect guidance or information on
how to develop the ideas—he or she is on his/her own.

☐ Becker, Joyce. *Bible Crafts*. Holiday House, 1982, 28 pp.
Primary listing under *Crafts and Hobbies*.
  A good collection of craft projects related to well-
known Old Testament stories.

☐ Gerston, Rich. *Just Open the Door*. Interstate Printers and
Publisher, 1982, 112 pp.
  Nearly three hundred lesson plans and activities that use
outdoor/environmental experiences, tying them in to
classroom curriculum, relating them to various specific
subjects, etc. Practical and useful. Entries are all short,
but much specific guidance is given briefly. Excellent.

□ Rowell, Elizabeth H. and Thomas B. Goodkind.
  Teaching the Pleasures of Reading. Prentice-Hall, 1982,
  256 pp.
  > The title of this resource book is somewhat misleading.
  > It is *not* a book that aids teachers/parents in getting chil-
  > dren involved in a specific list of recommended books.
  > What it does do is give hundreds of suggestions that
  > involve kids pleasurably in word-related activities in five
  > areas: humor, TV, art, music, the outdoors. The overall
  > concept is that if children's reading skills are developed
  > in diverse ways, and they find that using words can be
  > fun, they will do more reading and enjoy reading more.
  >   In the humor section, for example, puns, jokes,
  > riddles, paraphrasing, idiomatic expressions, writing
  > about a favorite humorous character, analyzing humor-
  > ous advertisements are just a few of the approaches
  > used. Without going into lengthy detail, it is difficult to
  > adequately describe the variety of activities covered, but
  > they are very extensive. A helpful, idea-generating hand-
  > book.

□ Shoemaker, Kathryn. *Creative Classroom*. Winston Press,
  1980 (all ages).
  > A well-done book full of great ideas for creative activi-
  > ties and projects children can do in the classroom.

□ Sisson, Edith A. *Nature with Children of All Ages:
  Activities and Adventures for Exploring, Learning and
  Enjoying the World Around Us*. Prentice-Hall, 1982,
  224 pp.
  > Information and suggested activities related to the nat-
  > ural world: trees, seeds, insects, fish, birds, mammals,
  > etc. Some of the activities involve hiking or games; oth-
  > ers are science experiments; still others give craft
  > instructions for making a variety of things. A bibliogra-
  > phy is at the end of each chapter.
  >   This is a secular book, and in some discussions the
  > evolutionary theory is implied. Parents/teachers should
  > be prepared to respond in the manner in which they
  > normally deal with this issue—one their children will
  > frequently encounter.

□ Swan, Malcolm D., ed. *Tips and Tricks for Outdoor Education*. Interstate Printers and Publisher, 1978.
> A fine source for outdoor activities. Its eighteen chapters focus on different areas: "Animal Studies," "Geology and Soils," "Interpretive Trails," "Measurement and Mapping" are a few of the chapter titles; others focus on water, weather, plants and more. Detailed instructions for many procedures are given.

Index